Facilitating Experiential Learning in Higher Education

This book provides evidence-informed and practical advice on how to design, teach, and facilitate hands-on, experiential learning in practical higher education settings.

With rich case studies and carefully considered analysis tasks, all underpinned by research evidence, it explores the functional aspects of teaching outside of regular classroom environments. Designed to enable university teachers to adapt strategies for teaching confidently and effectively, this must-read text focusses on enhancing learning and avoiding pitfalls whilst allowing students to develop and recognise the skills needed to excel in their chosen discipline.

This book also provides:

- *Reflection Points* to enable application of the ideas into teaching practice,
- *Action Summaries* that distil the main recommendations into easily applicable solutions,
- *Further Reading* sections to allow for deeper exploration of key ideas.

Practical and evidence-informed, the strategies within this book are useful for all educators teaching in practical settings including projects, labs, studios, in the field, and in practice placements.

Roland Tormey is a teacher and researcher in learning sciences and leads the Teaching Support Centre at the École polytechnique fédérale de Lausanne (EPFL), Switzerland.

Siara Isaac is a teaching advisor at the École polytechnique fédérale de Lausanne (EPFL), Switzerland.

Cécile Hardebolle is a teaching advisor and learning scientist at the École polytechnique fédérale de Lausanne (EPFL), Switzerland.

Ingrid Le Duc is a teaching advisor at the École polytechnique fédérale de Lausanne (EPFL) and teaches university pedagogy at the University of Bern, Switzerland.

Key Guides for Effective Teaching in Higher Education Series
Edited by Kate Exley

This indispensable series is aimed at new lecturers, postgraduate students who have teaching time, Graduate Teaching Assistants, part-time tutors and demonstrators, as well as experienced teaching staff who may feel it's time to review their skills in teaching and learning.

Titles in this series will provide the teacher in higher education with practical, realistic guidance on the various different aspects of their teaching role, which is underpinned not only by current research in the field, but also by the extensive experience of individual authors, and with a keen eye kept on the limitations and opportunities therein. By bridging a gap between academic theory and practice, all titles will provide generic guidance on the topics covered, which is then brought to life through the use of short, illustrative examples drawn from a range of disciplines. All titles in the series will:

- represent up-to-date thinking and incorporate the use of computing and appropriate learning technology
- consider methods and approaches for teaching and learning when there is an increasing diversity in learning and a growth in student numbers
- encourage readers to reflect, critique and apply learning in their practice and professional context
- provide links and references to other work on the topic and research evidence where appropriate.

Titles in the series will prove invaluable whether they are used for self-study, as reference material when seeking teaching recognition or as part of a formal taught programme on teaching and learning in higher education (HE), and will also be of relevance to teaching staff working in further education (FE) settings.

Enhancing Learning Through Formative Assessment and Feedback
Alastair Irons

Inclusion and Diversity Meeting the Needs of all Students
Sue Grace and Phil Gravestock

Giving a Lecture From Presenting to Teaching, 2ed
Kate Exley and Reg Dennick

Using Technology to Support Learning and Teaching
Andy Fisher, Kate Exley and Dragos Ciobanu

Leading Learning and Teaching in Higher Education The Key Guide to Designing and Delivering Courses
Doug Parkin

Small Group Teaching Seminars, Tutorials and Workshops, 2ed
Kate Exley, Reg Dennick and Andrew Fisher

Developing Your Teaching Towards Excellence, 2ed
Peter Kahn and Lorraine Anderson

Examining Doctoral Work Exploring Principles, Criteria and Processes
Jerry Wellington

Assessing Students' Written Work Marking Essays and Reports
Catherine Haines

Facilitating Experiential Learning in Higher Education Teaching and Supervising in Labs, Fieldwork, Studios, and Projects
Roland Tormey and Siara Isaac with Cécile Hardebolle and Ingrid Le Duc

For more information about this series, please visit: www.routledge.com/Key-Guides-for-Effective-Teaching-in-Higher-Education/book-series/SE0746

Facilitating Experiential Learning in Higher Education

Teaching and Supervising in Labs, Fieldwork, Studios, and Projects

Roland Tormey and
Siara Isaac

with Cécile Hardebolle
and Ingrid Le Duc

LONDON AND NEW YORK

First published 2022
by Routledge
2 Park Square, Milton Park, Abingdon, Oxon OX14 4RN

and by Routledge
605 Third Avenue, New York, NY 10158

Routledge is an imprint of the Taylor & Francis Group, an informa business

© 2022 Roland Tormey, Siara Isaac, Cécile Hardebolle and Ingrid Le Duc

The right of Roland Tormey, Siara Isaac, Cécile Hardebolle and Ingrid Le Duc to be identified as authors of this work has been asserted by them in accordance with sections 77 and 78 of the Copyright, Designs and Patents Act 1988.

All rights reserved. No part of this book may be reprinted or reproduced or utilised in any form or by any electronic, mechanical, or other means, now known or hereafter invented, including photocopying and recording, or in any information storage or retrieval system, without permission in writing from the publishers.

Trademark notice: Product or corporate names may be trademarks or registered trademarks, and are used only for identification and explanation without intent to infringe.

British Library Cataloguing-in-Publication Data
A catalogue record for this book is available from the British Library

Library of Congress Cataloging-in-Publication Data
Names: Tormey, Roland, author. | Isaac, Siara Ruth, 1977- author. | Hardebolle, Cécile, author. | Le Duc, Ingrid, author.
Title: Facilitating experiential learning in higher education: teaching and supervising in labs, fieldwork, studios, and projects / Roland Tormey and Siara Isaac; with Cécile Hardebolle and Ingrid Le Duc.
Description: Abingdon, Oxon; New York, NY: Routledge, 2022. | Includes bibliographical references and index.
Identifiers: LCCN 2021013354 (print) | LCCN 2021013355 (ebook) | ISBN 9780367562977 (hardback) | ISBN 9780367620325 (paperback) | ISBN 9781003107606 (ebook)
Subjects: LCSH: College teaching–Methodology. | Experiential learning.
Classification: LCC LB2331 .T575 2022 (print) | LCC LB2331 (ebook) | DDC 378.1/25–dc23
LC record available at https://lccn.loc.gov/2021013354
LC ebook record available at https://lccn.loc.gov/2021013355

ISBN: 978-0-367-56297-7 (hbk)
ISBN: 978-0-367-62032-5 (pbk)
ISBN: 978-1-003-10760-6 (ebk)

DOI: 10.4324/9781003107606

Typeset in Perpetua
by Deanta Global Publishing Services, Chennai, India

Contents

Series editor introduction vii
About the authors x
Acknowledgements xi

PART I 1

1 Introduction 3
2 How students develop disciplinary expertise 12
3 What students learn from labs, studios, projects, and fieldwork 40

PART II 71

4 Teaching, not telling: Using questions 73
5 Providing feedback on students' practical work 100
6 Explaining and demonstrating to students in practical settings 125
7 Managing relationships with a class 157

PART III 193

8 Research findings about the thinking that gives rise to learning 195

9	Research findings about the contexts of learning	217
10	Becoming a better teacher for practical settings	240
	Index	266

Series editor introduction

THE SERIES

The Key Guides for Effective Teaching in Higher Education were initially discussed as an idea in 2002, and the first group of four titles was published in 2004. New titles have continued to be added and the series now boasts 12 books (with new titles and further new editions of some of the older volumes in the pipeline).

It has always been intended that the books would be primarily of use to new teachers in universities and colleges. It has been exciting to see them being used to support postgraduate certificate programmes in teaching and learning for new academic staff and clinical teachers, and also the skills training programmes for postgraduate students who are beginning to teach. A less anticipated, but very valued, readership has been the experienced teachers who have dipped into the books when reviewing their teaching or referenced them when making claims for teaching recognition or promotion. Authors are very grateful to these colleagues who have given constructive feedback and made further suggestions on teaching approaches and shared examples of their practice, all of which has fed-forward into later editions of titles.

In the UK, the work of the Higher Education Academy (HEA), now part of Advance HE, in developing a Professional Standard Framework (UKPSF), on behalf of the sector, has also raised the importance of providing good quality guidance and support for those beginning their teaching careers. It is therefore intended that the series would also provide a useful set of sources for those seeking to gain professional recognition for their practice against the UKPSF.

KEY THEMES OF THE SERIES

The books are all attempting to combine two things: to be very practical and provide lots of examples of methods and techniques, and also to link to

SERIES EDITOR INTRODUCTION

educational theory and underpinning research. Articles are referenced, further readings are suggested, and researchers in the field are quoted. There is also much enthusiasm here to link to the wide range of teaching development activities thriving in the disciplines, supported by the small grant schemes and conferences provided by Advance HE, the Society for Research in Higher Education, professional bodies, etc. The need to tailor teaching approaches to meet the demands of different subject areas and to provide new teachers with examples of practice that are easily recognisable in their fields of study is seen as being very important by all the series authors. To this end the books include many examples drawn from a wide range of academic subjects and different kinds of higher education institutions. This theme of diversity is also embraced when considering the heterogeneous groups of students we now teach and the colleagues we work alongside. Students and teachers alike include people of different ages, experience, knowledge, skills, culture, language, etc., and all the books include discussion of the issues and demands this places on teachers and learners in today's universities.

In the series as a whole there is also more than half an eye trying to peer into the future – what will teaching and learning look like in 10 or 20 years' time? How will student expectations, government policy, funding streams, and new technological advances and legislation affect what happens in our learning spaces of the future? What impact will this have on the way teaching is led and managed in institutions? You will see, therefore, that many of the books do include chapters that aim to look ahead and tap into the thinking of our most innovative and creative teachers and teaching leaders in an attempt to crystal-ball gaze. So these were the original ideas underpinning the series, and my co-authors and I have tried hard to keep them in mind as we researched our topics and typed away. We really hope that you find the books to be useful and interesting, whether you are a new teacher just starting out in your teaching career, or you are an experienced teacher reflecting on your practice and reviewing what you do.

Facilitating Experiential Learning in Higher Education: Teaching and Supervising in Labs, Fieldwork, Studios, and Projects

I cannot tell you how long I have wanted this book to be included in the series. Designing and supporting hands-on, experiential learning and teaching has been an obvious gap in the the Key Guides since they were conceived in 2003. Practical teaching clearly places such specific demands on teachers and learners alike that it very much warrants and deserves this title. Siara

SERIES EDITOR INTRODUCTION

and Roland, with Cécile and Ingrid, have provided a volume that was worth the wait. They explore the many functional aspects of providing good contextualised and positioned learning in the lab, the field, or the studio, whilst explaining the underpinning theory behind the examples and case studies they share.

I am sure if you have found your way to this book that you need little convincing of the value of experiential learning within the curriculum. You will already be aware of the impact it can have on the development of skills and knowledge and indeed one's academic identity within many disciplines. The authors further illuminate this significance whilst exploring the many ways teachers can interact with their students, in practical environments, to both enhance learning and avoid common pitfalls. The book certainly offers much in the way of concrete advice and useful tips, applicable across a range of learning settings, but what characterises this book is the accessible way educational research is used to justify the recommendations given.

Designing and running a set of Year One laboratory classes was my first ever teaching job and I wish I had had this book then – I very much hope you find its pages useful and stimulating now.

Kate Exley

About the authors

Roland Tormey is a sociologist who worked in teacher education in Ireland for almost two decades. He is currently head of the Teaching Support Centre, as well as a teacher and researcher in learning sciences, at the École polytechnique fédérale de Lausanne (EPFL).

Siara Isaac trained as a chemist and is currently pursuing a degree in educational research at Lancaster University. She has worked in higher education in Canada, China, France, and Switzerland. She is currently a teaching advisor at the École polytechnique fédérale de Lausanne.

Cécile Hardebolle is an electrical engineer and computer scientist. She has taught at several grandes écoles in France, and she is currently a teaching advisor and learning scientist at the École polytechnique fédérale de Lausanne (EPFL).

Ingrid Le Duc is a social psychologist, who graduated from the London School of Economics and Political Science. She has worked in higher edu- cation in Mexico, the United Kingdom, and Switzerland. She is currently a teaching advisor at the École polytechnique fédérale de Lausanne.

Acknowledgements

We are grateful for the many people who shared their stories and experiences with us, enabling us to create richer and more contextualised examples of teaching in practical settings. Thank you all, with particular appreciation for Anne-Sophie Chauvin, Gwen Moore, and Loreta Castro Reguera Mancera.

Our thinking about teaching in higher education has benefitted from discussion with, and learning from the ideas of, many colleagues, including Roisin P. Corcoran, Simone Deparis, Julien Delisle, Dieter Dietz, Pierre Dillenbourg, Marcel Drabbels, Barbara Grisoni, Patricia Guaita, Simone Henein, Ivan Istomin, Patrick Jermann, Helena Kovacs, Marc Laperrouza, Oliver McGarr, John McKinney, John O'Reilly, Cyril Picard, Dominique Pioletti, Oriane Poupart, Vivek Ramachandran, Mark Sawley, Jürg Schiffmann, and Pascal Vuilliomenet. The teachers, doctoral assistants, and student assistants who have participated in our teaching development activities, as well as the students in the How People Learn course, have also significantly advanced our thinking. These interactions and discussions have allowed us to prototype, revise, reflect, and improve our teaching strategies for practical settings.

We would also like to recognise our families who provide support and understanding on all the late nights, early mornings, and weekends that we go missing to write.

Roland would like to thank Christine Farget and his children Charlotte, Olivia, Eloïse, and Neassa, who put up with missing weekends and distracted half conversations, and still find time to teach him new things about how people learn.

Siara is grateful for everything she learned about teaching from her parents, Soo Newberry, who always teaches with questions, and John Isaac, who put tools in her hands. And for the continued support of her husband, Jean-Philippe Roy, to keep learning new things. Siara would like to thank Mary Newberry for creating the index for this book.

Ingrid would like to thank her husband Pascal Paschoud and her children David and Laura for their encouragement and patience. And Ann Bless for her guidance and for being an inspiration.

Cécile is grateful for the support of her husband, Thierry Debleds, and for the daily inspiration of watching her son Antoine as he learns and develops new skills.

Finally, the ongoing conversations with our colleagues Ludovic Bonivento, Sylvie Bui, Ilya Eigenbrot, Isabelle Sarrade, and Nadine Stainier in the Teaching Support Centre provide fertile ground for ideas to mature and sprout into projects that encourage us all to stretch beyond our comfort zones, to fail, and to try again. Thus, we assume full responsibility for any mistakes, inaccuracies, or errors contained in this book. Writing it has been a great opportunity to learn.

Part I

Chapter 1
Introduction

EXPERIENTIAL LEARNING IN HIGHER EDUCATION

Practical, hands-on settings create opportunities for students to engage with ideas, tools, and other people in ways that can be pivotal for developing the knowledge and skills of their chosen discipline. Experiential learning in labs, studios, fieldwork, practice placements, and projects is therefore often highly impactful for students. For teachers, it can allow us to work more closely with students in a contextualised way that enables us to accompany important aspects of their development. Teaching in these settings is valuable, busy, challenging, rich, and interesting. It can be highly rewarding, but also, sometimes, frustrating. It can be time-consuming and complicated to organise, and can lead to disappointment when the results do not fulfil the promise of what could be learned.

This book is about how to teach effectively in these settings. There are as many good ways to organise practical learning as there are teachers and disciplines, so our approach here is not to propose to you a *correct* way of organising practical learning that will require you to revise the structure of your course or educational programme. Instead, we focus on the ways that teachers interact with students and look at how these interactions can help to maximise students' learning, whatever the practical setting or discipline in which you teach.

Students' experiences of practical learning in higher education can be as varied as teachers', with both strong positive and negative aspects. We start by introducing some key themes of this book with some students' accounts in their own words.

Experiential learning in labs, projects, field experiences, and studios can give students a sense of what it is like to connect to their discipline *for real* – a sense that they will rarely be able to get from lectures and readings:

DOI: 10.4324/9781003107606-1

PART I

> I'm very glad I had chosen to do the project assignment as it gave me a rough idea on what a real life project out on site would look like. The project based work enabled me to better see how the theoretical principles we have learned in class actually translate into the real world.
>
> (A student in an engineering soil mechanics course project, cited in Gratchev and Jeng [2018, 795])

It was our second experiment we extracted three components from um Excedrin. We extracted aspirin, caffeine, and acetaminophen. And I just thought that was really interesting. I felt like I was kind of like more in like the medical field like last year all we did was titrations. Like we added acids and bases and like what is this? But now the stuff we are doing is actually dealing with medicine and like separating things.

(Phyllis, a student in an organic chemistry lab, cited Galloway et al. [2016, 231])

When participating in a field activity ... I found myself becoming far more involved and emotionally attached than I would be in a lecture and Being let "loose" as it were, and being left to discover an area on our own [reconnaissance day] without influence from tour guides or those in the know (lecturers) ... allowed us to effectively bond with ... [our locations].

(Two geography students on an international field experience, cited in Simm and Marvell [2015, 606–612])

It kinda shows you the chemist perspective of chemistry. You know, like you have, when you think of like a scientist, you know, exploring stuff.

(Anna, describing participation in a chemistry lab, cited in Sandi-Urena et al. [2011, 439])

But because it is unlike learning from more familiar lectures, exercises, and reading, experiential learning poses new challenges to students as they deal with the unfamiliar complexity of real-life practice and of working in teams in their discipline:

> When you get into the classroom, there's always somewhat of a disconnect between all these idealistic theories and what's actually going on. There's just certain things you just don't even get to because you also have to deal with students ... and there are so many management issues.
>
> (Céleste, a student teacher in a fourth-grade class [nine- to ten-year-old pupils], cited in Anderson and Stillman [2010, 122])

> Some are shy, insecure ... am I selfish to wish I didn't have those people in my group? Because it's really hard to work if a group member keeps repeating she doesn't want to be here and OK, after starting off so well this morning collecting our data for the cape weavers and analysing all the data, we got to the point of writing it up which has proved absolutely impossible with lots of conflicting ideas from lots of different professors.
>
> (Two biology students describing their field work project, cited in Cotton [2009, 171])

> I was very intimidated the first, uh, project that we had, just because. I felt like we were kind of thrown in, and we had to try to swim to the surface to try to figure out what to do.
>
> (Zoey, describing participation in a chemistry lab, cited in Sandi-Urena et al. [2011])

And because it is often new, complex, challenging, and because the stakes can be high, experiential learning can generate strong positive and negative emotions that seem unfamiliar to students and which students may struggle to process:

> At the start I was fairly emotional ... Your brain is just so full of stuff like and stuff you want to talk about ... There were some instances in my class and I just used to write for pages ... I didn't want to be going home every evening, going on about it because some stuff you shouldn't be talking about outside of school.
>
> (A final year student teacher, cited in Corcoran and Tormey [2012, 164])

> It is in my mind, always in my mind. It really touched my heart. I was stressed and vulnerable.
>
> (A social work student after discovering that a client he had seen the week previously had taken his own life, cited in Barlow and Hall [2007, 403])

> Um, honestly, I hate chemistry lab. Uh, I really like my lab group and I like my TA a lot, but the chemistry lab sucks.
>
> (Anna, who was quoted above, again describing her chemistry lab, cited in Sandi-Urena et al. [2011])

> Our beds are kind of gross, they should have warned us to bring a bed spread as well as a sleeping bag and We went for a look round, saw a strange rodenty creature with green eyes which was pretty cool, a locust, and an owl and some other things which I'm not quite sure what they are

or they might have been a figment of my imagination. Doesn't matter, it was still very exciting.

(Two more biology students describing their field work project, cited in Cotton [2009, 171])

I enjoyed everything, but especially the river work and walk in the Cairngorms. It was a lot more fun than I thought it would be.

(A first-year geography student describing fieldwork, cited in Boyle et al. [2007, 312])

These accounts from students report positive and negative aspects, often mixed together. Viewed like this, from the student perspective, it is easy to see why practical learning is challenging for both students and teachers. It introduces complexity, exploration, and uncertainty. It puts students in situations where they are working at the very limits of their capabilities. It generates strong emotions like joy, hate, anxiety, disgust, stress, and pride. This richness means that teachers have an important but complex role in guiding students to encounter, engage, and learn from these experiences on multiple levels. This requires teachers to manage, in addition to the core disciplinary aspects, questions of health, safety, and general well-being that typically do not arise in lectures, tutorials, exercises, or in the library.

At the same time, these students' perspectives also make it easy to see why practical learning in labs, projects, field experiences, and studios is such an important part of learning in higher education. In lectures, students will hear about things, but in experiential learning they will hear, see, smell, touch, and taste them. Reading will often provide students with neat, ordered lists of concepts, ideas, principles, and strategies, but practical learning will help students to build connections between it all and therefore develop their ability to recall the right information at the right time to solve the problem they are facing right now. As Chapter 2 will explore, practical experiences in the field, labs, studios, and projects are central to how learners go from being a *student of* a discipline to starting a trajectory towards developing *expertise in* a discipline.

But despite its absolute centrality to students' learning of what it means to act, think, and feel like an expert in their chosen discipline, practical-based learning is still sometimes viewed as an uncomfortable appendage to students' learning in higher education. For some higher education managers this may be because of the high costs involved when compared to the false economies of lecture-based teaching. But the issue also probably goes deeper than just cost, and may relate to the social value that is placed on *head*, *hands*, and *heart* in contemporary societies and to the unfortunate tendency to see *theory* and *practice* as being separate domains. That universities tend to value *thinking* over *acting* and *feeling* is evident in, for example, the centrality of Bloom's cognitive learning outcomes to so many discussions of higher education reform and development, and the comparative neglect of learning in the affective and psychomotor domains, which are often treated as an afterthought, if they are treated at all (this is an idea we will return to in Chapter 2).

A key idea underpinning this book is that practical learning should not be an afterthought assigned marginal status in our educational programmes and in our understandings of what it means to be a teacher in higher education. Rather it should be central to how we teach our students the disciplinary competence that we want them to develop, and how we put them on a pathway towards expertise.

WHO IS THIS BOOK FOR?

This book is intended to help both novice and more experienced teachers in practical settings to develop their teaching skills.

By *practical settings* we specifically mean settings which place students *doing* or *experiencing* at the centre of the course, such as projects, labs, field work, professional practice placements, and studios. Many of these settings look different in different disciplines, for example field experiences are different in geography and in teacher education, while labs may well be dissimilar in electronic engineering and psychology. Although each of these settings is quite different, however, they typically share an underlying focus on learning through unifying – rather than separating – experience, thought, feeling, and acting. To avoid being too repetitive, we will use the terms *learning by doing*, *experiential learning*, *hands-on learning*, and *learning in practical settings* as synonymous in this book.

THE STRUCTURE AND APPROACH OF THIS BOOK

One aim of this book is to explore *what to teach* in practical settings. It may seem that the answer to this is obvious: you want students to learn the skills of your discipline. But research on the differences between experts and novices highlights both the breadth of things which are implicit in expertise and also helps to illuminate the process of learning towards expertise. This suggests some key ideas for how to learn effectively in practical settings. This is addressed in Part I.

Chapter 2 explores the big goals of learning in higher education, and suggests that ultimately your goal is to help students on the pathway towards *expertise* in your discipline. It looks at what it means to think, act, and feel like an expert across a range of disciplines and explores what the research evidence says about the importance of experiential learning for helping students to develop expertise.

Chapter 3 looks at teaching and learning in a range of practical settings, and highlights some features which are common across different types of experiential courses. It highlights that, in experiential learning, students learn from not only having experiences, but from reflecting on them, generalising from them, and from trying to reapply those generalisations to practice. The ideas in Part I are important to set up the following chapters, since how to teach depends a lot on what is being taught.

The central aim of this book is to provide concrete and practical advice on *how to teach and facilitate learning* in practical settings. The heart of this book is Part II, which focuses on helping teachers to develop their capacity to teach using four skills which can be applied in a range of settings. The teaching practices presented are:

- prompting students to think for themselves through asking questions (Chapter 4),
- responding effectively to students' work (Chapter 5),
- providing good explanations (Chapter 6),
- managing the learning environment to minimise disruption and maximise learning (Chapter 7).

These central chapters are both evidence-informed and practical. The structure of each of the chapters in Part II is intended to replicate in some small way how students learn in practical settings. As such, each of these chapters starts with an *experience* (in this case a vicarious experience in the form of a case study for you to analyse), before introducing some concepts and ideas which can help to make sense of the experience. These concepts and ideas are illustrated with examples drawn from labs, studios, field experiences, and projects, and you will be encouraged to apply them to your own practice via Reflection points. At the end of each chapter in Part II, you will have the chance to test your learning through analysing a final case study.

A third aim of this book is to clarify *why we recommend some approaches to teaching* and not others. Underpinning the teaching approaches we describe is the idea that *good teaching* is not the same as *good telling*. Perhaps the most fundamental finding of decades of research in learning sciences is that learning is an effortful process which occurs when learners actively process information. So unless the student is thinking about experiences and ideas, applying them, trying to use them, trying to see how they relate to other experiences and ideas, and revisiting them again and again, they are probably not learning, even if the teacher or the teaching assistant is explaining really well. The evidence which underpins the teaching methods we propose is explored in Part III.

Chapter 8 summarises the findings of cognitive sciences research as it applies to teaching in practical settings in higher education, and Chapter 9 presents an overview of research about how social contexts influence and support students. Any investigation of higher education teaching will normally look at *what* you want to achieve, *how* to do so, and *why* the approach is likely to work. That is the order in which we have presented these things in this book. Those who are interested in understanding why particular teaching approaches work before going on to apply them in practice may want to start with Part III before going back to Parts I and II.

The final chapter in Part III serves to draw together key ideas from the book by looking at how you can apply what you have learned about expertise to your own development of teaching skills. It approaches learning to teach in practical settings as being an example of practical learning, and shows how you can apply the principles and ideas described in the book to develop your own teaching.

We noted above that experiential learning in practical settings typically shares an underlying focus on learning through unifying experience, thought, feeling, and acting. This concern underpins not just the content of this book but also how we have written it. Throughout the book, but especially in Part II, we try to ensure that the ideas presented are clearly linked to examples drawn from real-life teaching and learning. In addition to examples in the text we also do this in two other ways:

- *Case studies* are accounts of lab, studio, project, or field experience situations that contextualise and illustrate key ideas and practices. The defining characteristic of case studies is that you do not simply read them, you *study* them, using the case analysis questions provided. Case studies are based on interviews by the authors or on our own experiences. In some cases the interviewee is named, and in others the case is a fictionalised composite of multiple teachers' experiences (these more fictionalised accounts are identified in the text).
- *Spotlight* boxes provide examples of how particular ideas or practices can be applied in context. They are similar to case studies; however they do not include case analysis questions. Most are based on previously published research, and a few come from author interviews and experiences.

Alongside seeing clear illustrations of how the ideas in this book look in practice, it is also important that you can apply these ideas to your own practice. Throughout the book we do this in three other ways:

- *Reflection Points* ask you to apply the ideas found in the text of this book, often to your own life and teaching practice.
- *Action Summaries* at the end of Chapters 4–7 and 10 distil the main findings from learning research on a particular teaching skill into a few readily applicable ideas.
- *Further Reading* sections highlight a couple of references for readers who would like to deepen their exploration of key ideas from the chapter.

As Chapter 2 will explore, one of the challenges in education is that everyone has some experience of it and everyone has some theory about how it does or should work. In order to emphasise that the approach we propose here is not just one more theory among many, we generally avoid referring to *educational theories* and focus instead on *evidence about learning*. Of course, there are many areas in learning where the evidence remains unclear, and we do not want to suggest that there is no space left for debate and discussion. But we do suggest that when there is clear research evidence on a particular topic, it would be better if teachers drew on it when planning how to support students' learning in practical settings. This book will help you do exactly this – it is a practical guide to implementing evidence-informed strategies for teaching in experiential settings. So let's get started.

REFERENCES

Anderson, L., and Stillman, J. (2010). Opportunities to teach and learn in high needs schools: Student teachers' experiences in urban placements, *Urban Education* 45(2): 109–141. https://doi.org/10.1177/0042085909354445.

Barlow, C., and Hall, B.L. (2007). 'What about Feelings?': A study of emotion and tension in social work field education, *Social Work Education* 26(4): 399–413. https://doi.org/10.1080/02615470601081712.

Boyle, A., Maguire, S., Martin, A., Milsom, C., Nash, R., Rawlinson, S., Turner, A., Wurthmann, S., and Conchie, S. (2007). Fieldwork is good: The student perception and the affective domain, *Journal of Geography in Higher Education* 31(2): 299–317. https://doi.org/10.1080/03098260601063628.

Corcoran, R.P., and Tormey, R. (2012). *Developing Emotionally Competent Teachers; Emotional Intelligence and Pre-Service Teacher Education*. Oxford: Peter Lang.

Cotton, D.R.E. (2009). Field biology experiences of undergraduate students: The impact of novelty space, *Journal of Biological Education* 43(4): 169–174. https://doi.org/10.1080/00219266.2009.9656178.

Galloway, K.R., Malakpa, Z., and Lowery Bretz, S. (2016). Investigating affective experiences in the undergraduate Chemistry Laboratory: Students' perceptions of control and responsibility, *Journal of Chemical Education* 93(2): 227–238. https://doi.org/10.1021/acs.jchemed.5b00737.

Gratchev, I., and Jeng, D.-S. (2018). Introducing a project-based assignment in a traditionally taught engineering course, *European Journal of Engineering Education* 43(5): 788–799. https://doi.org/10.1080/03043797.2018.1441264.

Sandi-Urena, S., Cooper, M.M., Gatlin, T.A., and Bhattacharyya, G. (2011). Students' experience in a general chemistry cooperative problem based laboratory, *Chemistry Education Research and Practice* 12(4): 434–442. https://doi.org/10.1039/C1RP90047A.

Simm, D., and Marvell, A. (2015). Gaining a "sense of place": Students' affective experiences of place leading to transformative learning on international fieldwork, *Journal of Geography in Higher Education* 39(4): 595–616. https://doi.org/10.1080/03098265.2015.1084608.

Chapter 2

How students develop disciplinary expertise

INTRODUCTION

It might seem that the goal of higher education is obvious: we want students to learn the things we teach, whether that is geography, dance, accountancy, management, or another discipline. Generally, we want students to do more than just learn things; however, we want them to be able to use the things they learn after they leave higher education. And, since we know that students' learning has not finished on the day they graduate, we also want them to be able to continue to improve after they leave higher education. This chapter provides a way of thinking about these questions of learning, using learning, continuing to learn, and about how they apply in specific disciplines. It does this by exploring what it means to become an *expert* in a particular domain.

There are a number of ways in which those interested in teaching and learning have approached the question of what happens when people learn. One way is to carry out research on people while they are learning. This kind of research is valuable in giving a picture of what happens *during* the process of learning (as you will see, Chapters 8 and 9 rely heavily on such studies). But such studies typically cannot follow people for months or years, and can only tell us about relatively short-term learning of very specific skills or knowledge. Since, in higher education, it is expected that people will learn lots of inter-related knowledge and skills over an extended period of time, there is a lot of important learning that we cannot see from such studies. A second way to carry out research on learning is to look at those who *have learned* a lot about a given domain (experts) and to compare them with those who have learned little in the same domain (novices). The idea is that if we better understand what makes experts different from novices, we can gain an understanding of how to help learners develop expertise and about the role of experiential learning in labs, studios, fieldwork, and projects in that process. That is the focus of this chapter.

It is important to note that expertise takes a long time to develop – the figure of 10,000 hours is sometimes presented in popular psychology as an estimate of the time taken to become an expert. While, as this chapter will explore, it would be misleading to rely too heavily on the idea of 10,000 hours, it nonetheless does provide a good indication of the order of magnitude involved in developing expertise. To put this in more everyday terms, 10,000 hours translate into roughly 3 hours practice per day for 10 years. This is far more than the amount of time most students spend studying in a higher education degree. This means that we should not expect that students will be experts in our domain by the time they finish their degree. Nonetheless, studies on expertise can provide interesting insights into how people begin the process of becoming experts and can shed some light on how we can develop students' current level of competence and set them on the road towards developing expertise.

The goals of this chapter are:

- to clarify what is meant by *expertise*,
- to describe the differences between expert performance and novice performance,
- to explore how people develop and become experts,
- to apply these insights to look at how higher education students can and should learn in practical settings such as fieldwork, labs, projects, and studios.

It is worth pointing out that the focus on *expertise* in this chapter is a little unusual for a book on learning in higher education. Many books on higher education focus on the idea that the goal is that students will develop *understanding* of the content by engaging in *deep* (as opposed to *surface*) approaches to learning. This idea is made explicit, for example, in the title of a 2009 book by the highly influential UK scholar Noel Entwistle called *Teaching for Understanding at University: Deep Approaches and Distinctive Ways of Thinking* (2009), but is equally present in the work of other highly cited writers of higher education texts including Paul Ramsden (2003) and John Biggs (2003). Indeed, the *deep/surface* model has become so widespread and so deeply rooted that it has entered into the folk culture of higher education and become almost a common-sense assumption. It may seem strange, therefore, that this chapter (indeed this book as a whole) eschews the use of the *deep/surface* model for thinking about learning in higher education. It does this for a number of reasons.

First, the *deep/surface* distinction originally arose in part from studies of how students learn from reading and in part from studies of how people memorise and recall information. Although the *deep/surface* model has generally been applied much more widely to refer to a broader set of learning situations, researchers have questioned the applicability of the *deep/surface* approaches model to learning in settings other than learning in a lecture or by reading. For example Jennifer Case and Delia Marshall (2004) have highlighted that the exclusive focus on *understanding* and *thinking* in the *deep/surface* approaches model seems to be a bad fit for disciplines which are focused on learning skills which require the development of routines, such as mathematical problem solving (in their case, in engineering). They suggest that the model does not pay sufficient attention to the kinds of procedural or algorithmic learning that are important in many disciplines. Learning in practical settings typically includes a focus on practising and improving both physical behaviours and problem-solving routines. The *deep/surface* metaphor is, therefore, not a great fit for making sense of the full range of things that students are expected to learn in practical settings, which include changes in perceptual abilities as well as physical and intellectual skills and emotional competences. This is not to suggest that students don't learn to *know* and *understand* in practical settings (indeed, while this chapter doesn't use the *deep/surface* approaches to learning model we do refer to deeply processing information). The point here is simply that practical learning includes (but is much wider than) thinking, knowing, and understanding.

A second reason for eschewing the use of the *deep/surface* model is that, although it is often presented as a research-based model, the research evidence to support the idea that deep approaches to learning are associated with increased student attainment is actually quite thin. Roland Tormey (2014), for example, has reviewed the empirical evidence to support the approaches to learning models and has found many of them show only a weak and inconsistent association between deep approaches and actual measures of learning. This is possibly because, as the previous paragraph notes, a deep and integrated conceptual understanding of content knowledge is only one of the things we expect students to develop in higher education. Because there are different things we want students to learn, there are different learning processes that are relevant in different settings. Put simply, a *surface* approach may be the most appropriate in some situations and a *deep* approach more useful in others. What is probably more important than having a *deep* or *surface* approach to learning is choosing the right approach for the learning goals in question. Within the approaches to learning model, this is sometimes called having a *strategic approach* to learning and is generally something that is not promoted within the approaches to learning model. As this chapter will explore, being strategic is not a bad thing for learners to do. In Chapter 3, we will explore the related idea of *metacognition* as being something that is regarded as generally quite important in practical learning.

A third reason for eschewing the *deep/surface* metaphor is that there are powerful alternative ways of thinking about learning which tend to get hidden by the dominance of the *deep/surface* metaphor in higher education writing. In education studies more widely, writers on teaching and learning have over the last 20 years turned to the notion of *expertise* as a way of thinking about the goals of education (Bransford et al. 2000). While this focus on *expertise* has not become prominent in higher education texts, as this chapter will explore, it actually provides a good fit for thinking about the kinds of skills that students are generally expected to develop in higher education labs, studios, fieldwork, and projects. It also integrates ideas about the importance of metacognition and of the social dimensions of learning. *Expertise* also provides a useful framework for thinking about how students learn and develop those skills over time.

When defending the approaches to learning model over two decades ago, Noel Entwistle wrote that the approaches to learning framework would have to suffice until "other theories emerge which provide equally valid and useful descriptions of the teaching-learning process in higher education" (1997, 217). This chapter focuses on the concept of expertise as providing a more pertinent description of the teaching-learning process for higher education fieldwork, labs, studios, and projects.

Although this chapter does draw on lots of examples of expertise in different domains, it is not possible for one chapter to describe how the idea applies to every domain. We have, therefore, included a series of reflection activities in this chapter (and throughout this book) that invite you to think about how the concept applies in your own domain. It is worth taking some time to think about each of these Reflection points and perhaps to write down your answers and discuss with colleagues. As we will explore in Chapters 3 and 10, you will get more out of reflection activities such as these if you invest some time in them.

WHAT IS EXPERTISE?

The ultimate goal of educating people is that they become good at performing the kinds of tasks that are required in their discipline. This is what is generally referred to as expertise. Expertise can then be defined as referring to "superior reproducible performance on representative tasks" (Ericsson 2018, 4).

Although short, this definition contains a number of important features that are worth identifying.

First, experts are not simply *better* or *more clever* people: they are better than other people at the specific types of tasks that are associated with a given discipline. For a nurse this might mean assessing the level of bleeding in a patient after a surgery, and identifying if that is a cause for concern, given the profile of the patient in question and the surgery they have undergone. For a school teacher it might mean being able to rapidly identify the type of thinking a student will need in order to solve a particular problem and to automatically ask the right questions to elicit this kind of thinking in the student. For a musician, it may mean being able to perform, without errors, technically complex pieces of music in highly pressurised *one-shot* performances.

Research on expertise shows that while differences in performance on these kinds of tasks by novices may be associated with measures of *intelligence* or *talent*, the role of talent or intelligence seems to diminish over time, and the learning process which a person has undergone becomes more important than *natural talent* in determining expertise (Ericsson et al. 1993). For educators, this is a heartening finding: experts are not born, they are formed through the way they learn. This, in turn, means teachers and teaching can make a difference. It is worth bearing in mind, however, that the corollary of this is that being an expert in one domain does not make one an expert in all domains: expert chemists still think like novices when faced with problems in political science, for example (Voss and Post 1988).

A second feature of the definition above is the idea that expertise is defined in terms of ability to complete *representative tasks*. As will be evident from the *representative tasks* described in the previous paragraph, expertise does involve knowing and understanding one's discipline, but it also involves:

- Bringing to mind without effort the right information in the right context (like the nurse who needs to juggle many contextually specific variables when deciding how much bleeding is problematic for a specific patient after a specific surgery but is able to do so fluently because the right information comes to mind in the right context).
- Responses which have become so automated that they can happen before we have time to think about them (like the school teacher who thinks of the right question without having to stop and weigh up the situation because pausing to think about everything when you are in a lab managing both 25 young people and the subject matter while the clock is ticking is simply not an option).

- An ability to perform intricate or physically complex and demanding tasks (like the musician's faultless playing of a guitar or piano or the nurse's deft touch when examining a patient).
- Being able to perform under the kinds of pressure which would elicit extreme stress and other strong emotions for non-experts (something which is evident in all three of these examples).

Expertise then means going beyond knowing and understanding, to also include physical skill, habituated automated processes, an ability to respond to one's context, and situationally specific emotional competence. Expertise is a whole-person – often a whole-body – experience.

HOW EXPERTS DIFFER FROM NOVICES

Early studies of the differences between experts and novices tended to focus on areas like chess, music, classical dance, or sport. These are all areas in which it was quite easy to identify which people consistently performed better than others. Later on, researchers also looked at other kinds of domains (like computer programming, medicine and surgery, nursing, teaching, design, and social research) in which there is no simple metric for what constitutes expertise but in which, nonetheless, other experts in the domain tend to *know it when they see it*. While there are differences between expertise in these two types of domain, there are also considerable similarities.

Experts see important patterns

Experts in a domain perceive the world differently to novices in that domain. One of the first studies of expertise looked at how expert chess players' observations of chess games differed from merely good players. While it was hypothesised that experts would be more analytical in assessing the full range of potential moves, what the researchers found in fact was that experts didn't just consider a lot of moves and consider them carefully, they also tended to *see* better quality moves. This is also evident when watching experts play lightning chess – they identify good moves that merely good players do not see.

This superior ability to perceive meaningful patterns of information is not limited to expert chess players but, it turns out, is a more general attribute of experts. Indeed, as Spotlight 2.1 shows, experts can literally see things that novices do not. Studies with expert and novice teachers, for example, have found that when asked to watch videos of class activities, experts and novices differ in what they see (Sabers et al. 1991). While novices focused on student behaviour and misbehaviour, for example, experts tended to notice how teacher behaviour contributes to the underlying reasons for student misbehaviour which in turn meant that expert teachers were able to describe potential solution strategies. Similar findings emerge from other studies on expertise in domains like electronic circuit design, radiography, and physics – experts perceive meaningful patterns where novices do not.

> ## SPOTLIGHT 2.1 – HOW DOES THE PERCEPTION OF VISUAL ARTISTS DIFFER FROM THAT OF ART NOVICES?
>
> How are visual artists cognitively different from other people? This is the question posed in a study by Aaron Kozbelt (2001) which looked at how art or design students differed in their perception of visual stimuli when compared to students who were majoring in other domains.
>
> Participants in the study were given out of focus photographs and incomplete line drawings for which they had to identify the subject of the picture (what is referred to as a *Gestalt* task). They were also asked to look at geometric shapes where they had to identify an embedded simple shape, or which they had to mentally rotate in three dimensions. The art and design students clearly outperformed art novices on all four tasks. For example, while novices were less able to recognise the subject of a drawing in which some of the lines has been removed, visual art majors were able to recognise the *hidden pattern* that allowed them to identify the subject of the drawing.
>
> The superior performance of art and design students then was not only their better ability to draw or represent an image, but also in their ability to visually analyse the image. While the art and design students' ability to draw involved additional skills alongside visual processing (such as fine motor control skills), their perceptual ability was highly linked to their ability to draw.
>
> Kozbelt concludes that the reason why the art experts outperformed novices so much is probably because of the vast experience in processing visual information which they had built up over years of practising drawing and other artistic activities.

Experts recall knowledge from their domain quickly, and they complete representative tasks fluently

It is perhaps obvious to say that experts know a lot about their domain; however it is nonetheless important to restate because it is sometimes assumed that in a networked age when a vast supply of knowledge is available at a student's finger tips, the student no longer needs to learn *stuff* but rather be able to navigate and find *stuff* when they need to. But experts don't just see and think differently to novices, they also know more and recall what they know with greater fluency.

One difference between how novices and experts remember disciplinary knowledge is that experts' recall tends to retrieve a group of related pieces of information together. For example physics experts are likely to remember multiple kinematics formulae together, whereas novices remember them one at a time. This gives some insight into how experts store knowledge: for experts information is typically organised and interconnected. So, the expert physicist's memory has a built-in link between the kinematics equation for displacement and those for velocity, and when they are recalled the connections between each make it easy for the expert to navigate between them. For the novice, these are stored as multiple separate pieces of information that are recalled one by one. For the novice it is more difficult to toggle between different pieces of information because each one ends up being treated separately.

In addition to quickly recalling what they know, experts also complete physical and mental tasks in their domain with greater fluency. Expert typists type more quickly and with fewer errors than novices, and expert school teachers generally generate better questions to ask students without having to think too much about it. For experts, the characteristic physical and mental processes of their domain can be thought of as like learning to ride a bicycle: in the early stages of learning to ride a bicycle the cyclist needs to pay a great deal of attention to how they pedal, steer, and shift their weight. After some time, however, the physical processes become automated and the cyclist no longer needs to pay attention to perform the task and they can cycle fluently while observing the traffic or enjoying the scenery. Likewise, because experts have had a great deal of practice at doing the things that are characteristic of their domain, these processes have become automated to such a degree that they can be performed fluently and automatically, leaving the expert with more free mental space.

The automation of processes like this moves experts beyond the realm of knowing and understanding: just as the cyclist will typically find it very hard to explain exactly how much pressure they put on each pedal at each moment in a single revolution of their pedals, experts will often find it very difficult to describe their intuitive decisions and automated processes.

> **REFLECTION POINT 2.1**
>
> In your discipline, what kinds of patterns do experts perceive that novices do not?
>
> What are some of the *representative tasks* of your discipline, that is, the things that people in your discipline can do fluently that novices to your discipline cannot?
>
> What are the opportunities for students learning your discipline to practice (even in a simplified way) these representative tasks?

Experts have characteristic ways of thinking about problems in their domain

Experts approach problems in their domain in a way that is different to how non-experts approach them. This can be seen, for example, by looking at how social scientists problem solve. In James Voss and colleagues' study, social scientists and social science novices (a group which included both undergraduate students and expert chemists) were asked to solve the problem of improving crop productivity in the former Soviet Union (1983). Social scientists tended to draw on their domain knowledge to provide an analysis of the potential causes of low productivity, to decompose the problem into a small number of contributing factors, and to convert the analysed problem into one that could be solved. In identifying solutions they also analysed what problems may be encountered in those solutions. Experts also tended to explain and justify their solution as part of the problem-solving process (perhaps in recognition that there are multiple contested solutions available to social scientific problems and, as such, justification of a solution is itself part of the solution process). Social science novices on the other hand tended to describe the causes for the problem at a very concrete and specific level and tended not to analyse or elaborate the initial problem to any real extent. Being a problem-solving expert in a different domain (such as chemistry) did not really make a difference in performance in social scientific problem solving (Voss et al. 1983). However, chemistry experts do engage in expert problem-solving strategies within their own discipline (Randles and Overton 2015). In short, expertise does not readily transfer from one domain to another.

Although experts remember things and perform the characteristic processes of their discipline quicker and with greater fluency than novices, they paradoxically often spend longer analysing problems in their domain than do novices. While novices will often *jump in* to a problem and quickly generate solutions which they then try out, experts will typically spend more time building a mental representation of the problem which allows them to choose more productive solution strategies. This is what was evident in the study of social scientists cited in the previous paragraph, but the same pattern is found in looking at other domains such as engineering or physics (this is further explored in Spotlight 2.2). Experts know how to analyse problems in their domain, and they have the habit of doing so without really having to remind themselves to do so. Novices tend to *rush in where angels fear to tread*.

> ## SPOTLIGHT 2.2 – EXPERTISE AS DECISION MAKING IN SCIENCE AND ENGINEERING
>
> How do experts in science and engineering work, and what does this tell us about how we should teach science and engineering students? This was the question asked by a research team led by the Nobel Prize-winning physicist Carl Wieman at Stanford University. While higher education teaching often emphasises the *content knowledge* of disciplines, their intuition was that the practice of experts in a discipline could be described in terms of a reasonably small number of *decisions* which experts take when solving problems.
>
> In their study, they interviewed 31 expert professionals from ten different science, engineering, and medicine disciplines about how they solved authentic problems in their work. These problems were typically quite different from textbook problems in that they had no clear solution method and typically involved making judgements based on limited information.
>
> What emerged from the analysis conducted by Argenta Price and her colleagues was that expertise across these different domains involved making a limited set of decisions (they identified 29). These decisions could be organised under the headings that are often used in textbook descriptions of research or problem solving, such as selecting the goals, framing the problem, planning the solution process, interpreting information, and so on. However, the research team noted that the reality is far messier than the linear or cyclical way in which these stages are often presented:
>
>> the process is far less orderly and sequential than ... any characterization of an orderly "scientific method". There are flexible connections between decisions and repeated iterations – jumping

back to the same type of decision multiple times in the solution process, often prompted by reflection as new information and insights are developed.

(Price et al. 2020)

Their focus on *decisions* did not mean that they saw *disciplinary knowledge* as being unimportant: while the same decisions are seen in different disciplines, they may look very different because these decisions are shaped by the predictive framework provided by the theory and knowledge of the discipline in question. It is this which allows the experts to identify what is important, to run *mental simulations*, to make predictions, and to interpret information.

The researchers also noted that, while they focused on decisions, experts themselves drew attention to the importance of teamwork and interpersonal skills in advancing their problem solving. These skills are sometimes ignored by cognitive researchers but in fact represent important elements of problem solving, as was strongly emphasised by the experts in this study.

Price and her colleagues propose that their model of *expertise-as-decision-making* can be used to improve the education of scientists and engineers by highlighting a failure of traditional programmes to engage students in complete problem solving. They propose that alongside the focus on knowing and understanding, education should provide "concentrated practice, with feedback, at making the specific decisions identified here in relevant contexts" (Price et al. 2020). They suggest that it is the practice students have had making decisions, rather than simply the content they have seen, that ultimately shapes how students learn to solve problems like experts.

REFLECTION POINT 2.2

What kinds of problems do experts in your discipline solve?
Can you identify differences between the approaches used by experts and novices in your discipline to solve these kinds of problems?
What opportunities do students in your discipline have to practice these distinctive approaches to problem solving?

Experts remember the right information in a given context

Experts know a lot and can remember it quickly but only a small subset of what an expert knows is relevant in any given situation. If an expert had to search through all their knowledge to find which information was relevant at any given time, this would take time and mental effort. But this is not generally what happens. Instead, experts typically call to mind the information they need for their situation. Studies on chess experts, for example, have found that expert players do not necessarily consider more moves than do novices but they do consider *better* moves, that is, moves which are more likely to be appropriate for the circumstance in which they find themselves. This suggests that when knowledge is stored by experts it is linked not simply to other ideas and concepts but also to memories of particular contexts in which that knowledge is used. This is referred to as knowledge being *conditionalised*. While a student may learn a great deal of knowledge from a lecture or from reading, it is in practical learning environments that the knowledge becomes conditionalised and linked to contexts which in turn transforms the knowledge from abstract learning to practically useful learning.

Such conditionalisation of knowledge means that it can be readily remembered in contexts like those in which the knowledge or skill was previously used or practised. However, a corollary is that people often find it harder to remember relevant knowledge if they are in a situation other than the one in which they have learned or practised it. This is seen, for example in a study from the early 1990s at a time when microsurgery techniques (that is, surgery in which the operation is guided visually with the use of a microscope) were being introduced. In this study a surgeon who was experienced in open surgery did not perform better than a surgical trainee when they were asked to perform in the microsurgery environment. Although the experienced surgeon had a wealth of experience and rich knowledge about the suturing or stitching procedure, this was not transferable to the microsurgery environment because it had been developed and used with particular reference to open surgery (Starkes et al. 1993).

One of the implications of the contextualised nature of knowledge for learning in higher education is that it is difficult for students to take what they have learned in a lecture or a book and to recall, apply, or use it in the kinds of situations where experts need to practice. Experiential learning in labs, studios, fieldwork, exercises, and projects is often crucial for enabling students to move from knowing what experts know, to performing like experts perform.

> **REFLECTION POINT 2.3**
>
> In your discipline, what are the contexts where graduates are expected to perform after leaving higher education?
> Are there opportunities for students to experience performing your disciplines' representative tasks in these kinds of contexts during their studies?

Experts monitor themselves better than novices

When experts make mistakes they tend to be more aware of it than are novices. In studies of experts in scientific domains, for example, experts tended to be better at judging how difficult a problem is likely to be, they are better at knowing when their solution is and is not going to work, and they are better at checking their solutions. When they don't understand something, experts are typically better than novices at identifying why they don't understand. When faced with challenging texts, experts typically ask more questions than novices, who tend to ask more questions when faced with less challenging texts. This self-checking is seen in domains other than sciences: studies that have looked at how people develop expertise in piano playing (Oura and Hatano 2001) have found that among those learning the piano, successful learners tended to check and refine their performance with the perspective of the audience in mind. Less successful learners (who were still at novice level despite similar amounts of practice time) focused on performing accurately and smoothly without taking the audience into account.

This self-monitoring of their own learning and performance is part of metacognition, an idea that will be explored in the next chapter. The increased metacognitive capacity of experts seems to reflect the depth of the experts' knowledge and experience, in that the expert has already seen more problems like the one they are facing and so has more experience against which to judge how difficult the problem will be and may be more aware of potential difficulties that may be encountered. The enhanced metacognitive capacity also seems to reflect the discipline-specific problem-solving processes, in that experts seem to include error checking as a habitual and normal process when solving problems in their domain.

Experts feel differently than novices

So far, this section has dealt primarily with cognitive (*knowing*) and procedural (*doing*) dimensions of expertise. This, in a sense, reflects the fact that many studies of expertise originated in cognitive psychology and this discipline had little interest in emotions. For example, in the 470-page collection called *The Nature of Expertise*, edited by leading expertise researchers Michelene Chi et al. (1988), the word *emotion* appears only five times and in each case it refers to the emotions of a client or a patient and not the emotions of the expert in question. This perhaps reflects a broader trend in everyday, common sense, or folk theories which tend to link expertise and learning to *thinking and doing* rather than to *feeling*.

But, for many experts, their expert performance involves considerable emotional work. Studies on professional writers, for example, show that they experience considerable frustrations and anxieties. Professional writers need to produce thousands and tens of thousands of words of text and to do so even when it is not fun or enjoyable. When working on challenging writing tasks, writers need to develop the capacity to tolerate negative emotional states as well as the ability to enjoy positive emotional experiences. Professional writers typically use a range of strategies for managing the emotion of writing, such as following particular routines and schedules, managing work in relation to realistic deadlines, and avoiding becoming too emotionally engaged by their own writing (Kellogg 2018).

While professional writers manage their own emotional process, other disciplines also require managing the emotions of others. In disciplines such as physiotherapy, nursing, teaching, or social work, for example, expert performance depends in part on managing other people (see Spotlight 2.3). However, the role of experts' emotions extends beyond managing relationships because experts are often in positions of power and therefore must take responsibility for decisions which affect the lives of others. In nursing or physiotherapy, for example, mistakes can have real and sometimes serious consequences for the patient or client. Research with nurses at different stages in their learning has found that unless nurses stay emotionally engaged and accept both the joy of a job well done and the remorse of mistakes, they stagnate in their practices and have an increased risk of burnout (Benner 1984).

Nor are emotions confined to the *creative* and *caring* professions: technical professions are also replete with emotional practices (even if the dominant narrative in those disciplines is often that that they are rational and *not* emotional). The mathematician Andrew Wiles (2016), famous for solving a centuries-old mathematical problem called Fermat's Last Theorem, has put it like this:

> what you have to handle when you start doing mathematics as an older child or as an adult is accepting this state of being stuck. People don't get used to that. Some people find this very stressful. Even people who are very good at mathematics sometimes find this hard to get used to and they feel that's where they're failing. But it isn't: it's part of the process and you have to accept [and] learn to enjoy that process. Yes, you don't understand [something at the moment] but you have faith that over time you will understand – you have to go through this.

Indeed, participants in technical or scientific projects often experience an emotional process which starts with excitement at a new project, and which turns to frustration as the complexity of the task becomes more apparent, then depression or anger as the complexity of the task leaves them feeling lost and unsupported, before finally moving back towards pride in their achievement. Higher education teachers with project courses may well be familiar with this emotional journey from what they read in student course feedback – midterm feedback to teachers on semester projects is often far more negative than the student feedback at the end of the semester when the students have re-emerged from the swamp of despair and are often satisfied with what they have achieved.

We noted above that power and emotion go hand in hand (a theme we will return to in Chapter 7). Disciplines like engineering, for example, are often involved in designing solutions which can have extremely negative impacts on the lives of others. Sometimes this negative impact may be due to accidental but avoidable design failures, such as the 1998 German Intercity express train crash which killed 101 people and which was caused by a wheel design that was not adequately tested at high speeds and by safety norms not adapted to the wheel design in question. Sometimes the negative impact is *by design*, such as the low overpasses built over the parkways on Long Island in New York between the 1930s and 1970s which were designed to prevent busses and the people who travelled on them (who were more likely to be African-American) from accessing the beaches (Van de Poel and Royakkers 2011). There is a growing recognition within the engineering profession that one factor in reducing these engineering failures is to improve the extent to which engineers experience the emotions associated with the risks they generate, and empathise with those affected by their designs (Roeser 2012; Tormey 2020).

SPOTLIGHT 2.3 – MANAGING EMOTIONS WHEN LEARNING TO TEACH

Students who are learning to be school teachers are not simply learning to develop content knowledge in their pupils but also learning how to develop the pupils' motivation and social and emotional skills. In addition to managing the emotions of their students, teachers are also managing their own relationship with the students. As James Stigler and Kevin Miller put it,

> teachers cannot achieve their goals without the cooperation of students. Chess experts don't require the cooperation of the chessboard. The chessboard, the musical instrument, and so on are invariants in many domains of expertise. But in education, teachers are in a very real sense at the mercy of students, and policy-makers and curriculum designers.
>
> (2018, 431)

On top of these extremely complex activities, student teachers are also themselves learners and so are struggling to apply what they have learned in education lectures to the complex and changing mosaic of the classroom. While experienced teachers have generally developed a set of automated responses and contextualised memories which mean they can generally act appropriately without thinking too much about what they are doing, student teachers are often faced with the extremely frustrating challenge of trying to figure out what knowledge they need to apply in which situation and how to do so. As if this was not enough, student teachers are also being judged and graded on their performance in this setting. And these judgements are not simply like other grades because, unlike in traditional courses, they are now being judged on how they perform the representative tasks of the profession they have chosen. While other grades may feel like a judgement on their intellect, their performance on teaching practice can feel like a judgement on their whole identity.

Student teachers, then, bear the double emotional weight of managing the responsibility for the emotional life of students while at the same time managing their own considerable emotional turmoil. Research by Roisin Corcoran and Roland Tormey (2012) on the teaching practice experience of advanced beginner teachers found they often described it as a rollercoaster of emotions and that they described the experience as being marked by anger, anxiety, boredom, disgust, sadness, and fear, as well as by positive emotions such as love and joy.

They found that advanced novices regulated the emotion in their practice using a range of strategies. For example, they specifically designed lessons with a view to managing what emotions the lessons might generate, and sometimes adapted lessons on the fly depending on the emotional state of their class. Recognising that students had not been able to go outside during the break due to bad weather, for example, led one of the students to adapt the afternoon's lessons to take account of this – something which, he noted, he had never considered as a novice student teacher. Other advanced beginner teachers highlighted the need to manage the way they conveyed their emotions in class, while some discussed the way in which emotional responses were often reciprocal and that a teacher's frustration was likely to be mirrored by an equivalent response from pupils. Quite a few of the advanced beginner teachers described using emotion regulation strategies such as using relaxation techniques, self-talk, or rethinking a situation to see if it could be reconsidered in a more positive or constructive way (an approach called *cognitive reappraisal*).

Expertise is social

If the emotional dimensions of expertise were typically overlooked by cognitive scientists, so too were the social dimensions. Yet expertise is an intensely social phenomenon. Harry Collins and Robert Evans (2018, 25) for example identify that while *primary source knowledge* can be attained from watching lectures or reading textbooks and articles, this will not lead to the kinds of procedural fluency, contextualised knowledge, and emotional competences that are characteristics of expertise. Reaching expertise, they note, depends on "immersion in the relevant community as this is the only way to acquire the specialist tacit knowledge needed to become a more complete expert" in a domain. While this feature of expertise was often not emphasised in early studies on expertise it was nonetheless present: chess experts did not develop their expertise by simply developing approaches and strategies based on their knowledge of the rules – rather they developed their skills by watching, listening to, and studying the actions of other chess players.

Etienne Wenger (1998), who has studied the development of expertise in a range of different settings, has highlighted that as people learn, they become more active participants in their particular social community and they develop an identity associated with that community. Students do not simply learn chemistry, teaching, or dance; instead, they *become* a chemist, a school teacher, or a dancer. This happens not simply by reading or listening in a lecture, but by engaging in the practices of the discipline in what Wenger calls a *community of practice*. As such, when students engage in practical learning activities in labs, fieldwork, studios, and projects we need to consider not just the behaviour of the individual learners, but the way in which the community around them helps them to develop and refine the ways of thinking and acting that are characteristic of that expert community (see Spotlight 2.4).

REFLECTION POINT 2.4

Are there times during their learning when students are likely to experience the emotions arising from the practice of your discipline? Is this explicitly addressed as part of the learning experience, or are students left to deal with it by themselves?

Do experts in your discipline have to take responsibility for decisions that might impact on the lives of others? If so, do students in your discipline have opportunities to experience at least part of what that is like, and to reflect on that experience?

Do higher education students in your discipline have opportunities to interact with experts in the discipline (other than their teachers)?

To summarise, experts in a domain see, know, think, feel, and interact differently to novices.

- Experts perceive things that novices don't, they remember more and remember more quickly than novices, and they can perform the procedures associated with their discipline with greater ease and fluency. These differences are often seen to be linked to the fact that experts have spent a long time practicing their discipline, and so have built both fluency and contextualised knowledge which cannot be achieved through learning from lectures and texts alone.
- Experts can rapidly recall whole blocks of relevant information. This is seen to be linked to deeply processing the content knowledge

of their discipline and building connections between ideas, and between ideas and situations in which the idea might be applied.
- Experts tend to monitor their learning and performance better than novices in ways that make sense within the discipline in question. While self-monitoring may look different in physics than in music, in both cases, learning to implicitly check their own performance against some standard is part of becoming an expert, and will be learned in the times when learners are enacting the problem-solving routines of their discipline. Often this happens in experiential learning settings.
- Experts experience and regulate emotions in productive ways to allow them to continue to function in contexts that are often characterised by strong emotions. This is true in domains as different from each other as the arts, the caring professions, and engineering and technology. Again, learning to regulate ones' own emotions is unlikely to happen in lectures and reading alone but rather from having emotional experiences and from having opportunities to reflect on those experiences.
- Experts develop expertise through opportunities to develop tacit knowledge and skills in interaction with other members of an expert community. Without opportunities to try things out and get feedback in social settings, people are unlikely to develop expertise.

SPOTLIGHT 2.4 – THE STAGES OF BECOMING AN EXPERT NURSE

Long processes, like the process of becoming an expert, are sometimes described in terms of stages. One particularly influential model for thinking about becoming an expert is the five-stage adult learning model, developed by Stuart Dreyfus and Hubert Dreyfus (Dreyfus 2004). The model has been applied by Patricia Benner (2004) to thinking about how nurses become experts.

Stage 1 Novice: the novice knows very little about their domain and has little experience upon which to base their practice. In nursing, people enter their training at the novice stage. Early in their training they typically learn only the most general ideas and concepts relevant to their domain and the most general guidelines to direct their practice. For example, when thinking about the fluid balance in a patient, the novice is given very clear parameters and guidelines which they are to follow in all cases. Learning at this stage typically takes the form of applying judgement rules in tightly controlled environments (you will see this again in the next chapter in the case of Anne-Sophie's chemistry labs where students feel like they have to make a lot of decisions, but these take place within a narrow range of safe tasks which she had carefully designed).

Stage 2 Advanced Beginner: by the end of their nurse training, a nurse has typically reached the stage of advanced beginner. Advanced beginners have seen a number of different examples from different contexts and, as such, start to be able to recognise some situational factors which factor into their judgement. Benner describes the graduate nurse as starting to be responsible for their actions and consequently recognising that professional judgement does not simply mean applying rules but rather paying attention to context and situation. Because they can now take decisions in many situations, the advanced beginner feels greater freedom. They still rely heavily on more experienced clinical nurse specialists to know when they can and should take independent decisions, and may feel exhilarated at how much they are learning.

Stage 3 Competence: after one to two years in practice, following rule- or guideline-bounded behaviour in situations which the nurse recognises as being increasingly complex eventually becomes exhausting. As one nurse cited by Benner says after realising that an error had been made,

> I'm feeling like I have things straight now, and I can handle the situations, and when something like this happens, I think, well, I still have a lot of learning to do. I can handle the situations that are *status quo*; it's the unexpected that I have to learn to deal with now.

Benner sees nurses at this stage starting to plan more so that they have pre-considered likely outcomes based on their prior experience. The nature of the emotional experience also changes. For novices and advanced beginners, there was a generalised stress and anxiety. For competent nurses their emotions become more tailored to their specific situation, and so they may be encouraged to pay attention to vague feelings of foreboding or anxiety as being useful indicators when there are no rules to guide them. A sense of confusion or questioning when things do not go *according to plan* also drives the competent nurse to continue to learn.

Stage 4 Proficiency: after some years of practice, the nurse is aware that the diversity of contexts means that they cannot simply follow rules to make good decisions. They also recognise that uncertainty means that their planning has limitations. Benner describes proficient nurses as experiencing a qualitative leap in the way they do their job: they are now perceiving information that others cannot, and are making decisions which synthesise that information in a way that has become so automated that it is hard for them to put into words. Rather than trying to predict and control the situation, they are responding to what they perceive in an open-minded way. Again, there is a strong emotional dimension to this. Whereas a less experienced nurse may experience this open-minded approach as being prone to suggestibility and confusion, the proficient nurse is ready to correct their judgements in light of new information.

Stage 5 Expertise: the expert practitioner rapidly sees not just what needs to be done but also how to do it. The expert is able to discriminate between situations which may well appear identical to a novice but in which subtle variations mean a different response is required. While the proficient nurse made decisions analytically, the expert nurse makes them intuitively. For the expert nurse, says Benner, action, thought, and feeling are fused.

THE JOURNEY TOWARDS EXPERTISE

As was noted at the outset of this chapter, becoming an expert takes time, and so it is unlikely that many higher education students will have become expert by the end of their degree. So it is worth asking what can we reasonably expect from students by the time they are finishing their initial higher education studies.

It is worth noting where a student's degree fits into their trajectory towards expertise, as there are significant differences between disciplines. For example:

- The art and design students studied by Aaron Kozbelt (see Spotlight 2.1) showed at least some signs of expertise in that their perception was notably different from that of art novices. In fact Kozbelt did not find differences between first- and fourth-year art students. It appeared as though the first-year students already showed signs of expertise, or at least competence, possibly due to the fact that they had many opportunities to practice before entry to higher education (and indeed may have needed to demonstrate competence before being allowed to enter an art or design programme). The same may well be true of other disciplines where students have already had exposure to the area prior to entering higher education.

- The nursing students and practitioners studied by Patricia Benner (see Spotlight 2.4) did not come to higher education with a lot of nursing expertise or experience. In fact, they typically had no prior experience of clinical nursing situations. In this sense, they are genuine novices when they begin their programme and are realistically only advanced beginners by the time they graduate.
- Teacher education students do have considerable experience of learning situations before they begin training, in that they have well over 10,000 hours as students in classrooms before they ever enter teacher education programmes. This experience is, however, likely to be misleading (Stigler and Miller [2018] refer to it as *pseudo-expertise*). Indeed, Stigler and Miller suggest that one of the things that makes it hard for people to develop expertise in teaching is that most people think they already know what an expert teacher does, without ever having considered any of the research about teaching and learning. Teacher education programmes often have to start, therefore, by helping learners to question and deconstruct their internalised assumptions about teaching before they can begin on a pathway towards expertise (we will return to this issue in Chapter 10).

BECOMING AN EXPERT

It should be evident by now that developing expertise takes a long time. Early studies with chess experts found that it typically took more than ten years from first learning the rules of chess to becoming an internationally recognised grandmaster. Similar timeframes are found in studies of musicians, composers, and scientists. As was evident in the case of expert nurses (Spotlight 2.4), the development of expertise requires constant exposure to a large range of different situations in which the expert develops. However, as we will explore in Chapter 3, it is not experience itself that people learn from, but rather how they process information from that experience. As one of the world's leading expertise researchers K. Anders Ericsson has remarked, expertise "in a given domain is not attained automatically as a function of extended experience, but the level of performance can be increased even by highly experienced individuals as a result of deliberate efforts to improve" (Ericsson et al. 1993, 366).

Ericsson and his colleagues have argued that in order to improve in a discipline:

- A learner needs to have opportunities to practice the skills of the discipline that they cannot already perform – they need to *stretch* themselves.
- *High-stakes* situations, where failure will have serious costs for the learner, have a negative impact on learning because people are more likely to perform what they already know how to do well and avoid attempting challenging new skills (i.e. *practice* is not the same as *work*).
- The learner needs to pay attention to what they are doing and to how it can be improved – their performance needs to be monitored and the learner needs to get feedback on their performance of the skills.
- The learner needs opportunities to repeat doing the skill correctly so that they can develop some degree of automation (as the Olympic swimmer and swim coach Tracey McFarlane Mirande puts it "practice doesn't make perfect; perfect practice makes perfect" [2005, 17]).
- The learner may well experience frustration and other negative emotions during the learning – their motivation to engage in these kinds of challenging tasks comes not from the enjoyment of the activity itself but rather from the trust that they will improve their performance (i.e. *practice* is not the same as *play*).

Ericsson and his colleagues (1993) called this kind of practice *deliberate practice*. This particular way of describing effective practice was originally developed during their studies with musicians (violinists and pianists). They found that the principal difference between good violinists and the best violinists is the amount of time they have spent engaging in this kind of practice: the best had about 10,000 hours by the time they were 20 years of age, as compared to good ones who had about 8,000 and competent ones who had about 4,000 hours. Because this figure of 10,000 hours is neat and easily understandable, it has rapidly entered into the public discourse and consciousness. But 10,000 hours is not a magic number. Indeed if the measures were taken with older or younger violinists the figure would have been different, and the figure is also different for other types of expertise (singers, for example tend to practice less than other musicians).

Ericsson's description of deliberate practice is clearly applicable for developing expertise in domains that require physical skills, like music, dance, art, and sport. However, the same principles also apply to learning in other domains which require different types of skills. In teaching, for example, the *lesson study* practice which developed in Japan and has become increasingly popular in Western countries can be seen as a type of deliberate practice. In lesson study, teachers work in teams to collaboratively plan, implement, observe, and improve specific lessons. This requires teachers to *slow down* their thinking and invest time in first examining and understanding the teaching situation. Once the situation has been analysed and a lesson has been planned, one member of the team then teaches the lesson while the other team members observe. The team then share and analyse these observations, paying particular attention to where their predictions were wrong and focusing on the lesson itself (rather than on critiquing the teacher who has been observed). The lesson study approach provides teachers with opportunities to practice the skills of observation and analysis of learning in a low-stakes setting while collecting evidence which allows for wrong assumptions, mistaken hypotheses, and other errors to be identified.

REFLECTION POINT 2.5

At what stage in the development of expertise do you expect students to be when they take your course? What kinds of representative tasks should they be practicing at that stage in their development?

Do students' practical experiences include characteristics of deliberate practice such as:

- stretching their ability in particular skills?
- low-stakes opportunities to practice, fail, and try again?
- monitoring of their performance on those skills?
- rapid feedback directed at improvement?
- opportunities to repeat and develop automaticity in the correct performance of skills?
- emotional supports that enable them to regulate and process their frustration, to experience their joy, and to recognise how these emotions are linked to performance in their discipline?

CONCLUSION

In order to help students learn as much as possible in practical settings, it is useful to have an idea about the specific competences of the discipline that we want them to develop. The *expertise* concept is helpful in this, because it draws our attention to a number of key features of what high performance looks like in any given discipline:

- Experts know a lot.
- Experts have practised their skills to a degree that they have become automated.
- Experts remember the right information in the right situation because they have experience in using their knowledge in practice.
- Experts adopt problem-solving approaches characteristic of their discipline.
- Experts make good intuitive judgements about how to act in a range of different situations because they have experienced a wide range of different settings.
- Experts plan and monitor their own learning and thinking.
- Experts pay attention to the information coming from their emotions and can regulate their emotions to help them perform.
- Experts learn and operate in social settings.

Since expertise involves linking knowing and thinking to doing, interacting, and feeling, experiential learning is central to its development. It is typically through practical learning experiences like labs, fieldwork, studios, and projects that students have the opportunity practice linking knowing to doing, feeling, interacting, and to relevant contexts.

The next chapter will focus on some specific examples of practical teaching and identify that, while each discipline and type of practical teaching is different, there are often common goals that underpin these divergences.

FURTHER READING

This small number of sources is intended to provide further useful information for those who wish to explore the chapter topic in more detail. A full reference list for the chapter is provided below.

Experts and novices

Bransford, J. D., Brown, A. L., and Cocking, R. R. (2000). Chapter 2. How experts differ from novices. In: *How People Learn, Brain Mind Experience and School*. Washington, DC: National Academy Press. https://doi.org/10.17226/9853.

Expertise in specific disciplines

Benner, P. (2004). Using the Dreyfus model of skill acquisition to describe and interpret skill acquisition and clinical judgment in nursing practice and education. *Bulletin of Science, Technology and Society* 24(3): 188–199. https://doi.org/10.1177/0270467604265061.

Hardebolle, C. (2018). Learning to design solutions to complex problems [Video]. *SwtichTube*. https://tube.switch.ch/download/video/07fdbbd6.

Stigler, J. W., and Miller, K. F. (2018). Expertise and expert performance in teaching. In: K. A. Ericsson, R. R. Hoffman, and A. Kozbelt (eds.), *The Cambridge Handbook of Expertise and Expert Performance* (pp. 431–452). Cambridge: Cambridge University Press. https://doi.org/10.1017/9781316480748.024.

Wiles, A. (2016). Andrew Wiles: What does it feel like to do maths? *+Plus Magazine*. https://plus.maths.org/content/andrew-wiles-what-does-if-feel-do-maths.

Wiles, A. (2017, December 4). Andrew Wiles talks to Hannah Fry [Video]. *Youtube*. https://youtu.be/uQgcpzKA5jk?t=2590.

Deliberate practice

Ericsson, K. A., Prietula, M. J., and Cokely, E. T. (July-August 2007). The making of an expert. *Harvard Business Review*. https://hbr.org/2007/07/the-making-of-an-expert.

Hambrick, D. Z., Oswald, F. L., Altmann, E. M., Meinz, E. J., Gobet, F., and Campitelli, G. (2014). Deliberate practice: Is that all it takes to become an expert? *Intelligence* 45: 34–45. https://doi.org/10.1016/j.intell.2013.04.001.

REFERENCES

Benner, P. (1984). *From Novice to Expert: Excellence and Power in Clinical Nursing Practice*. Reading, MA: Addison-Wesley.

Benner, P. (2004). Using the Dreyfus model of skill acquisition to describe and interpret skill acquisition and clinical judgment in nursing practice and education. *Bulletin of Science, Technology and Society* 24(3): 188–199. https://doi.org/10.1177/0270467604265061.

Biggs, J. B. (2003). *Teaching for Quality Learning at University 2nd edition*. Buckingham: Open University Press/Society for Research into Higher Education.

Bransford, J. D., Brown, A. L., and Cocking, R. R. (2000). *How People Learn; Brain Mind Experience and School*. Washington, DC: National Academy Press. https://doi.org/10.17226/9853.

Case, J., and Marshall, D. (2004). Between deep and surface: Procedural approaches to learning in engineering education contexts. *Studies in Higher Education* 29(5): 605–615. https://doi.org/10.1080/0307507042000261571.

Chi, M. T., Glaser, R., and Farr, M. J. (eds.) (1988). *The Nature of Expertise*. New York: Psychology Press. https://doi.org/10.4324/9781315799681.

Collins, H., and Evans, R. (2018). A sociological/philosophical perspective on expertise: The acquisition of expertise Through socialization. In: K. A. Ericsson, R. R. Hoffman, and A. Kozbelt (eds.), *The Cambridge Handbook of Expertise and Expert Performance* (pp. 21–32). Cambridge: Cambridge University Press. https://doi.org/10.1017/9781316480748.002.

Corcoran, R. P., and Tormey, R. (2012). *Developing Emotionally Competent Teachers; Emotional Intelligence and Pre-Service Teacher Education*. Oxford: Peter Lang Press.

Dreyfus, S. E. (2004). The five-stage model of adult skill acquisition. *Bulletin of Science, Technology and Society* 24(3): 177–181. https://doi.org/10.1177/0270467604264992.

Entwistle, N. (1997). Reconstituting approaches to learning: A response to Webb. *Higher Education* 33(2): 213–218. https://doi.org/10.1023/A:1002930608372.

Entwistle, N. (2009). *Teaching for Understanding at University: Deep Approaches and Distinctive Ways of Thinking*. London: Palgrave Macmillan.

Ericsson, K. A. (2018). An Introduction to the second edition of the Cambridge Handbook of Expertise and Expert Performance, its development organisation and context. In: K. A. Ericsson, R. R. Hoffman, and A. Kozbelt (eds.), *The Cambridge Handbook of Expertise and Expert Performance* (pp. 3–20). Cambridge: Cambridge University Press. https://doi.org/10.1017/CBO9780511816796.001.

Ericsson, K. A., Krampe, R. T., and Tesch-Römer, C. (1993). The role of deliberate practice in the acquisition of expert performance. *Psychological Review* 100(3): 363–406. https://doi.org/10.1037/0033-295X.100.3.363.

Kellog, R. (2018). Professional writing expertise. In: K. A. Ericsson, R. R. Hoffman, and A. Kozbelt (eds.), *The Cambridge Handbook of Expertise and Expert Performance* (pp. 413–430). Cambridge: Cambridge University Press. https://doi.org/10.1017/CBO9780511816796.022.

Kozbelt, A. (2001). Artists as experts in visual cognition. *Visual Cognition* 8(6): 705–723. https://doi.org/10.1080/13506280042000090.

McFarlae Mirande, T. (2005). *Championship Swimming: How to Swim Like a Pro in Thirty Days or Less*. Frankfurt: McGraw-Hill Education.

Oura, Y., and Hatano, G. (2001). The constitution of general and specific mental models of other people. *Human Development* 44(2–3): 144–159.

Overton, T. L., and Randles, C. A. (2015). Beyond problem-based learning: Using dynamic PBL in chemistry. *Chemistry Education Research and Practice* 16(2): 251–259. https://doi.org/10.1039/c5rp00114e.

Price, A., Kim, C., Burkholder, E., Fritz, A., and Wieman, C. (2020). A detailed characterization of the expert problem-solving process in science and engineering: Guidance for teaching and assessment. arXiv.org Pre-Print: arXiv:2005.11463v5 [physics.ed-ph].

Ramsden, P. (2003). *Learning to Teach in Higher Education*. London: Routledge Falmer.

Roeser, S. (2012). Risk communication, public engagement, and climate change: A role for emotions. *Risk Analysis: An International Journal* 32(6): 1033–1040. https://doi.org/10.1111/j.1539-6924.2012.01812.x.

Sabers, D. S., Cushing, K. S., and Berliner, D. C. (1991). Differences among teachers in a task characterized by simultaneity, multidimensional, and immediacy. *American Educational Research Journal* 28(1): 63–88. https://doi.org/10.3102/00028312028001063.

Starkes, J. L., Payk, I., Jennen, P., and Leclair, D. (1993). Chapter 12 A stitch in time: Cognitive issues in microsurgery. *Advances in Psychology* 102: 225–240. https://doi.org/10.1016/S0166-4115(08)61473-9.

Stigler, J. W., and Miller, K. F. (2018). Expertise and expert performance in teaching. In: K. A. Ericsson, R. R. Hoffman, and A. Kozbelt (eds.), *The Cambridge Handbook of Expertise and Expert Performance* (pp. 431–452). Cambridge: Cambridge University Press. https://doi.org/10.1017/9781316480748.024.

Tormey, R. (2014). The centre cannot hold: Untangling two different trajectories of the 'approaches to learning' framework. *Teaching in Higher Education* 19(1): 1–12. https://doi.org/ 10.1080/13562517.2013.827648.

Tormey, R. (2020). Towards an emotions-based engineering ethics education. In: Engaging Engineering Education Proceedings of the European Society for Engineering Education 48th Annual Conference 2020 (pp. 1128–1138). Twente, 20–24 September 2020. https://www.sefi.be/wp-content/uploads/2020/11/Proceedings-2020-web.pdf.

Van de Poel, I., and Royakkers, L. (2011). *Ethics, Technology, and Engineering: An Introduction*. Hoboken, NJ: Wiley.

Voss, J. F., and Post, T. A. (1988). On the solving of ill-structured problems. In: M. T. H. Chi, R. Glaser, and M. J. Farr (eds.), *The Nature of Expertise* (pp. 261–285). Mahwah, NJ: Lawrence Erlbaum Associates, Inc. https://doi.org/10.4324/9781315799681.

Voss, J., Green, T., Post, T., and Penner, B. (1983). Problem solving in the social sciences. In: G. H. Bower (ed.), *The Psychology of Learning and Motivation: Advances in Research and Theory* (vol. 17, pp. 205–232). New York: Academic Press.

Wenger, E. (1998). *Communities of Practice, Learning, Meaning and Identity*. Cambridge: Cambridge University Press. https://doi.org/10.1017/CBO9780511803932.

Wiles, A. (2016). Andrew Wiles: What does it feel like to do maths? +Plus Magazine https://plus.maths.org/content/andrew-wiles-what-does-if-feel-do-maths.

Chapter 3

What students learn from labs, studios, projects, and fieldwork

INTRODUCTION

The previous chapter looked at how students develop expertise with disciplinary content in higher education. It highlighted that experiential or practical learning is absolutely central to the process through which students work towards developing expertise in their discipline. This chapter focuses more closely on what happens in labs, studios, projects, and fieldwork, and looks in particular at the diversity of ways in which they are organised, what students are expected to learn, and how teachers teach these things. As with the previous chapter, a central question here remains what students need to learn from practical activities in higher education. In Chapter 2 we looked at the more obvious answer to this question: students should learn to use and apply the content knowledge that makes up their discipline and learn to perform the discipline's representative tasks, whether that means playing the violin, designing electrical circuits, teaching children, or analysing business data. However, one of the key themes of this book is that focusing only on the explicit content knowledge and process skills of a course can mean failing to develop the thinking skills that students are also expected to learn in higher education.

Underpinning the vast array of things students learn in practical courses are a number of *ways of thinking*. These ways of thinking include:

1. being able to use things they have learned in one context (such as in a class) in a different context (such as in the world outside of higher education),
2. investigating the world using the skills and approaches of their discipline,
3. finding solutions to problems which are often ill-defined or open-ended and may involve a range of constraints (including financial, technical, legal, and ethical constraints),

DOI: 10.4324/9781003107606-3

4. professional skills like project management or working effectively in teams and alongside others,
5. managing their own learning to be able to continue to adapt to situations and challenges after they leave higher education.

Learning by doing situations are often expected to develop these skills by creating opportunities for students to connect real-life experience with the concepts and ideas from a discipline. These connections help students to make sense of those experiences and to develop the perspective and skills of experts in that discipline. This chapter takes a similar approach to a practical class in that it starts with lived experiences and then links them to concepts and ideas. The chapter is structured around a number of examples that are used to illustrate how the underlying thinking skills associated with practical work are brought to life in labs, studios, fieldwork, and projects.

ORGANISING LABS, STUDIOS, PROJECTS, AND FIELDWORK

Learning by doing takes place in a wide variety of settings. The following examples give a feel for the diversity of the settings where students can engage in practical learning in higher education. Since we use these examples to illustrate the concepts and ideas throughout this chapter, it is worthwhile to read all of them carefully, even if some of them may seem on the surface to be less directly relevant to your discipline or learning goals than others.

SPOTLIGHT 3.1.A – LEARNING IN THE MUSIC STUDIO

Gwen teaches a practical course in *musical composition* to student teachers who are learning to teach music in primary schools. In the course, students first work as a class of 30 to practically explore ways to compose, using a range of sounds including *found sounds* and body percussion. After this induction, students begin to work in groups to complete an initial composition activity which involves responding to a stimulus such as composing a piece of music to accompany a film or piece of visual art. After the seventh week of the term, the students work in groups to develop an original musical composition that they perform at the end of the semester.

Previously, Gwen has also taught an *advanced performance* studio in classical guitar on a bachelor's degree in music. The studios were based on a *conservatoire* model, where a teacher works with an individual student to help them develop the skills to deliver an end of semester recital, which ranges in length from 30 minutes to over an hour depending on the year of the student. In this course, students are focused on developing the technical ability, stamina, and musical and mental skills required to deliver an elite-level performance in a one-off, highly pressurised situation.

SPOTLIGHT 3.2.A – LEARNING TO DESIGN IT SYSTEM ARCHITECTURE

For a number of years, Cécile (one of the authors of this book) taught a course in *service-oriented architecture* to computer scientists. Although the course was taught to master's-level students, many of the students did not have much prior knowledge of IT architecture and so needed to learn about some of the basic concepts and ideas. The course was an optional one and was popular with some students because they liked the topic, and with others because *service-oriented architecture* was a *buzzword* in the industry at the time and students wanted to work as consultants in the field.

As part of the course, students completed a design project – their goal was to design an IT architecture that met a particular set of client needs. The exercises of the course were structured in such a way as to walk students through the stages of a design project. At each phase, students could use different tools (such as system modelling tools), and the exercises in the course allowed students to practice using these tools.

SPOTLIGHT 3.3.A – LEARNING TO MANAGE OPEN-ENDED PROJECTS

Roland (another of this book's authors) teaches a course in the social and behavioural sciences of learning. The course, which runs over a full academic year and is taught as an elective to a class of about 60 natural science and engineering students, begins by exposing students to both the key concepts in learning sciences as well as to the mechanics of relevant research techniques (like psychological experiments and social surveys) and to their associated statistical techniques. In the second semester, students are required to apply what they have learned by working on a team project.

The projects (which can be either research projects or design projects) are structured as *ill-defined problems*: students are given a broad problem statement and a *client*, and are asked to explore the problem statement with the client before clarifying exactly what problem they are going to solve. They then solve the problem by either completing some social scientific research or by designing an educational tool. Roland creates heterogeneous teams because learning to work with people from other walks of life and disciplinary backgrounds is one of the goals of the project.

SPOTLIGHT 3.4.A – CARRYING OUT SCIENTIFIC INVESTIGATIONS IN A LAB

Anne-Sophie runs chemistry labs for more than 300 students and manages dozens of teaching assistants. The labs have multiple goals: at one level students learn to physically enact particular procedures, following a set of instructions when working with a piece of lab equipment in order to answer a particular question. However, Anne-Sophie says, there is a lot more to the labs than just mechanically following instructions:

> If they just replicate the procedure, they aren't thinking and they forget everything quickly. They need to be thinking, to be making

> connections with the theory, and checking to see if it makes sense. This is something students have difficulty with – does their result make sense physically? Even if they end up working as quality control in a production line, it is quite automatic, but they need to know what a result means, how to interpret it, and how to test their interpretation.

As can be seen from the four cases above, practical learning in university covers a great diversity of settings. The size of practical learning classes ranges from one-to-one classical music studio tuition to an enormous pedagogical system involving hundreds of students and dozens of teaching assistants in a chemistry lab. The location ranges from a highly controlled lab to meeting with clients, potentially outside the university. The things that students learn and practice in practical courses range from physical acts like playing music or accurately manipulating lab equipment, to cognitive processes like statistical testing and systems modelling. In some cases, practical learning takes place in a very open-ended context where students create their own music or generate their own research and design questions. In other cases the tasks themselves are more tightly defined, such as following a particular procedure for manipulating lab equipment, or correctly applying particular statistical tests. In some cases the practical activity is a project within a course which also includes lectures: in other cases the practical is the whole focus of the course.

Despite these differences, there are evident similarities too. In all cases students are *doing*, whether that means designing something, playing something, composing something, or investigating something: they are not, for example, only reading about experiments in chemistry or in learning sciences, they are actually designing and carrying them out. In doing so, they are taking ideas, concepts, and techniques that they are hearing about in other courses and they are seeing how they look, feel, and smell, and what they sound like, in real-life settings. They are linking their physical movements to concept and ideas, and vice versa. This process of making connections between the meaning of different ideas (known as *deep processing of information*) and between ideas and real-world sights, smells, and feelings (known as *rich encoding*) is central to how learners form long-term memories that they will be able to recall when they need them. That is, they are central to effective learning.

It is also evident in all of the cases above that the students are learning things that they should be able to apply and use outside of the university classroom or lab. This is really explicit in Gwen's classes (when students are learning composition in order to teach it to primary school children, or are learning musical pieces in order to perform in public) and in Cécile's class (where at least some students are taking the class in order to work as consultants in the field). In the case of Roland and Anne-Sophie's classes, the specific contexts in which students may end up using these skills are perhaps less clearly defined, but it is nonetheless intended that students will be able to apply what they have learned. This ability to use what was learned in one situation in a different situation is known in learning research as *transfer*. Transfer, it turns out, is a major challenge for university teaching. Some 30 years ago, research in university physics teaching highlighted that students can learn the concepts, formulas, and algorithms they need to pass physics courses but then fail to use this knowledge when faced with questions which are phrased as *practical problems* and which don't require calculation (Hake 1998). Over the last three decades, research in other disciplines has found that this problem is not confined to physics or, indeed, to natural sciences. To put this in more straightforward terms, it is not easy to turn *book learning* into *practical knowing*. In each of the cases described above, experiential learning is intended to provide something of a bridge between the ideas learned in traditional classes and the ways in which students will use them in practice in the world outside the university.

LEARNING IN PRACTICAL SETTINGS

If the organisation of experiential learning is diverse, so too are the range of skills and the knowledge that students are expected to develop. As we saw in Chapter 2, knowledge and skills are typically deeply embedded in the specifics of the discipline. But there are also commonalities in learning goals that cut across different disciplines and across a range of different practical learning settings. These differences and similarities are explored below in the second part of each of the case studies.

SPOTLIGHT 3.1.B – LEARNING IN THE MUSIC STUDIO

Gwen's musical composition course provides a practical setting for students to apply a range of musical concepts like structure, dynamics, and timbre, as well as developing performance skills and listening skills such as being able to think in sound (called *audiation*).

Gwen says,

> The big challenge with the course is that the students are grappling with the idea of being *the composer*. Some have little prior musical experience but even those who do are sometimes at a disadvantage because their prior experience is often based on reproducing pre-existing musical works, in other words, playing pieces written by Beethoven or Bach or whoever. It is easy for those students to fall back into adapting and re-creating pieces in a pastiche style rather than fully engaging in the process of creative music-making.

This notion of *process* is central to this practical course. The process operates at four, inter-related, levels. At a micro-level, is the process of playing or making music. Gwen says "music is a temporal art – it passes through time". Unlike, for example, a painting which exists and can be experienced after it has been created, the experience of music is intrinsically tied to the process of *making* music. "Of course music can be recorded, but sometimes when music is being made in that moment there is a sense of what Csikszentmihalyi (1990) has called *flow* – a bit of magic – they're completely present in the performance". Learning the capacity to *be present* in the performance is part of what students need to learn in the course. The second-level process is the process of composing. Students who have prior musical experience in particular run the risk of imposing their implicit sense of *what works,* and so getting students to engage without preconceptions in the process of composing can sometimes be a challenge.

This challenge is associated with what happens at the third level of process: the level of group work. "Sometimes", Gwen says, "the really successful groups are those who are not experienced musicians. Because they have no prior expectations they find it easier to engage in the process. Prior experience is welcome, but it is not an advantage". Experienced musicians can end up short-circuiting the composing process, and this can cause tension and impact on the work of the group. Playing and listening as part of an ensemble is part of the skill set in music and is one of the activities of this practical. Hence, learning to work in a team is also a learned skill: "Students develop a whole series of extra-musical skills through the practical's teamwork, like skills in cooperating with others, patience, negotiation, empathy and leadership", says Gwen. While working within the group can be challenging, those who learn to work well in a group find it improves their work. The fourth level of process is the process of each student learning to manage their own thinking. Sometimes students are impeded by their prior misconceptions and beliefs about music:

> There are a lot of strange assumptions about what music means and about what it means to learn it. It is seen as elitist and sometimes people think it requires innate abilities in order to learn it. Sometimes people have to kind of unlearn this kind of thinking.

Since these students are not only learning to compose but also learning to teach composing, thinking about how and what they are doing, while doing it, is central to the skill set of the course.

The learning goals in the musical composition practice are quite different to those in the *advanced performance* studio. In the studio, the explicit focus is on developing the technical skills required to perform in the student's recital. Alongside this come other skills and abilities, such as developing the stamina to be able to memorise and engage in a physically demanding performance. More implicitly, the studio also teaches the student the mental skills required for their performance. Learning a piece of music is not just in the hands, it is also a cognitive process of understanding the structure of a piece of music, thinking about it, and recognising where you are within that structure at any given time. In the studio, the student doesn't just learn to behave like a musician but to think like a musician. The student needs to have strategies for how they will handle mistakes during the performance in order to "not fall apart completely", Gwen says. "You can help the student prepare for this mentally".

SPOTLIGHT 3.2.B – LEARNING TO DESIGN IT SYSTEM ARCHITECTURE

Although Cécile's IT system architecture course was an advanced one, many students had not been previously exposed to the ideas and concepts of the field. The course therefore introduced key ideas like the range of functions present in even relatively simple architectures, the different ways in which a system can be modelled, and how to use these models to identify flaws or to determine how to implement new functionalities in the system.

Designing an architecture to solve a problem for a client that will work in the specifics of that client's situation can be thought of as involving a number of steps: first deep understanding of the client's situation and needs (analysis phase), imagining possible solutions (divergent design phase), choosing an approach, and then refining it (convergent design phase). It was important for students to identify where they were in the design process and what was expected in that phase: "Some students did poorly because of a lack of depth in the analysis phase. They didn't see it as important: maybe it was seen as boring compared to the exciting work of designing something", says Cécile.

In each of these phases students could draw on specific approaches and tools of the field. The challenge for students was to understand and be able to use these techniques, but also to be able to understand at what stage and in which context particular techniques and tools could be used. "It was a complex course", Cécile says:

> I really enjoyed how applied it was, that the students learned and used real-world skills. Students had to learn content, how to follow a design process, how to work with each other, they had to practice using a whole series of different tools but also understand when and where to use them.

SPOTLIGHT 3.3.B – LEARNING TO MANAGE OPEN-ENDED PROJECTS

Although the content of Roland's course focuses on learning sciences, the goal of the project itself is to teach students how to use what they had learned to frame, to understand, and to solve an ill-defined problem. Roland says,

> The students take the course because they are interested in how they themselves learn and how they can help other people learn, but I am really explicit with them that the particular problem that they will solve in their project is a problem they will probably never face again in their professional lives. So while they may or may not find it interesting to solve this particular problem, what is more important is that they learn skills in problem solving that they can use to solve other problems.

Many of the *problems* students have encountered in their studies up to this point are very well-defined: the students are given an exercise statement which contains all the information they need to solve the problem, and there is usually only one or a few correct answers. At the end, students will know that they got the answer either right or wrong. "Mostly the problems they will face in real-life are not well-defined", Roland continues.

> Often the problem itself is not clear, they don't have all the information they need, and there are a range of things they need to take into account like resources, ethics, legal constraints and so on. So the first task for them is learning to take an ill-defined problem and turn it into a problem they can solve. This is a major challenge for some students.

Some students immediately imagine a solution to a problem and set about building that solution. Often when they build it, it can't be used because it needs too much maintenance, or is too fragile, or too expensive, or because the problem it solves is not the one that their client actually has. Those who take the time to understand the client's needs, resources, and constraints will generally produce more successful solutions. Similar problems can occur for those who work on research projects: many groups imagine a research study which can't be operationalised because it would take too long, cost too much, use data in unethical or illegal ways, or because participants can't be recruited. Roland says,

They often have unrealistic ideas as to what is possible in social science research – they find it to be messy and unpredictable. Because the results are rarely as neat as in a textbook they sometimes struggle to interpret what the data actually means.

Students work in teams of three or four to solve the problem, and these teams are chosen to be heterogeneous. "I try to make sure that students in each group come from different departments, and that students who did their undergraduate studies elsewhere are mixed with those who did their bachelor degree here", says Roland. The goal, again, is to enable students to learn things that they will be able to use thereafter. Since their professional life as engineers will see students interacting with clients, with other professionals, and with those who will use the products and processes they design, learning to work effectively with diverse people is a useful professional skill.

SPOTLIGHT 3.4.B – CARRYING OUT SCIENTIFIC INVESTIGATIONS IN A LAB

Anne-Sophie's labs address a range of different skills that students need to develop, including

> manipulations and equipment handling, using software to analyse data, and communicating results effectively. But ultimately it is like the training from a PhD – you need to be able to transfer what you learned, the ways of working and thinking in the lab, into different contexts which require analysis and innovative thinking.

In addition to the specific tasks that students learn to perform in any given lab session, there are also skills that are transversal across the whole course: these include learning to work safely in a lab and to link the concepts seen in lectures to the experimental procedures they are enacting. At a deeper level, students are also learning to determine if the experiment was successful or not, how to adapt the

> experimental design to be more precise, and how to present their results such that they are clear to others.

PROBLEM SOLVING

On one level it is clear that the learning goals in these courses are radically divergent. While Anne-Sophie wants students to learn to apply chemistry knowledge and use software, Cécile is focused on her students learning techniques in IT system design, while Gwen is teaching the physical and mental skills required to perform challenging pieces of music in public.

And yet, at the same time, some common patterns emerge. Roland, Gwen, and Cécile, each in their own way, are concerned with making explicit for students a process which they will use to solve a problem in their discipline. While the problems are as different as composing a piece of music and designing an IT system architecture, the idea that there is a process for solving problems of this type is shared across these different examples of practical learning. Indeed, there are even some similarities between the different processes: in Gwen's case students start by investigating the world through exploring found sounds. In Roland's case too, students also explore the problem space they are presented with and work to understand the goals, constraints, and resources which are in front of them. Cécile's case also involves the student in first analysing the client's situation and needs before turning to designing solutions. These similarities are not coincidental: as Spotlight 2.2 explored, studies of problem solving in a range of different domains suggest that there is often a common underlying process to problem solving which involves:

- understanding, reviewing, or analysing the problem and its context,
- laying out or designing an approach for solving the problem,
- building or applying the solution,
- evaluating or reviewing the effectiveness of that solution.

The idea that problem solving can be represented in terms of these stages is one that is found in disciplines as diverse as mathematics (where the Stanford mathematician George Polya described problem solving as following the stages of *understanding-planning-solving-looking back* [1945/1957]), engineering design (which is often described in terms of *scoping-planning-designing-testing-deploying*), and social studies (where the action research cycle of *review-plan-implement-evaluate* is widely used as a model). Listing these steps is not intended simply as a description of how people *do* solve problems in these domains. A key idea underlying these descriptions of problem solving is that students will be better able to solve problems if teachers make explicit to them that there is a process and if they are explicitly taught the skills and approaches relevant at each stage in the process. Again, there is good evidence to support this idea: a statistical review of studies of learning carried out by the educational researcher John Hattie found that explicitly teaching students problem-solving processes was far more successful an educational strategy than the more traditional strategy of expecting them to implicitly see the how to solve problems by simply solving lots of problems (2009, 210). As both Cécile and Roland note, for example, students who fail to understand or analyse their context adequately typically perform less well than those who do.

Disciplinary inquiry

A second common feature across the learning goals of these case studies is the idea that students are learning the investigatory techniques of their discipline. For Anne-Sophie, for example, students are not simply learning to use chemistry lab equipment but also learning how to investigate phenomena using that equipment, to frame or adapt experimental designs, to analyse their results using software, to determine if the experiment was successful or not, to draw conclusions, and to present their results findings such that they are clear to others. For Roland too, students are learning to design ethical and valid sociological and psychological studies which draw on the approaches and statistical techniques of these disciplines. While the statistical techniques and analyses are different, designing effective studies which can isolate the desired focus of attention, collecting data, interpreting it, and drawing conclusions are equally important here.

Just as with problem solving, carrying out investigations can be thought of as a stepwise process (although, just as with problem solving, the process is rarely linear in reality). Although these stages are given a range of names by different writers, broadly speaking they include the following (Pedaste et al. 2015):

- an *Orientation* stage where the question to be addressed is identified and clarified,
- a *Conceptualisation* stage where general questions are turned into a study design and where concepts and ideas are operationalised in ways that can be investigated quantitatively or qualitatively,

- an *Investigation* stage where data is collected, recorded, and where decisions are taken to ensure the validity and applicability of the study,
- an *Analysis* or *Conclusion* stage where conclusions and inferences are drawn from the data recorded,
- a *Communication* or *Discussion* stage where findings are framed (often in writing) so they can be communicated, and where the limitations of the study are explored.

As with problem solving, an awareness of where one is in the investigation process can help to clarify the different skills to be learned as well as helping students (and their teachers) decide what questions need to be addressed and when.

PROFESSIONAL SKILLS

A third common theme that emerges from these teaching Spotlights is that students learn professional skills. These skills might include managing a project, making team decisions, or managing resource constraints. In the Spotlight teaching situations above, there are numerous examples of students learning the professional skills of working effectively with other people. For many higher education students, their traditional courses are designed to be quite solitary activities – while they are in class alongside others and may study with them, they are assessed essentially as individuals and their performance is not dependent upon others. Practical work is often organised quite differently: for Gwen, students learn a range of social and interpersonal skills in the composition class including skills in cooperating with others, patience, negotiation, empathy, and leadership. While these are described as *extra-musical* skills, she also makes explicit that these are not simply *nice to have* optional extras: being able to work and perform in an ensemble is a key requirement for musicians. Roland also highlights the extent to which taking account of others is a professional skill, both in the sense that students have to learn how to work alongside others in teams composed of diverse people, but also in the sense that they have to be able to take into account the needs and rights of other people who are not in their immediate social environment, that is, people like clients, research participants, or those who will use the products they make.

As with problem solving and investigating, it is sometimes assumed that students will learn to work in teams simply by having the experience of working in teams. Research on student teams, for example, has found that they are often challenging and frustrating for students (Isaac and Tormey 2015) and that students struggle with questions of leadership, conflict, managing egos, and in dealing with *free-riders* or *slackers* (Colbeck et al. 2000). Ford and Morice identify that, for "students already struggling with the pressures of university life in general, the added burden of trying to work within a seemingly dysfunctional team was often the *last straw*" (2003, 269). Research on what happens within diverse teams suggests that experiences in groups can be influenced by social factors such as gender or ethnicity, as well as by discipline: research on speech dynamics within small groups, for example, has found that engineering students tended to be harsher in their judgement of female-typical speech acts when compared to non-engineering students (Wolfe and Powell 2009), while Prisca Aeby and colleagues (2019) found that male students were significantly more likely than female students to report that they were confident that their opinions or suggestions about a project would be valued as much as anyone else's in the group. It is not all that surprising, then, that Carol Colbeck and colleagues concluded that without "faculty guidance, it seemed that only a few student teams developed positive goal or role interdependence" (2000, 78). It is not enough to put students in teams; teachers also need to be explicit about the way functioning teams should operate and about the interpersonal skills required for effective teamwork.

LEARNING TO THINK AND TO MANAGE THEIR THINKING

A fourth pattern that emerges from the case studies is that practical learning often involves students learning to manage their own thinking and learning process. For Gwen, students often brought with them problematic prior knowledge and assumptions (linked to their knowledge of music composed by other people), which caused them to short-circuit the composing process and as a result to produce less optimal work. Being able to identify their own problematic beliefs and to work on changing them is central to becoming successful. Gwen also described how during musical performances, students can lose focus and, if they got lost in a piece of music, could *fall apart completely*. Having the mental skills to recognise and manage that situation is part of what they need to learn in their performance studio. Like Gwen, Roland and Cécile also identify students short-circuiting the process, whether that means investing less in the analysis stage of an IT architecture design project or following their initial intuition as to how to design an experiment without adequately considering the goals, constraints, and resources. Students who can recognise this problematic thought pattern can take a step back and manage their own thinking processes to ensure that they can learn and perform more effectively. But this is not something that happens spontaneously without help.

This ability to think about and to plan, monitor, debug, and evaluate one's own thinking or learning was referred to in Chapter 2 and is known as metacognition. Metacognition has been defined as "knowledge about the nature of people as cognisers, about the nature of different cognitive tasks, and about possible strategies that can be applied to the solution of different tasks" (Flavell 1999, 21). Metacognition can be thought of as a kind of internal conversation in which students ask themselves questions like *What is my goal?*, *How do I know if I am doing well in achieving that goal?*, *What resources do I have to help me?*, *What sort of strategies or practices are likely to work?*, *Is my strategy working?*, *How could I do things differently?*, and *How well did I do?* Metacognition is something that can be learned. Marcel Veenman (2011, 247) has identified three principles which underpin effective teaching of metacognitive skills. They are:

- Explicit or informed instruction: learners should know that they are trying to develop metacognitive skills, and that these skills are likely to help them perform better.
- Embedded instruction: metacognition should not be taught as a stand-alone activity but intrinsically integrated into the ways of doing and thinking in the students' discipline.
- Prolonged instruction: students will not learn metacognitive skills through a one-time intervention, but rather through having repeated exposure over time which will allow them to develop the ability to use these skills fluently and smoothly.

Experiential learning provides just such an opportunity for students to learn to manage their own thinking in ways that are explicitly linked to their discipline.

Thus far, this chapter has looked at the organisation of practical learning as well as its learning goals. Alongside the disciplinary knowledge and skills of music, chemistry, computer science, psychology, and sociology, the Spotlights suggest that practical learning also has other (often implicit) goals. These include:

1. being able to use things you have learned in higher education when you are outside higher education (the problem of *transfer*),

PART I

2. finding solutions to problems which are complex and for which a solution is not already known (*problem solving*),
3. using the skills and approaches of their discipline to find out things about the world (*investigating*),
4. professional skills like managing a project or working effectively alongside others (for example, *working in heterogeneous teams*),
5. managing one's own thinking and learning to be able to respond to novel situations and challenges (*metacognition*).

The next section considers effective strategies for teaching these, often implicit, skills in practical settings.

TEACHING IN HANDS-ON SETTINGS

In this final section, our focus shifts from what students need to learn, to how teachers set about teaching the skills and competences of practical learning. The continuation of the case studies below illustrates how teachers' instructional choices reflect the target skills of each practical setting.

> ### SPOTLIGHT 3.1.C – LEARNING IN THE MUSIC STUDIO
>
> Both of Gwen's practical music courses are organised so that students are centrally engaged in making music. Beyond that, however, since the goals of learning are so different, the methods of teaching are also different. While both of them rely on students actually producing music, the musical composition course relies heavily on group interaction and reflection. Students work together to generate and test ideas and sounds, and discuss with each other what they are doing and why. They are asked to think about their role in the group and their contribution to the process of composition. They regularly reflect on what they would do differently if they had to do the same process again. Working together, they identify the musical and extra-musical skills they have learned. And they reflect on how to apply what they have learned to the primary classroom, and how to integrate it with other art subjects addressed in the school curriculum.
>
> Since the process is so central to the learning, students are assessed continuously, and their end of semester performance is not

assessed. Students do, however, still take the performance very seriously — the sense of camaraderie in their group means that they do not want to let each other down. But the decision not to evaluate the final performance means that students are not solely focused on the performance and thus are free to pay attention to the process.

Part of that process means focusing on improving their own skills in composition and performance. Students are encouraged to record their performances during the term and to review them in order to make decisions on how to improve. Gwen says,

> Once they start working in groups, my role becomes that of facilitator. My job is to debrief with them about what they did and about what they learned from that. I'm continually assessing their work and giving them feedback within the class.

If the group is central to teaching and learning in the musical composition practical, the advanced performance studio is focused on the relationship between the teacher and the student.

> Historically, the *conservatoire* model was very top-down with a lot of inscribed authority on the role of the teacher. The teacher was the master and the student was the apprentice, and the student was there to learn to play in the way the master played, to mirror and hone the master's technique,

Gwen says. Even if this has changed, the teacher still retains considerable power in the relationship since it is the teacher who determines what the student needs to know and so, it is the teacher who decides what the student needs to do to learn these things. If a student needs to work on stamina, for example, the teacher will select appropriate exercises and instruct the student to work on them. Within this, feedback remains as crucial in this setting as in the musical composition class. Students need to know what they need to do, how close they are to doing it, and how to close the gap.

As well as modelling and giving feedback on technique, the teacher also focuses on the mental dimensions and demands of performance. Talking to the student about cognitively understanding the structure of a piece, locating *hooking points* to help them pick back up if they have a problem, and so on. Discussion and explaining are therefore also important in the pedagogy of the performance studio.

SPOTLIGHT 3.2.C – LEARNING TO DESIGN IT SYSTEM ARCHITECTURE

In Cécile's course, the exercises that students complete were designed to walk them through the different stages of the design process and the kinds of tools and approaches they could use at each stage in the process. While this approach gave them both an overview of the design process as well as drilling down to specific tools and competences, not all students found it easy to zoom out and see how it all fitted together. Cécile says,

> For example, when learning a particular approach to representing a system, students could follow a series of steps to completion but not be able to step back and say "Ah! I can now represent a system in this way; I can use that in this situation or in that situation".

SPOTLIGHT 3.3.C – LEARNING TO MANAGE OPEN-ENDED PROJECTS

For Roland, learning in his project is based on students doing and on reflecting on what they have done.

> Students will only learn new things if they try to do new things. A lot of the project is designed to push them outside their comfort zone. Students are assigned to groups, for example, and the groups are chosen to include a mix of disciplines and backgrounds. Some students have never spoken to a client

before, or recruited participants for an experiment. The conditions for learning are created by asking them to do things which are new to them.

This gives rise to a lot of student questions, which Roland says, he tries not to answer.

> One year a team came to me with two different designs and explained they could not choose between them so they asked me which they should pursue. I asked them why they couldn't decide. After a while, it became apparent that they didn't know any strategies that could help them make a decision. I explained two strategies to them, a decision matrix and multi-voting. I suggested they use a strategy and come back to me to let me know what they decided. I think they would have preferred if I had just told them which design was better, but I don't think they would have learned much from that.

Alongside their final report students also complete a learning portfolio documenting the process of doing the project which accounts for 20% of the marks. At set times during the term, they are asked to collect data on how they are managing their project and on how they are working as a team. Each team has to analyse this data and make suggestions as to how they could work more effectively. At the end of the semester each person lists all the changes that their group had proposed, which ones actually got adopted, and which ones they would try to use in future team projects. The portfolio activities shift the focus a little away from the product and towards understanding the process.

> They'll probably never have to solve this same problem ever again, so the solution they arrive at isn't all that important to them. But understanding the process is. Even if their solution doesn't work, I'm not going to worry, so long as they understand why it didn't work and how they could manage the process better next time.

> **SPOTLIGHT 3.4.C – CARRYING OUT SCIENTIFIC INVESTIGATIONS IN A LAB**
>
> Developing independence in the lab is important for Anne-Sophie,
>
> > Our graduates aren't employed to just follow protocols – they need to be able to tackle novel problems and figure out how to design experiments that meet specific needs. To develop this ability, students need to have the experience of making decisions.
>
> However, Anne-Sophie also has to manage significant logistic and safety concerns related to having hundreds of novice chemists in the lab each week.
>
> > I want students to feel that they are making the decisions, that they have to figure out what needs to be done and how to do it. But in fact, I have set up sort of a corridor for them, even though their decisions make them zigzag along rather than running straight through. For example, students might be told they can synthesis a particular product any way that they choose. But once students have narrowed their options in terms of the chemicals I've made available to them, they will end up with one relatively safe option. There is a lot of guidance that they don't really see.

As with other aspects of practical learning treated above, it is evident that there is a great deal of differences between the teaching approaches. In some cases, like Gwen's performance studio, the teacher is highly directive. In this case, the teacher is demonstrating and directing and the student is an apprentice, mirroring and *learning from the master*. In Roland and Anne-Sophie's cases, the course activities are designed to build the learner's autonomy and ability to deal with uncertainty. To achieve this, the teaching is organised so that the student is much more in control. Indeed, even when the students ask for direction, Roland sometimes tries to avoid giving it to them, preferring instead to nudge them into making their own decisions. Cécile's situation is somewhat between these two: students are working on their own project and have to make their own decisions, but they also have the teacher's input both in the form of lectures and in the form of highly structured exercises which *walk them through* the processes they need to master.

WHAT STUDENTS LEARN IN PRACTICAL SETTINGS

FIGURE 3.1 Who directs students' activities in experiential classes and with what goals?

Rather than being simply student-led or teacher-led, then, experiential learning can be thought of as being along a continuum ranging between those two positions. This continuum is illustrated in Figure 3.1. This is not simply a function of the teacher's preferences or personality. For example, Gwen's two practical courses have very different organisational approaches to learning activities: her composition studio is substantially student-led, and her role there is often that of facilitator, while in the performance studio her role is more that of master who leads the student-apprentice. More important than teacher personality or preference are the learning goals which ultimately determine whether the teacher is modelling, explaining and directing, or facilitating.

EXPLAINING, QUESTIONING, GIVING FEEDBACK, AND MANAGING THE LEARNING CLIMATE

Underneath this divergence in the *big-picture* organisation of the practical class, some patterns stand out. In all cases there are times when the teacher needs to demonstrate or explain to the students. In some cases, like Cécile's course, this may be seen in pre-planned and highly structured explanations in the form of lectures and solved exercises to accompany a project. In Roland's case the explanations are not pre-planned but rather arise in response to students' questions. In this case, even if Roland doesn't want to explain to students which design is better, he still needs to explain to them different strategies which they could use for making their own decision. *Effective teacher explanations* are, then, central to practical learning.

A second strategy which emerges is *asking questions or posing problems* for students. When Roland is asked a question by students, he responds with a question. For Anne-Sophie, labs are structured so as to avoid giving all the answers to students – their instructions are deliberately structured to include gaps which the students themselves have to fill. Students' processing of information is central to their learning; she says, "If they just replicate the procedure, they aren't thinking and they forget everything quickly. They need to

PART I

be thinking, to be making connections to the theory, and checking to see if it makes sense". Being able to formulate appropriate questions or thinking tasks – often in response to student questions – is central to practical teaching.

A third teaching strategy that is evident in multiple case studies is that of *giving students feedback* on the work they produce. For Gwen, for example, her teaching approach is described as "continually assessing their work and giving them feedback within the class". Since feedback means responding to something a student has produced, and since practical work is centrally concerned with students producing something, feedback is an absolutely central teaching activity in labs, fieldwork, projects, and studios.

Finally, it is clear that in all these cases, students are being asked to try things they are not comfortable with, to fail, to get feedback, and to improve. Students are only willing and able to do this if the class climate is one that makes them feel secure and where they think that the teacher is genuinely concerned with their learning. Managing the learning climate of the class is, therefore, a fourth important strategy.

Chapters 4–7 of this book are structured around these four strategies. Whatever the learning goals, being able to explain, give feedback, ask good questions, and manage learning relationships are teaching strategies that can be used to help achieve these goals.

DOING, REFLECTING, THEORISING, AND TESTING

It is obvious that practical courses typically involve the student in *doing*. However what the Spotlights above also clarify is that *reflecting on doing* is central to learning in experiential courses. For Gwen, students work together to generate and test ideas and sounds; then they discuss together (i) what they are doing and why, (ii) how they are working together and how they would work together differently if they had to do a similar task again, and (iii) how to apply what they have learned to the primary classroom. For Roland too, students are asked to reflect as part of a portfolio which they develop alongside working on their project. In this case, students collect data on their own processes and decide what they would like to change in how they are working. As with Gwen's case, they discuss these reflections with teammates.

One frequently used way of thinking about the relationship between *doing* and *reflecting* in practical learning is the experiential learning cycle model, originally proposed by David Kolb (1984).

For Kolb, "Learning is the process whereby knowledge is created through the transformation of experience" (1984, 38). In order to learn then, students need four different kinds of abilities to transform experience into knowledge:

- concrete experience abilities: to be able to be open to fully experience, without bias, their actual experience,
- reflective observation abilities: to be able to observe this experience and to think about it from different perspectives,
- abstract conceptualisation abilities: to be able to see regularities in these experiences and to link them to logically sound concepts and theories,
- active experimentation abilities: to be able to use these concepts and theories to make decisions and solve problems in the real world.

These four abilities are represented graphically in Figure 3.2.

Kolb identified that, for learning to take place, it is not sufficient for a learner to employ only one of these abilities – rather experiential learning needs to be understood as a holistic and cyclical process in which learners can draw on all of the required learning abilities one after another. In this way, students cycle through a series of steps: having an experience, thinking about it, using that to build their concepts and understandings, and using those concepts to solve problems and ask questions of the world.

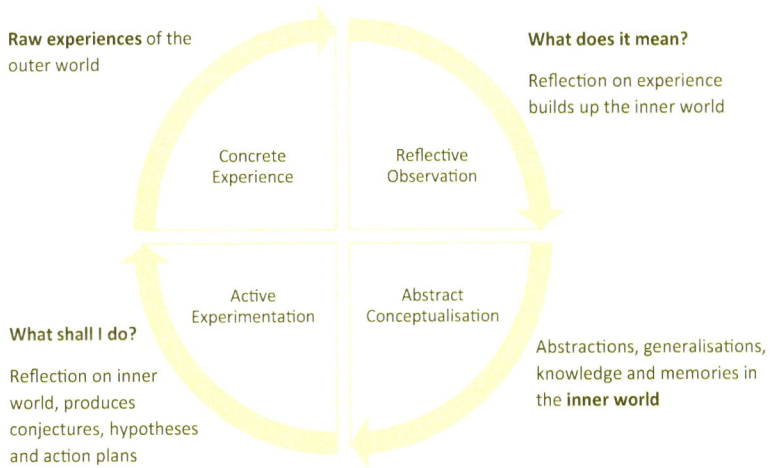

FIGURE 3.2 Kolb's experiential learning cycle (1984)

(Adapted from Exley et al. 2018, 17)

Kolb's ideas have been hugely influential. Later work has simplified his language a little to suggest that the four skills of experiential learning can be framed as four stages which can be called *experience*, *reflect*, *generalise*, and *test*. It may not be necessary for a learner to follow this particular order, though they are often presented as four sequential steps.

Mick Healey and Alan Jenkins (2000) describe the application of Kolb's ideas to a range of different geography courses, including a fieldwork course. In their case, before the field experience, students began by reading competing theories regarding the geography of post-industrial society (AC – generalise) and then worked in teams to define how they would collect interview data from the field study which would allow them to test these models (AE – test). Once in the field, students went through a cycle of conducting initial field interviews (CE – experience), discussing them and journal writing (RO – reflect), making tentative hypotheses based upon their interviews and reflections (AC), adapting their interview schedule in light of their emerging theorisations (AE), and then carrying out further interviews (CE).

They note that Kolb's learning cycle provided a useful way to think about the sequence and structure of the activities that they built into the course in order to maximise student learning. They also note that the model typically does not require a complete revision of existing hands-on activities – it is a useful framework for thinking about and tweaking practical classes, rather than one which requires massive restructuring of them.

It is worth noting that, although Kolb's work has also been extended into a highly influential *learning styles* model, this idea is not explored in this chapter. Although *learning styles* theories are very popular they are also highly controversial among learning researchers. Indeed they may constitute an example of what is sometimes called pop psychology or *neuromyths*, that is, ideas about the brain and the mind which have been so widely shared that they become popularly accepted despite a lack of evidence to support them. In the case of learning styles, there is actually little empirical evidence to support the idea in general (Pashler et al. 2009) or Kolb's learning styles approach in particular (see [Coffield et al. 2004, 60–70] for a review). We present Kolb's experiential learning cycle solely as a useful way to think about practical learning and do not promote linking it to learning styles.

This section began with a recognition that doing alone was not sufficient for learning – it seems likely that students will need to engage in a mix of doing and reflecting (as well as generalising and testing). However, it is worth noting that, although the term *reflection* is widely used, it is not always evident to students what they are expected to actually do when being asked to reflect (indeed, as we will return to in Chapter 10, the same can often be said of higher education teachers). Writing in the context of students' field experiences in a teacher education programme, for example, Oliver McGarr and Orla McCormack (2014) note that, while the term *reflection* is so widespread that it has effectively become a dominant paradigm in teacher education, many students do not seem to have a clear idea as to what they are expected to do when reflecting. Students typically use reflection as a kind of diary (recording day-to-day events), or as a form of confession (avowing responsibility), but rarely as a form of critical inquiry into their own practices and those of others. They note a number of factors which may enable students to engage in the kinds of deep reflection which would be associated with learning:

- The timing of reflective activities is likely to be important: reflection involves "detachment from an activity followed by a distinct period of contemplation" (Hatton and Smith 1995, 34). Reflections may therefore require some time to detach and pause for thought.
- Treating reflection as a dialogue: when people discuss their impressions with others, it often becomes apparent that the way they interpreted a situation is not the same as how others interpreted it. As such, they start to see their own perspective as being just that – *their own* perspective, and one of *potentially many* perspectives. As such, they move from "this is how it was" to "this is how I saw it". This, in turn, opens up the possibility to reinterpret or rethink the situation. Building opportunities for dialogue is likely to be important in supporting reflection.
- The intended audience is likely to be important: McGarr and McCormack note that students seem to sometimes write reflections as if they are following a distinct narrative in which they demonstrate their perseverance and commitment by overcoming obstacles. They suggest that, in writing in this way, the student may be performing to a script which matches what they think the tutor wants to see. If the students are to be given space to be more honest in their reflections, perhaps at least some of those reflections need to be for their own eyes only.

You may want to apply these ideas to reflecting on your own experiences. This is why, in Chapter 2, we suggested that you may wish to set aside time to work through the Reflection point activities, to write down your answers, and to discuss them with colleagues.

PART I

THE IMPORTANCE OF CLEAR LEARNING GOALS

One final key pedagogical dimension is implicit in much of the discussion in this chapter: for problem solving, investigations, professional skills like teamwork, and metacognitive competences, it was pointed out that students learn these skills best when the skills are made explicit to students.

This is an important point, because it is sometimes assumed that if one creates opportunities for students to have practical experiences, then they will learn from those experiences. This approach is sometimes referred to as *discovery learning* (but could be more precisely called *unguided discovery learning*). Discovery learning is often characterised as encouraging students to explore a given situation with minimal guidance with the assumption that students will learn by having their curiosity unleashed and spontaneously recognising patterns (such as that particular ways of working in a team are effective and others are not).

A commonly used analogy is the idea that infants can learn to swim simply by being immersed in water and allowing their natural reflexes to take over. While infants have reflexes that sometimes make it look like they can naturally swim, the reality is that infants cannot *naturally* swim: indeed, drowning is a leading cause of death among young children. Similarly, it is not realistic to expect that a natural curiosity and an innate ability to recognise patterns will mean that students are able to learn to solve problems, or to manage teams simply by being dropped into a team and asked to solve problems.

This is not simply a question of philosophy or of competing educational theories: this issue has been subject to exhaustive research over an extended period of time. In their review of quantitative studies of learning, John Hattie and Gregory Donoghue (2016) found that making the success criteria or learning goals explicit to students increased their average attainment very substantially. Hattie and Donoghue note that,

> when students learn how to gain an overall picture of what is to be learnt, have an understanding of the success criteria for the lessons to come and are somewhat clear at the outset about what it means to master the lessons, then their subsequent learning is maximised.

(2016, 6)

CONCLUSION

This chapter looked at a range of practical work settings in higher education including a chemistry lab, a music studio, geography fieldwork, a research project, a teacher education field experience, and computer science and education projects. The diversity of organisation, of learning goals, and of teaching strategies across these different forms of practical work is evident. At the same time, it is clear that there is a high degree of commonality shared across these practical learning settings. While practical courses are central to teaching students the knowledge and skills of their discipline, they also generally share a focus on certain underpinning *ways of thinking*. These ways of thinking include:

1. being able to transfer what has been learned in their course, project, or lab into real-world contexts,
2. carrying out investigations using the skills, approaches, and tools of the discipline,
3. solving problems which are often ill-defined or open-ended,
4. working as professionals, including interacting professionally with others,
5. being metacognitive – that is, managing one's own learning and thinking in order to be able to adapt as situations change.

Because the goals are so varied, the ways of teaching in experiential settings are also varied. But, once more, there are some underlying similarities across these learning settings. Central to practical learning is Kolb's idea that "Learning is the process whereby knowledge is created through the transformation of experience" (1984, 38); in other words, it is not enough for students to *have* experiences in practical classes, they also have to *transform* that experience into concepts and ideas by reflecting on and discussing the experience. Their classmates, labmates, and project team members are central to this in that they can provide a space for exchange and discussion. But so too are teachers, who will:

- *explain* ideas to students that help them to make sense of their experience,
- *pose challenges* and ask questions of students that will encourage them to think through their experience,
- *clarify goals for and give feedback to* students which will help them understand what they are aiming to achieve and how they can achieve it,
- *create a class environment* that supports students to engage in the various activities identified above that contribute to learning.

These four ideas are addressed in each of the chapters in Part II of this book.

FURTHER READING

This small number of sources is intended to provide further useful information for those who wish to explore the chapter topic in more detail. A full reference list for the chapter is provided below.

Learning in groups

Cohen, E.G., and Lotan, R.A. (2014). *Designing Groupwork: Strategies for the Heterogeneous Classroom*, 3rd edition. New York: Teachers College Press.

Exley, K., Dennick, R., and Fisher, A. (2018). *Small Group Teaching, Tutorials Seminars and Workshops*. London: Routledge. https://doi.org/10.4324/9780429490897.

Isaac, S. (2018). Supporting project teams: How do students learn team skills? [video]. *SwitchTube*. https://tube.switch.ch/download/video/344430f1.

Inquiry teaching

Pedaste, M., Mäeots, M., Siiman, L.A., de Jong, T., van Riesen, S.A.N., Kamp, E.T., Manoli, C.C., Zacharia, Z.C., and Tsourlidaki, E. (2015). Phases of inquiry-based learning: Definitions and the inquiry cycle. *Educational Research Review* 14: 47–61. https://doi.org/10.1016/j.edurev.2015.02.003.

Volkman, M.J., and Abell, S.K. (2003). Rethinking laboratories, tools for converting cookbook labs into inquiry. *Science Teacher* 70(6): 38.41.

Explicit learning goals

Butcher, C., Davies, C., and Highton, M. (2019). Chapter 3. What are your students supposed to learn and be able to do? In: *Designing Learning: From Module Outline to Effective Teaching* (pp. 47–66). London: Routledge. https://doi.org/10.4324/9780429463822.

D'Andrea, V.M. (2003). Chapter 3. Organizing teaching and learning: Outcomes based planning. In: H. Fry, S. Ketteridge, and S. Marshall (eds.), *A Handbook for Teaching and Learning in Higher Education*, 2nd edition (pp. 26–41). London: Routledge.

Sá, M.J., and Serpa, S. (2018). Transversal competences: Their importance and learning processes by higher education students. *Education Sciences* 8(3): 126. https://doi.org/10.3390/educsci8030126.

Experiential learning in practical classes

Abdulwahed, M., and Nagy, Z.K. (2013). Applying Kolb's experiential learning cycle for laboratory education. *Journal of Engineering Education* 98(3): 283–294. https://doi.org/10.1002/j.2168-9830.2009.tb01025.x.

Mazur, E. (2016, March 28). Flat space, deep learning, Monday. Physics colloquium [video]. *YouTube*. https://youtu.be/X64TfzDIOAg?t=90.

Raschick, M., Maypole, D.E., and Day, P.A. (1998). Improving field education through Kolb learning theory. *Journal of Social Work Education* 34(1): 31–42. https://doi.org/10.1080/10437797.1998.10778903.

Teaching metacognition

Tanner, K.D. (2012). Promoting student metacognition. *CBE—Life Sciences Education* 11(2): 113–120. https://doi.org/10.1187/cbe.12-03-0033.

University of Waterloo's Centre for Teaching Excellence also has a valuable website: https://uwaterloo.ca/centre-for-teaching-excellence/teaching-resources/teaching-tips/metacognitive.

Vanderbilt University's Centre for Teaching has a useful website on teaching metacognition. https://cft.vanderbilt.edu/guides-sub-pages/metacognition/.

REFERENCES

Aeby, P., Fong, R., Vukmirovic, M., Isaac, S., and Tormey, R. (2019). The impact of gender on engineering students' group work experiences. *International Journal of Engineering Education* 35(3): 756–765.

Coffield, F., Moseley, D., Hall, E., and Ecclestone, K. (2004). *Learning Styles and Pedagogy in Post-16 Learning; a Systematic and Critical Review*. London: Learning and Skills Research Centre.

Colbeck, C.L., Campbell, S.E., and Bjorklund, S.A. (2000). Grouping in the dark: What college students learn from group projects. *Journal of Higher Education* 71(1): 60–83. https://doi.org/10.2307/2649282.

Csikszentmihalyi, M. (1990). *Flow*. New York: Harper and Row.

Exley, K., Dennick, R., and Fisher, A. (2018). *Small Group Teaching, Tutorials Seminars and Workshops*. London: Routledge. https://doi.org/10.4324/9780429490897.

Flavell, J. (1999). Cognitive development: Children's knowledge about the mind. *Annual Review of Psychology* 50: 21–45. https://doi.org/10.1146/annurev.psych.50.1.21.

Ford, M., and Morice, J. (2003). How fair are group assignments? A survey of students and faculty and a modest proposal. *Journal of Information Technology Education: Research* 2(1): 367–378. https://doi.org/10.28945/335.

Hake, R.R. (1998). Interactive-engagement versus traditional methods: A six thousand-survey of mechanics test data for introductory physics courses. *American Journal of Physics* 66(1): 64–74. https://doi.org/10.1119/1.18809.

Hattie, J. (2009). *Visible Learning: A Synthesis of over 800 Meta-Analyses Relating to Achievement*. London: Routledge. https://doi.org/10.4324/9780203887332.

Hattie, J., and Donoghue, G. (2016). Learning strategies: A synthesis and conceptual model. *npj Science of Learning* 1: 16013. https://doi.org/10.1038/npjscilearn.2016.13.

Hatton, N., and Smith, D. (1995). Reflection in teacher education: Toward definition and implementation. *Teaching and Teacher Education* 11(1): 33–49. https://doi.org/10.1016/0742-051X(94)00012-U.

Healey, M., and Jenkins, A. (2000). Kolb's experiential learning theory and its application in geography in higher education. *Journal of Geography* 99(5): 185–195. https://doi.org/10.1080/00221340008978967.

Isaac, S., and Tormey, R. (2015). Undergraduate group projects: Challenges and learning experiences. In: Proceedings of Engineering Leaders Conference 2014 on Engineering Education (p. 19). Doha, Qatar. https://doi.org/10.5339/qproc.2015.elc2014.19.

Kolb, D.A. (1984). *Experiential Learning: Experience as the Source of Learning and Development*. Englewood Cliffs, New Jersey: Prentice Hall.

McGarr, O., and McCormack, O. (2014). Reflecting to conform? Exploring Irish student teachers' discourses in reflective practice. *Journal of Educational Research* 107(4): 267–280. https://doi.org/10.1080/00220671.2013.807489.

Pashler, H., MacDaniel, M., Roher, D., and Bjork, R. (2009). Learning styles: Concepts and evidence. *Psychological Science in the Public Interest* 9(3): 105–119. https://doi.org/10.1111/j.1539-6053.2009.01038.x.

Pedaste, M., Mäeots, M., Siiman, L.A., de Jong, T., van Riesen, S.A.N., Kamp, E.T., Manoli, C.C., Zacharia, Z.C., and Tsourlidaki, E. (2015). Phases of inquiry-based learning: Definitions and the inquiry cycle. *Educational Research Review* 14: 47–61. https://doi.org/10.1016/j.edurev.2015.02.003.

Pólya, G. (1945). *How to Solve It*, 2nd edition, 1957. Princeton: Princeton University Press.

Veenman, M.V.J. (2011.). Learning to self-monitor and self-regulate. In: R. E. Mayer and P. A. Alexander (eds.), *Handbook of Research on Learning and Instruction* (pp. 197–218). New York: Routledge.

Wolfe, J., and Powell, E. (2009). Biases in interpersonal communication: How engineering students perceive gender typical speech acts in teamwork. *Journal of Engineering Education* 98(1): 5–16. https://doi.org/10.1002/j.2168-9830.2009.tb01001.x.

Part II

Chapter 4

Teaching, not telling
Using questions

> **CASE STUDY 4.1.A – ANALYSING RISK IN EMERGING MARKETS**
>
> *Read this case study and complete the analysis questions below.*
>
> Mila* teaches a course called *Investing in Emerging Markets*. In the course, the students complete a project in which they research and produce a detailed report on an investment outlook for a specific company. One of the tutorial sessions accompanies a lecture on risk assessment, and students are told to prepare for the tutorial by reading the relevant chapter in their textbook. She starts the tutorial with a short review of the principles of risk assessment from the course. About half way through her explanations, Mila has the feeling several students may not be following. Mila asks "Is everything clear so far?" and most students respond with an affirmative nod or indifferent shrug. When she reaches the end of her review, Mila asks "Does anyone have any questions?" One student, Janna, asks if they need to present the risk assessment for their report in the same format as the one in the book. Mila explains that the project brief does not require this. There are no other questions. After the students submit the risk assessment component of their project, however, Mila is frustrated to notice that quite a few of them made errors which she had addressed in her tutorial introduction.

PART II

> **Case analysis questions**
>
> Write down and keep your answers to the following questions; you will need them in Case study 4.1.B. Suggested answers can be found at the end of the chapter.
>
> 1. What two questions does Mila ask? For each question: what is the goal of the question? And is it achieved?
> 2. Does Mila explain material that students are already familiar with? How well does her introduction prepare students for the exercise?
>
> * This case is a fictionalised account
of teaching experiences.

INTRODUCTION

One of the most fundamental ideas in teaching is that learning happens because of the activity of the learner. As Chapter 3 explored, learning in practical classes requires the student to use the skills of being open to experiencing things, of reflecting on and thinking about this experience from different perspectives, of seeing the regularities and patterns in experiences, and linking them to concepts, theories, and ideas, and of drawing on these concepts and theories to make decisions and solve problems. While teachers will often naturally focus on what they themselves are doing in a class (i.e. on their own *performance*), it is the learner's activity that is crucial. This chapter focuses on how teachers can shift the focus of activity from themselves to learners through the simple strategy of asking questions at times when they might be tempted to offer an explanation.

Questions are fundamental to the communication between teachers and students, but as for Mila in Case study 4.1.A, they do not always lead to stimulating interactions or indeed to learning. This chapter explores what makes a question a *good* question to ask students, and how our responses to students' questions can foster increased cognitive effort by them. The goal of this chapter is to assist you in constructing good questions that (i) engage your students in meaningful learning activity, (ii) structure your interactions with students to increase their participation, and (iii) respond to students' questions in a way that maximises learning.

There is a broad consensus among educational researchers and practitioners that students learn most effectively when they have frequent opportunities to actively construct their own understanding, rather than simply listening to a lecture or to a series of instructions. Asking students questions, rather than simply explaining things to them, takes more time but it is often ultimately a more efficient use of time. If you do all the explaining yourself,

- Students may walk away feeling like everything was clear but not actually be able to explain it to someone else or use it in practice.
- You may waste students' time by telling them what they already know, yet miss addressing the particular case or application that is problematic for them.
- You deprive students of the opportunity to practice and to get feedback on the thinking they will be expected to demonstrate on the assessment tasks.

Questions are actually the second most frequently used teaching method (according to Hattie [2009, 182], lecturing is the first), although, as illustrated in Spotlight 4.1, not all questions are useful for learning. Several studies have found the majority of questions asked by teachers required only lower-level thinking from students, such as recalling facts (Gaspard and Gainsburg 2020; Tofade et al. 2013). Gaspard and Gainsburg (2020) label more cognitively challenging questions, such as asking students to explain a procedure, *unpredictable questions* because students' responses vary much more widely than for *predictable questions*, such as asking students to state the next step in a procedure. They found that, despite expressing sound pedagogical motivation for using questions and particularly for *unpredictable questions*, student-teachers asked fewer questions and a lower percentage of *unpredictable questions* as the semester progressed. It appears that the student-teachers' commitment to using questions was insufficient to persist in the face of the difficulties of actually using questions. This is unfortunate, as the evidence indicates that students show greater gains in learning when more cognitively challenging questions are used more frequently in teaching (Redfield and Rousseau 1981). More encouragingly, the evidence also suggests that teachers are able to improve their questioning strategies with appropriate practice.

It is sometimes hard to convince teachers and learners that less *telling* may be a more effective teaching strategy than *more telling*. Good *telling* can feel very satisfying for the learner and is also rewarding for teachers, who can bask in the warm glow of satisfaction after having clearly explained something complex. Nonetheless the evidence is clear. Research by Scott Freeman and his colleagues, for example, found 642 research papers on this subject, of which 225 were found to meaningfully compare *interactive teaching* (in which teachers pose questions and encourage students to discuss ideas) with *traditional teaching* in higher education settings. They concluded that, across the studies, on average, failure rates fell from 33.8% under traditional lecturing to 21.8% under active learning (Freeman et al. 2014, 8410). This effect was consistently found across a number of disciplines

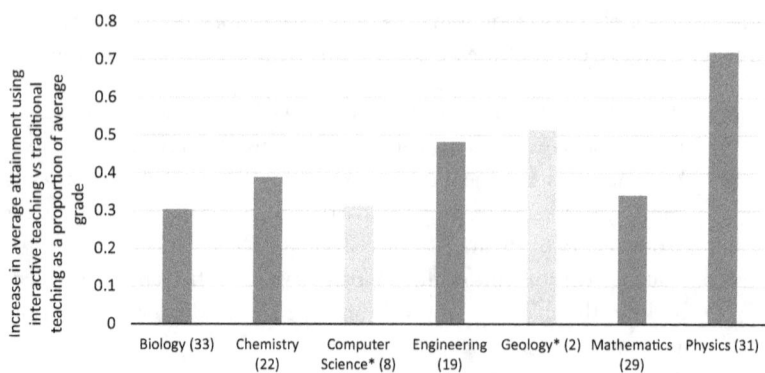

FIGURE 4.1 Increase in average attainment in active learning as compared to traditional teaching. Note: The number in brackets beside the discipline name is the number of studies included on that discipline. The chart represents 158 studies for which comparable examination or assessment data was available. *Lighter coloured bars indicate that the increase in attainment in these disciplines (computer science and geology) is not statistically significant (these disciplines have comparatively fewer studies than other disciplines listed).

(Graph adapted from Freeman et al. 2014)

(see Figure 4.1). There are, therefore, compelling evidence-informed reasons for teachers to try to *tell* less and *ask* more.

Before going further, it is worth recalling that all the chapters in Part II of this book are structured according to this experiential learning cycle described in Chapter 3: they first provide an opportunity for (vicarious) experience through a case study, before building through reflection towards identifying common patterns (i.e. theorising), and then using this to plan for trying things out in practice (i.e. testing). In short, you will probably learn more from this chapter if you take the time to read Case study 4.1.A and attempt the analysis questions before going further, if you have not already done so. You should also take some time to work on the Reflection point activities as you go through the chapter. You can also give yourself feedback, using the suggested responses to a selection of the chapter's activities, which can be found at the end of the chapter.

HOW TO ASK QUESTIONS

In addition to the phrasing of the question itself, how a question is asked will contribute to (or detract from) students' engagement. Even a well-crafted question can fail to elicit a response from students if the context isn't conducive to participation.

If students believe that good telling is good teaching, they may resist engaging with your questions and prefer that you directly tell them the best answer. Sharing your motivations for using frequent questions in your teaching, either in the form of an anecdotal story or the research evidence, may help students be more appreciative of a *teaching with questions* approach. By the time they reach university, students have more than a decade of experience with school and may be slow to change their learning habits without good reason. As Chapter 3 explored, getting students to think about how they are thinking and learning is an important feature of experiential learning and one that contributes to building expertise.

It is also important to consider the experience of students attempting to answer your questions. Revealing their thinking, their lack of knowledge, or their lack of skill in a particular practical task involves some risk. This can be heightened if the interaction is happening in front of the rest of their class. A desire to avoid laughter and scorn, from peers or teachers, is a powerful reason to avoid participating in class. As the teacher, you have the opportunity and responsibility to create a constructive classroom climate that encourages students to engage in deliberative practice by trying, failing, getting feedback, and trying again.

A primary way to create a question-friendly environment is to welcome every response from a student. How you respond to the first several answers students provide to your questions is very important, as it will set the tone for your interactions with the group. Phrases like, "I'm always glad when someone answers a question I ask; I'm never sure if my explanation was clear until I hear back from someone", communicate that student attempts to answer questions are welcome. You may even choose to make an explicit statement about the value of questions for learning. Having students actively process information is crucial for their learning, so be sure to express your appreciation when students contribute a question or answer.

One particularly challenging aspect for teachers is dealing with incorrect student answers. On one hand, the teacher doesn't want to embarrass the student as this just makes it less likely that students will try to answer in future. On the other hand, the teacher cannot pretend the answer is correct as this will hinder students' learning. As we noted in Chapter 2, a key feature of deliberate practice is that the student is able to try, fail, get feedback, and try again. Viewed from this perspective, getting things wrong in the low-stakes environment of your lab, project, studio, or field experience is a normal part of learning and is what helps make sure the student doesn't get it wrong when it really matters. There are a number of strategies that you can use to communicate to students that getting an answer to a question wrong is not really a bad thing:

- Ask them to elaborate on their response: it may be that they are actually closer to the mark than it first appears, and that they just had difficulty formulating a clear response; saying something like "Can you tell me more about that? I'm not sure I understand your answer" can be helpful.
- Don't try to fudge things: as Chapter 5 will explore, students learn a lot from finding out they are wrong when they thought they were right, so being clear that an answer is not correct is valuable to their learning.
- Make sure they don't feel alone: highlighting that their mistake is a common one (perhaps even one that you yourself made when you were first engaging with the material) can help them see their error as more acceptable.
- Highlight that wrong answers give useful feedback to the teacher: saying something like "That's not actually correct, but it is a really useful answer because it shows me my explanation was not clear", can take the focus off the student.
- Highlight that a wrong answer is not the end of the story, but part of the deliberate practice process: remind students that if they are to get something wrong, a low-stakes learning environment is the right time to do it.

A second important aspect of an environment that supports participation is adequate thinking time. A good question will require students to think, and you will need to create the temporal space for them to do this. It can be quite difficult for teachers to stop talking for long enough to allow students to really think, particularly with a performance-accelerated heart rate. Being willing to *live with the silence* for a few moments is important, because it conveys to the students that your question is not rhetorical and that you actually expect a response. Indeed, since many teachers do ask questions rhetorically, it may be necessary to clarify to students that you do expect a response to your question. When working with a group or a class, asking students to write down their answers to your question is a useful way to get feedback on *when* they finish the task (their pens stop moving) and it also takes their eyes off you, which can make waiting in silence more comfortable for you. When working with individuals or with a whole class, phrases like "I'm going to ask a question; you can take two minutes to consider you response and then I'll ask for an answer", can be useful.

Finally, it is appropriate to have prepared a debriefing strategy for students' responses. Debriefing provides an opportunity for students to get feedback on their learning, either directly from you or by comparing their own response to one shared by a peer. A good debriefing strategy makes use of what was produced through students' efforts and provides them with feedback on their learning. Techniques that make students' contributions more visible, such as reflecting back to them the key points you have heard them make, are valuable. While responding to questions one-to-one is challenging enough for students, responding when other students are watching can be even more daunting. In larger group settings you can make students' contributions visible by highlighting what interests you in their answer or by collecting responses from different people on the board. Reinforce a positive class environment by using debriefing strategies that allow students, not you, to choose *when* they share with the whole group; giving students this autonomy can decrease stress and foster trust. You also may want to use the three-part feedback structure, explained in Chapter 5, to give feedback to an individual or to a group. Table 4.1 summarises

TABLE 4.1 Fostering a participative environment

	Poor approach	Better approach
Creating an environment that welcomes questions	Imply that student participation is trivial or otherwise not worthy of class time.	Thank the student for participating or express interest in the thinking behind their contribution.
	Reject all responses that do not exactly match the answer you expected.	"That is part of the answer. Does anyone have something to add?"
Thinking time	Allow the first student who raises their hand to answer.	Ask students to write down their answers and allow time for half the class to finish before debriefing.
	Attentively watch students while they think, as though you are ready to start talking at any time.	Tell students how long they have to think and then take a step back (look away) to signal that you are not about to start talking.
Debriefing strategies	Present students with a perfect response you prepared ahead of time.	Use students' contributions to collaboratively build an excellent response.
	Spend five minutes correcting one student's incorrect answer.	Conduct a quick poll to see how many other students got the same answer.
	Respond by immediately characterising an answer as correct or incorrect.	Invite other students to share other answers or to explain their reasoning.

some of the points for creating a class climate that encourages student participation.

THREE TYPES OF QUESTIONS

The analysis questions in Case study 4.1.A asked you to consider Mila's goal for the questions she asked. Questions can be thought of as having a range of goals. For learning in practical settings, three types of goals are particularly important. First, *stimulating questions* that seek to engage students in really thinking about the course material and how to apply it. Second, *diagnostic questions* that provide feedback on what students have understood and the nature of any difficulties they have encountered. And finally, *hint questions* that are used to focus or direct students' attention on knowledge or a skill that would help them resolve a difficulty. These three goals for questions are illustrated in Table 4.2. Whichever of the

TABLE 4.2 Three common goals for asking questions

Type	Definition	Examples
Stimulating question	Poses a challenge that requires students to engage in a meaningful learning activity.	• "What theoretical models could you use to explain your field observations?" • "If the instrument output flatlines, what are the likely causes?" • "How could you formulate your recommendations so that the client is more likely to be receptive to them?"
Diagnostic question	Seeks information about the source or nature of a student's difficulty.	• "Can you show me what you have already done?" • "How are you feeling about what needs to be done?" • "What definitions did you need to establish for your study?"
Hints	Gentle, or more directed, reminders that focus students' attention on knowledge or a skill that will advance their current task.	• "What procedure do we usually perform after each acidification?" • "Have you seen a similar problem before? What process was used to solve it?" • "What does this type of reaction imply about a person's emotional state?"

three goals motivates a question, good questions will engage students in meaningful learning activity.

> ### SPOTLIGHT 4.1 – WHAT MAKES A GOOD QUESTION?
>
> Richard Felder (1994) notes that while questions are central to the learning process, most questions asked by teachers are not very useful because they fall into one of these two types of questions:
>
> 1. *If A decreases by 0.6 units per hour, how long until half of the initial amount of A is gone?*
> 2. *Do you have any questions?*
>
> The first type of question has a single correct answer, Felder notes, and involves only students' memory to repeat a definition or perform a numeric substitution. The second question is so broad as to rarely elicit much response from students. Felder writes that good questions "provoke curiosity, stimulate thought, illustrate the true meaning of lecture material, and trigger a discussion or some other form of student activity that leads to new or deeper understanding".

ASKING STIMULATING QUESTIONS

The effectiveness of stimulating questions can be judged against three criteria (indeed, these criteria can be applied more widely to other questions also). First, questions should engage students in relevant learning or thinking activity by posing a task that aligns with the target learning. Generating questions can be quite difficult, and teachers often ask a question that is easier to formulate or that has a clear answer, rather than a question that allows students to practice the most relevant thinking, feeling, or doing. Feldman's first type of question illustrates this short coming (Spotlight 4.1). If you would like students to develop critical thinking and problem-solving skills, for example, then you should ask questions that prompt the use of these thinking skills. As Chapter 2 explored, if you want students to develop into experts, then there is a range of different types of thinking, feeling, and acting that you might want to encourage:

- Experts perceive things that novices don't, so questions which ask students to safely look, listen, smell, touch, or taste can be helpful in building their ability to perceive; questions of this type might include "Who can describe to me what is happening here?" or "Can you tell me what you see?"
- Experts can rapidly recall whole blocks of relevant information, and can remember the right information in the right situation, so questions which ask students to link ideas to each other or to link ideas to situations can be helpful; examples of this kind of question include, "What principles apply in a situation like this?", or "Have you seen a situation like this described in the lecture?"
- Experts tend to be systematic in problem solving in their domain and to monitor their learning and their performance, and so questions which focus on self-monitoring can also be of value; this might include questions like, "What kind of factors should you consider before deciding how to proceed?" or "Is there any way you could check if you are on the right track in what you are doing?"
- Experts experience and regulate emotions in productive ways, and so questions which enable students to pay attention to their own emotional state are worth considering; examples of this kind of question might include, "Is there something that surprises you about your results?" or "You seem frustrated; how typical do you think it is for people at this stage in a project to feel frustrated?"

When working to develop the right kind of thinking there is nothing wrong with asking students factual or recall questions *per se*. Building expertise does involve being able to recall relevant information in context, and asking students to recall information that they have previously learned in a lecture or when reading, will help them to conditionalise that information in the lab, project, or field. Asking factual questions can also help them to focus on what is relevant when they are becoming overwhelmed by information and possibilities when they are working on projects or in the field. The problem with factual recall questions arises if they are the dominant question type used, rather than one of multiple question types. Since simple recall questions can often be formulated rapidly without prior preparation by the teacher, this type of question is asked more often (Wilen 1991) than other question types. But asking students to review a chapter via a decontextualised recall of information, for example (as illustrated in the first line of Table 4.3), does not in itself make the connections that will enable them to apply the information in context. Generating effective questions typically requires

TABLE 4.3 Characteristics of effective stimulating questions

Characteristics of effective questions	Poor example	Better example
Engage students in relevant learning or thinking activity.	"Can you list the types of forces presented in this chapter?" (where the goal is applying lecture material to a lab task)	"Looking at this illustration, what forces do you expect to be present?"
	"What did I tell you last class about how financial models are different from real situations?" (where the goal is comparing a mathematical model with a real-life phenomenon)	"How would you expect stock market values on the first day of the month to differ from our calculated model?"
Pose clear and specific questions.	"What are your ideas about how political regimes exert influence on the arts community?"	"What are three strategies political regimes use to exert influence on the arts community?"
	"Does anyone have any questions?"	"If the client lived in an urban environment, what is the major difference that you would expect to see?"
Offer an appropriate cognitive challenge, potentially as a series of tasks.	"How do you promote simultaneous movement in a group of dancers?"	• "What are the main gestures that contribute to the impression of synchronicity?" • "What cues can dancers use to initiate a movement?"

some advance planning, in the same way you prepare the introduction to a presentation.

A second feature of effective questions is that they clearly communicate the nature of the response you expect from students. Students will be more likely to engage if your question poses an explicit task. Taking the example in the third row of Table 4.3, students could misunderstand and think that you wanted them to tell you about *how* the arts community changes, or about historical examples, or about issues caused by the changes. The resultant uncertainty means that fewer students are thinking about what you want them to think about. Further, students may be hesitant to share their answer with the class due to the risk of exposing their misinterpretation. This leads to missed opportunities for you and your students to get feedback on learning. Returning to Case study 4.1.A, both of Mila's questions fall into the second of Felder's categories and suffer from a lack of specificity. While Mila's questions convey a desire for students to ask her questions, it is a difficult task for students to formulate a question that expresses their misunderstanding within a brief pause. Since students may not know whether or not they are alone in not understanding something, they may also be reticent to demonstrate their ignorance to their classmates. It is not uncommon, therefore, for the question "Do you have any questions?" to be met with silence. A better approach to checking understanding is to ask a question that allows students to check their own understanding (as shown in the example on the fourth line of Table 4.3). By asking students to respond to specific questions about the content of the session, teachers generate useful feedback for themselves and also for their students. Such questions can also stimulate students to respond by asking you more specific questions, as their misunderstandings and lacunae become clearer to them. Case study 4.1.B presents an example of what this might look like.

Finally, the question should pose an appropriate level of challenge. A question which is too easy does not engage students' curiosity and intellect. A question which is too difficult is equally demotivating and exposes students to the risk of derision from their peers. For more complex tasks, consider using a sequence of questions. For example, a series of specific questions can guide students to recall, compare, analyse, and then evaluate, for example, the relevance of a specific experimental protocol in a given context. Sequencing questions can also be useful in preventing students being overwhelmed by information or options. It can also support students to work more autonomously.

CASE STUDY 4.1.B – ANALYSING RISK IN EMERGING MARKETS

Read this case study and complete the analysis questions below.
   Mila has a second tutorial with a different group of project teams later in the week. Instead of starting with a review of the material on risk assessment, Mila has prepared a set of questions. Her first

sentence is "OK, thinking back to the last lecture, what are the key tools for performing a risk assessment?" Students contribute different methods and Mila writes them on the board, categorising them according to their focus. Next, she asks students to tell her about the potential effects of not performing an adequate risk assessment as part of their business outlook report. To check that students have understood the importance, she says "I think we have identified the big risks. So, to summarise, what are 3 most relevant risk mitigation strategies for companies in emerging markets?"

After a few students have responded, Thierry asks how to know if they have done the risk assessment correctly. Mila responds by deflecting the question back to the class "So, what does the project brief say about the requirements for the risk assessment?"

Despite the increased participation during Mila's introductory session, students encounter difficulties as they work through the risk assessment analysis. But Mila keeps asking her students questions to support them in figuring it out themselves, rather than relying on her to confirm each step.

Case analysis questions

Write down your answers to the following questions; you will need them later. Suggested answers can be found at the end of the chapter.

1. What questions does Mila ask in the second tutorial? For each question, what do you see as being the goal of the question? How are the goals different to her questions in the first tutorial?
2. Drawing on the three characteristics of effective questions, would you judge her questions in this second tutorial to be effective? How does this differ from your analysis of the first tutorial?
3. In this session, what does Mila explain that students should already know?

* This case is a fictionalised account of teaching experiences.

ASKING DIAGNOSTIC QUESTIONS

This section focuses on how to support students' thinking with *diagnostic questions* that seek to make the nature of the difficulty students are currently experiencing clear to them. Using diagnostic questions involves supporting students to develop the ability to tackle a similar issue autonomously in the future and should allow you to gain a better understanding of what students have understood.

Students' requests for help are often quite broad, for example "I can't do step #5", and thus do not provide much information about the obstacle they perceive. As experts, we tend to reply based on our own perception of what is difficult, but, as Chapter 9 explores, experts can find it hard to see what novices do not understand (Nathan and Petrosino 2003). Asking questions to get a clearer understanding of the students' thinking has advantages for teachers as well, such as getting feedback on your teaching and revealing students' misconceptions. While it is a challenge, attempting to put aside your assumptions and asking genuine questions will likely lead to more enlightening interactions for both you and the student (think, for example, of Roland's experience in trying to find out why students couldn't decide on which design they should pursue, described in Spotlight 3.3.C in Chapter 3).

We should also be careful to manage our tendency to focus our questions predominantly on content knowledge and to neglect the other skills outlined in Chapter 3, such as transferring learning to another context, finding solutions to ill-structured or open-ended problems, as well as professional skills like communication and life-long learning. Focusing only on disciplinary content may contribute to the invisibility of professional and transversal skills, while asking questions about them highlights to the students that they are important learning goals. These types of questions are useful to help students perceive the skills underlying the successful resolution of a particular activity or procedural step, and thus help students transfer their skills to future challenges. Spotlight 4.2 reports on a study that investigated the impact of teaching with questions in the lab.

It can be difficult to compose a question on the spot which targets higher level thinking skills, so having a few standard questions that you can use in a range of situations can be useful. Some examples of *diagnostic questions* are presented in Table 4.4, organised in terms of when during students' work on a specific activity they would be most relevant. However, it remains relevant to avoid imposing your assumptions on students. For example, a student may still be unclear about the goal of the lab despite having produced half a page of calculations. Any intervention on your part may be ineffective until the goal of the activity is clear for the student.

TABLE 4.4 Examples of diagnostic questions

Task progress	Poor questions	Better questions
Early	• "Why didn't you do X first?" • "Did you see that Y will determine the answer?"	• "What is the goal of this activity?" • "What looks difficult about this task?" • "What have you done so far?"
Mid	• "Did you try doing X instead of Y?" • "Have you completed phase 1?" • "You know you need to focus on X, right?"	• "What are the obstacles preventing you from moving forward?" • "Looks like good work. Show me what you've done so far, and where you are having difficulty." • "What are you trying to accomplish in this phase?"
Late	• "Did you check your results against the book?" • "Was this the way you were told to do this?"	• "How confident are you in your results? How could you check them?" • "What worked well and what worked less well in the approach you took?" • "Which step was most difficult for you personally?" • "Was there anything surprising or unexpected about this activity?" • "Would you be able to perform a similar task independently?"

If *diagnostic questions* are not sufficient to enable a student to overcome their obstacle, you may want to use a *hint*. *Hints* are more directed questions to help the students to recall specific procedural or content knowledge, and how to use these questions to guide students is explained in the next section.

SPOTLIGHT 4.2 – STUDENTS LEARN MORE IN THE LAB WHEN TEACHERS USE MORE QUESTIONS

P. Willam Hughes and Michelle Ellefson (2013) recruited 52 novice teachers (actually teaching assistants) to supervise the laboratory portion of an undergraduate biology course. While each one received

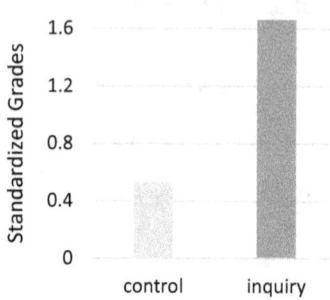

FIGURE 4.2 Students' grades increased when lab assistants were trained in inquiry teaching

two hours of training, they were randomly assigned to either the standard *best practices* training or a second training approach which focused on learning how to ask questions to guide students in the lab (called the *inquiry* group in the chart, see Figure 4.2). Despite the short intervention, being in a class in which the assistant had been trained to ask questions had a significant positive effect on what their students learned, as measured by students' grades and also their self-reports of learning.

QUESTIONS AND HINTS

If you have successfully diagnosed the nature of a student's difficulty, it may be that, rather than provide an explanation, you can help their thinking by providing a small nudge which prompts the student to focus on a particular aspect of the activity, or to remember strategies or information already known to them. Hints should be brief in formulation in order to keep the cognitive activity with the student rather than taking the form of a mini-lecture.

As illustrated by the examples in Table 4.5, hints can prompt students to recall specific procedural or content knowledge. Learning how and when to use their knowledge, and how to transfer their knowledge to novel situations, is a key goal of practical learning. A good hint stimulates the student to make conceptual connections, for example, "Given what you've told me about the molecular composition, what type of bonding do you expect?" A

TABLE 4.5 Examples of hint questions

Less directive hints	More directive hints
• *"What step of the method are you at now? What 'should' you do next?"*	• *"The first step is to understand your context. What kinds of things can you do to really scope out the problem?"*
• *"What approaches or options have you considered using?"*	• *"What tools or techniques are relevant in a situation like this?"*
• *"What concepts/models/principles seem relevant to you in this situation?"*	• *"Which perspectives have you included so far and which have you not included?"*
• *"Is there a way of testing that idea?"*	• *"Thinking in terms of power, what can you say about the relationship?"*
• *"You are making good progress. Keep at it – figuring it out by yourself is the best preparation for the field".*	• *"Where did your errors come from? How will you change your approach to avoid this in the future?"*

poor hint is an unrelated mnemonic riddle, for example "What type of bonding starts with the letter N?"

Hints are also useful to encourage students who are struggling with self-limiting beliefs or are only concerned with getting the correct answer right now and not developing skills for the longer term. Teachers in practical settings have a very important role in guiding students, without taking away their autonomy, to manage their own thinking processes. Asking hint questions that allow students to identify an inconsistency or an error themselves may appear less efficient than you pointing out the exact source of their difficulty, but your ability to see the error is a function of your expertise, and, for the student, part of the process of developing expertise is developing the ability to find their own errors.

While using hints can feel good for both the student and the teacher in terms of the progress on the current activity, this rapid progress should not be interpreted as effective learning. When we teach in practical learning settings, we need to create opportunities for students to apply their knowledge and to exercise their skills in increasingly autonomous ways. When you find yourself in dialogue with a student who requests a lot of guidance from you, it may be a good time to remind them about the big goals of the activity. Asking something like "Why has the professor assigned this report? Will she make investment decisions based on your analysis?" can be useful to remind the student that *learning how to do* the analysis is the essential aspect, rather than a final value or declarative statement.

It can also be useful to remind ourselves that the overuse of hints can decrease students' self-confidence and autonomy, as they come to rely on you to ease the way in particularly difficult steps. It is particularly important to consider how our implicit biases about the aptitudes of certain groups such as women or members of particular ethnic groups may influence our decisions about when to offer additional help. Extra *help* is sometimes a gentle, if unintentional, way of conveying lower expectations for particular students and is linked to lower academic outcomes by people who feel profiled in this way (Spencer et al. 1999). It was noted above that allowing students time to think through and respond to your questions is important. There is evidence which suggests that teachers can convey low expectations of students from some social groups by allowing them less time to think in response to questions. Being careful about how and when you use hints and guidance is, therefore, important.

An alternative strategy to *hint questions* is to get students to collaborate with their peers. Working with peers involves a high level of cognitive activity as students explain and interact with each other, and is particularly useful for metacognitive development, as it enables students to learn different ways of thinking and to assess their own approach. When setting up group work, be clear with students about the benefits for all students, rather than conveying that it will support less able students (this issue is explored in Chapter 9).

> ## REFLECTION POINT 4.1
>
> Make a record of the number and kind of questions you ask in your next interaction with students, using the questions below to guide your analysis. Making a record is probably most easily done by using a smartphone or other device to make an audio recording of what you say during the session.
>
> 1. What percentage of your interventions involve students receiving content information? What percentage of your interventions led to students actively constructing their own understanding?
> 2. How many of your questions were *stimulating questions, diagnostic questions,* and *hints*?

3. Which of your questions provided you or your students with useful feedback about student learning? Do these questions have anything in common?

RESPONDING WHEN STUDENTS ASK YOU QUESTIONS

Having students ask you questions is a great way to access the benefits of both active learning and of mutual feedback between students and teachers. Therefore responding to students' questions in a way that encourages them to keep participating is an important skill. Luckily, many of the strategies for asking questions in the preceding section are relevant here too.

The key idea underlying how you should respond to students' questions is that students should do the cognitive work themselves. While giving a clear and complete answer to a student's question may seem like a good response, it means that the teacher is doing the thinking instead of the student. A better response involves supporting the student, or the class, to figure out the answer. One effective approach is to collaboratively build an answer together as described in the debriefing strategies above. Another strategy is to respond by reformulating the question and asking it back to the student or to the group. If the question is quite difficult, consider breaking it into multiple questions or introducing constraints that serve to scaffold students' thinking. Reformulating a question to ask back to students is great for keeping students active, but take care not to discourage students from asking questions.

A highly effective question-based strategy for responding to students' questions is to ask a series of questions that enable them to clarify their own thinking. These questions are termed diagnostic questions and are explained earlier in this chapter. If you determine that it is appropriate for you to answer a student's question yourself, see Chapter 6 for advice on how to explain in ways that are effective for modelling thinking.

REFLECTION POINT 4.2

For each of the student statements below, formulate (i) a positive response that will encourage students to keep asking questions and (ii) several questions that you could ask the student to help them move forward.

1. I just don't understand the activity. Can you explain it to me?
2. I've never written a report like this before. What do I need to include?
3. I won't have enough time to finish before the session ends, just tell me the next step.
4. My answer is X, but my neighbour calculated Y. Which is correct?
5. I'm done. Everything was super easy.

TEST YOURSELF

Case study 4.2 and the analysis questions provide you with an opportunity to apply the concepts and ideas outlined in this chapter to a field placement scenario. Sample answers to the analysis questions are provided at the end of the chapter.

CASE STUDY 4.2 – QUESTIONING IN SOCIAL WORK FIELD PLACEMENTS

Read this case study and complete the analysis questions below.

Emil* is a university-based supervisor for social work team placements. Inspired by the impact of active learning reported in the research he has been reading, Emil has been working hard to use questions to guide students during his visits to their placements. In particular he has tried to respond to their questions with questions about how their experiences relate to their university courses. While it often felt more difficult to come up with a question rather than just telling students what they want to hear, he found it got easier with practice and that his students seemed to be becoming more autonomous.

However, when he received feedback from his students after the supervision, much of what they wrote was negative and Emil was completely unprepared for their responses. Students indicated that he didn't guide them enough, that they had to rely on their field-based supervisor to get clear solutions to their difficulties, and that he seemed to be focused on theory rather than practice. Emil feels discouraged and frustrated that his students didn't appreciate his effort to use effective teaching strategies. He is considering just going back to asking fewer questions and giving more directions.

Case analysis questions

Write down your answers to the following questions; you will need them later. Suggested answers can be found at the end of the chapter.

1. What would you say to Emil about using questions to teach? Do you have any experiences from your own teaching that could be relevant to his situation or any evidence he might want to consider?
2. How do you explain the difference between Emil's perception and his students' feedback?
3. How does the students' emotional and social environment impact on how they respond to Emil's questions?
4. Emil has decided to give it another try and will start by explaining *why* he uses questions to teach when the next group of students arrive. What are two to three things that you think he should communicate to students?

* This case is a fictionalised account of teaching experiences.

ACTION SUMMARY – TEACHING, NOT TELLING: USING QUESTIONS

- Create stimulating questions that engage students in a relevant thinking and learning activity, rather than presenting all of the instructions or background as a mini-lecture.
- Ask students questions so they practice recalling important concepts themselves, rather than presenting a review of material.
- Support students to develop their own trouble-shooting skills by using *diagnostic questions* and *hints*.
- Good questions get students to think – so slow down and allow them time to think.
- Create an environment in which students can feel able to try to answer a question, get it wrong, get feedback, and try again.

CONCLUSION

Using questions more often, and more effectively, in your teaching takes intention. It requires making new habits around how you interact with students and may also require an adjustment in how you see your role as a teacher. Many of us come to teaching having spent years watching other teachers explaining answers rather than asking questions. And explaining things can be quite personally satisfying for teachers. It can be difficult to avoid becoming more active than our students. But students learn because of what they do, and so the job of teaching in practical settings is often to try to get students to be active in doing, experiencing, reflecting, theorising, or testing. Using questions to engage and guide students may not be what people usually think of when we think of what higher education teachers do. But the research evidence suggests that it is often what higher education teachers should do – this research evidence is presented in more detail in Chapter 8.

The high level of student activity and one-to-one interactions with teaching staff during practical sessions such as projects, labs, and fieldwork makes these contexts an ideal place for teachers to develop good habits for active learning strategies. While clear explanations are a valuable teaching tool, teachers tend to overuse this strategy in practical settings when students should be actively generating their own understanding. This chapter presents strategies for using questions well and helping to forge new habits to temper our tendency to teach by telling. The next chapter addresses how to provide students with feedback on their learning.

FURTHER READING

This small number of sources provides further guidance on how to use questions effectively. A full reference list for the chapter is provided below.

Practical advice on using questions to teach

Davis, B. G. (2009). Part III. Discussion strategies. In: *Tools for Teaching*, 2nd edition (pp.95–132). San Francisco: Wiley.

Exley, K., Dennick, R., and Fisher, A. (2018). Chapter 4. The skills of facilitation. In: *Small Group Teaching, Tutorials Seminars and Workshops* (pp. 42–65). London: Routledge. https://doi.org/10.4324/9780429490897.

Nilson, L. B. (2016). Chapter 13. Leading effective discussions. In: *Teaching at Its Best: A Research-Based Resource for College Instructors*, 4th edition (pp.155–167). San Francisco: Jossey-Bass.

Tormey, R. (2018). Teaching with questions (STEM focus) [Video]. *SwitchTube*. https://tube.switch.ch/download/video/286ba775.

Research evidence on interactive teaching

Freeman, S. (2018). *An Overview of Active Learning Practices in STEM Disciplines with Dr. Scott Freeman* [Video] [Vimeo]. https://vimeo.com/253308837.

ANSWERS TO SELECTED CHAPTER ACTIVITIES

These sample answers are provided to allow you to generate some feedback for yourself. You should take time to complete the activities before comparing your answers with our ideas.

Case study analysis 4.1.A

1. Mila's first question is "Is everything clear so far?" Her goal for this question appears to be getting feedback from students about if they understand risk assessment. She concludes that they have understood, but later discovers that some clearly had not. Her second question is "Does anyone have any questions?" Her apparent goal seems to be to get feedback on what students find difficult or confusing about the topic. Again, it appears that this was not successful.
2. Given the lack of information from students, Mila doesn't know if she is repeating things they already know or skipping over points that they need clarified. Since it appears that some still had things they didn't understand, it does not look like her introduction was highly effective.

Case study analysis 4.1.B

1. Her first question is "what are the key tools for performing a risk assessment?" The goal is both diagnostic and stimulating thought: she is assessing what the students already know while also engaging them in recalling the information in a different setting. Her second question asks students to tell her about the potential effects of not performing an adequate risk assessment as part of their business outlook report. Her goal here is to move beyond recalling the steps to understanding why the steps are important. Her third question asks them to summarise the three most relevant risk-mitigation

strategies for companies in emerging markets. Her goal here is again to both diagnose what they know, and to get them to organise their thinking. Later she asks "So, what does the project brief say about the requirements for the risk assessment?" Here she is hinting to them about how to solve for themselves the difficulty Thierry has encountered.
2. The three characteristics are (i) engaging students in relevant learning or thinking activity, (ii) posing clear and specific questions, and (iii) offering an appropriate cognitive challenge. As noted above, these questions are engaging students in relevant thinking and learning activities. Her questions are also certainly more clear and specific than in the previous tutorial. By mixing recall and application questions, Mila also appears to be offering a challenge appropriate to the task at hand.
3. She diagnoses what students can and cannot recall, and directs them to find information that they already have at their disposal.

Reflection point 4.2

1. I just don't understand the activity. Can you explain it to me?
    a. Glad to help. Let's look at it together.
    b. What is the goal of this activity? Can you break it down into steps and tell me which ones aren't clear to you? Can you show me what you have done so far?
2. I've never written a report like this before. What do I need to include?
    a. This is a good question to be asking at this phase.
    b. Where could you find that information? How is this report different from other reports that you have written? What should this report communicate?
3. I won't have enough time to finish before the session ends, can you just tell me the next step?
    a. Yes, time management is definitely difficult.
    b. What is your procedure here? Looking at what you have done so far, what do you think still needs to be done?
4. My answer is X, but my neighbour calculated Y. Which is correct?
    a. Good to see that you are checking your answer.
    b. Have you compared your two approaches? Can there only be one correct answer or can both be right? Looking at the two results, what would produce such a difference?

5. I'm done. Everything was super easy.
    a. Great. Remember, though, it's not finished until it's checked. Have you checked that you've actually met the goals of the task?
    b. Do you know what skill we wanted you to learn by doing this activity? In what other contexts might you be required to use that skill?

Case study analysis 4.2

1. Given the clear evidence in favour of using questions and interactivity for learning, Emil should be encouraged to keep using questions.
2. It seems that his students may need to better understand his motivations for using questions. While on-site supervision often focuses on the direct work a student is undertaking on the site, the university placement supervisor is generally more focused on helping the student to apply what they have learned in their university courses to their practice placement. It appears that may not be clear to his students who seem to want him to provide clear answers to their on-site difficulties, and who are misunderstanding his questioning as being abstraction or evasion. Perhaps understandably, students want him to give them *the right answer* but, as Chapter 2 has explored, as novices move towards expertise they increasingly must learn to use their judgement rather than following rules of thumb. Emil may need to help students recognise that their expectation of having an answer for every situation is unrealistic and that by asking questions about their situation he is trying to help develop their perceptual skills and their ability to recognise patterns which will help them make judgements.
3. Learning in social work practice placements is a potentially emotionally challenging environment. Students will experience joy and satisfaction, but also be emotionally affected both by their clients' situations and by their own sense of responsibility. As Chapter 2 explored in relation to novice nurses, novice practitioners may well experience diffuse feelings of anxiety and confusion. It seems possible that Emil's questioning strategy may be adding to their confusion and anxiety. He may want to look at how he ensures that they recognise that it is OK to get the answers to his questions wrong, and that this is a normal part of the process of their learning. It may also be that he could consider questions which could draw their attention to their own emotional experiences and to how they are regulating

those experiences. The social context may also be relevant. Students on field placements can be confronted by a gap between theory and practice and can try to resolve this by rejecting theory and focusing on practice. Again, Emil may want to help students identify if they are implicitly thinking in this way and help them to rethink how they see the relationship between practice and theory (Kolb's learning cycle can provide a useful way of describing this to them).

4. Emil might want to be clear about his role as a university-based supervisor and about how it complements the role of the on-site supervisor, since it appears that this is not clear to some of his students. It may also be helpful to clarify that expert practitioners are able to see the links between theoretical frameworks and their real-life experiences, and that his job involves helping them make those links. Clarifying for students that his intention is not simply to help them solve current problems, but rather to develop thinking strategies which will help them solve future problems, may also be relevant.

REFERENCES

Felder, R. M. (1994). Random thoughts: Any questions? *Chemical Engineering Education* 28(3): 174–175. https://journals.flvc.org/cee/article/view/123656.

Freeman, S., Eddy, S. L., McDonough, M., Smith, M. K., Okoroafor, N., Jordt, H., and Wenderoth, M. P. (2014). Active learning increases student performance in science, engineering, and mathematics. *Proceedings of the National Academy of Sciences of the United States of America* 111(23): 8410–8415. https://doi.org/10.1073/pnas.1319030111.

Gaspard, C., and Gainsburg, J. (2020). Abandoning questions with unpredictable answers. *Journal of Mathematics Teacher Education* 23(6): 555–577.

Hattie, J. (2009). *Visible Learning: A Synthesis of over 800 Meta-Analyses Relating to Achievement*. London: Routledge. https://doi.org/10.4324/9780203887332.

Hughes, P. W., and Ellefson, M. R. (2013). Inquiry-based training improves teaching effectiveness of biology teaching assistants. *PLOS ONE* 8(10): e78540. https://doi.org/10.1371/journal.pone.0078540.

Nathan, M. J., and Petrosino, A. (2003). Expert blind spot among preservice teachers. *American Educational Research Journal* 40(4): 905–928. https://doi.org/10.3102/00028312040004905.

Redfield, D. L., and Rousseau, E. W. (1981). A meta-analysis of experimental research on teacher questioning behavior. *Review of Educational Research* 51(2): 237–245. https://doi.org/10.3102/00346543051002237.

Spencer, S. J., Steele, C. M., and Quinn, D. M. (1999). Stereotype threat and women's math performance. *Journal of Experimental Social Psychology* 35(1): 4–28. https://doi.org/10.1177/0146167203029006010.

Tofade, T., Elsner, J., and Haines, S. T. (2013). Best practice strategies for effective use of questions as a teaching tool. *American Journal of Pharmaceutical Education* 77(7): 155. https://doi.org/10.5688/ajpe777155.

Wilen, W. W. (1991). *Questioning Skills, for Teachers. What Research Says to the Teacher*, 3rd edition. Washington, DC: National Education Association.

Chapter 5

Providing feedback on students' practical work

CASE STUDY 5.1.A – DESIGNING A SOCIAL RESEARCH PROJECT

Read this case study and complete the analysis questions below.

Charlotte* is teaching a research lab in a sociology programme where students will learn to do survey research by collecting and analysing data within their university. Students begin with the following task:

> You are asked to research the relationship between student gender and integration in university. Define an appropriate hypothesis, and briefly describe a piece of survey research that could enable you to draw valid conclusions about this relationship, clarifying how the research will be designed and conducted ethically.

Noah, one of the students, submitted his hypothesis and survey design last week. Today, Charlotte returns the proposal to Noah as follows:

> H₀: There is no difference between the integration of female students in humanities courses and in science courses.
>
> H₁: Female students are more integrated in humanities courses than in science courses.
>
> Method: Class lists for female students in the Faculty of Arts and the Faculty of Sciences will be obtained. 100 Female students in each faculty will be selected at random. ✓
>
> Selected participants will be administered the Student Integration Survey ✓ [1]. Data on age, ethnicity, and social class will also be collected. The Social Integration Scores for each will be calculated. T-tests will be completed to assess if social integration is significantly higher in the arts/humanities students than in science students.
>
> The principal ethics issues are privacy and informed consent. Surveys will be anonymous, and students will be told they don't have to take part if they don't want.
>
> Grade: 6/10
>
> 1. Dowaloy et al. (1998) THE STUDENT INTEGRATION SURVEY: Development of an Early Alert Assessment and Reporting System. Research in Higher Education p. 518

"But is it ok?", Noah asks her.

"Yes, it's ok, ish", she replies. "You just need to be more detailed and more precise. You are missing some things that ideally you should have spotted".

"Ok. I'll look at it again", says Noah.

Case analysis questions

Write down and keep your answers to the following questions; you will need them in Case study 5.1.B.

1. Imagine you are giving Noah advice based on Charlotte's response to his research design. Based on her feedback, what things could you advise him to do to meet her expectations?
2. What specific advice could you give Charlotte to help her give better feedback to Noah? Try to list at least four things.

* This case is a fictionalised account of teaching experiences.

As with Noah in Case study 5.1.A, people learn when they have an opportunity to try things, to make mistakes, to get feedback on those mistakes, and to try again to get it right. Mistakes during a practical activity, seen in this way, are not a problem in themselves. They are just a part of the process of improving in order to avoid making such mistakes when it really matters. As the playwright Samuel Beckett famously wrote, "Ever tried. Ever failed. No matter. Try again. Fail again. Fail better" (Beckett 1984).

John Hattie, who carried out one of the largest ever statistical overviews of learning, found that feedback on students' work is one of the teaching strategies that has the strongest effect on student learning. He analysed 23 different reviews of quantitative data on feedback including over 1,200 studies involving almost 68,000 learners. His conclusion was that feedback is "among the most powerful influences on achievement" (Hattie 2009, 173). Although the research evidence shows feedback has huge potential in helping students learn, in many universities this potential is perhaps not being realised. In the UK, for example, the National Student Survey has found that the area of lowest student satisfaction across the higher education sector has consistently been feedback (Beaumont et al. 2011).

This chapter explores how higher education teachers can give feedback in ways that maximise the impact on student learning in practical settings. It identifies that good feedback clarifies what a great answer, product, or performance looks like, tells the student how well they are doing, and identifies how the student can improve. The chapter also looks at how feedback can be provided in ways that maximise the chances that the student will actually take it on board. And it addresses how feedback can be managed when student numbers grow and resources often do not.

Case study 5.1.A provides an opportunity for you to clarify your conceptions about what good feedback looks like. You will then be able to compare your preconceptions with the findings of research on feedback. It is important, therefore, to read Case study 5.1.A and attempt the analysis questions before going further.

HOW DO YOU HELP STUDENTS TO *FAIL BETTER*?

Research on efforts to help students *fail better* highlights that feedback is most effective when it addresses three different things:

- What does a good performance/answer/solution look like?
- How is the student actually performing?
- How can she or he improve?

We will take these three elements in turn.

What does a good performance/answer/solution look like?

First, one of the reasons a student may not achieve an excellent performance on a task is that they might not be clear as to *what a good performance looks like*. It may be that the teacher has told the students the criteria of evaluation, but that a given student, overwhelmed with information, has forgotten. It may be that the student remembers the criteria that the teacher explained, but has not yet realised what this means in the complexity of practice. It may be that the criteria for assessing the students' performances are so obvious to the teacher that the teacher feels there is no need to make them explicit to the students. Whatever the reason, it is frequently the case that students fail to perform well because they aren't fully aware of what *perform well* actually means.

Here are some examples of situations where students could have learned more or performed better if they had properly understood what was required of them (all are based on real examples the authors have encountered in working with teachers):

- Biology students gathered data from an experiment and carried out some exercises using the data. Many of them presented their answers to a precision of two figures after the decimal point (e.g. 4.16 or 314.51) because that was the level of precision they were required to have in previous courses in that department. However, in this experiment, the nature of the measurements used meant that this level of precision was unwarranted. The teacher expected students to report their results to a level of precision that matched the accuracy of measurements, but many students simply followed the procedure that had become their habit in previous courses in that department.
- Students in a teaching practice placement were required to complete a daily *critical reflection* on their experience during each day in school. For the practice supervisor, the term *critical* had a specific technical meaning: that is, that the students use information from peers, learners, and from literature to try to identify their own implicit assumptions about learning and learners (this approach is called *critically reflective practice* in the teaching literature – it will be discussed again in Chapter 10). For many of the students, however, the term *critical* implied first and foremost that they should criticise themselves. They therefore focused their daily critical reflections on what went wrong in that day, and failed to clarify how their own implicit assumptions were impacting on their practice. Their supervisor consequently described their reflections as *superficial*.

- Students studying social research worked in a team to design and carry out an experiment in a lab course. One of the course goals was for students to develop independence and so, when they asked specific questions about their proposed research design, the response from the teacher was often a variant on the phrase "You need to decide if you think that will work well". Some of the students produced experimental designs which lacked validity and ended up unhappy with their grade because they felt they weren't told that their project was problematic.

In each of these situations, part of the problem for a student is that they find it hard to produce a good answer or solution because they are not in fact clear as to what *good* actually means in this context. Part of helping people to improve performance, then, is to explain to them what a good performance looks like. It is really helpful to students if the person giving feedback clarifies the criteria *after the student has produced a piece of work* because this is an opportunity for the student to understand not just what the criteria are in abstract but what they actually mean in practice (this implies, of course, that the student should produce some work during the course and not only at the end).

REFLECTION POINT 5.1

Take an example of a student activity in a practical course you have been involved in teaching. Can you identify the criteria that would be used to assess this activity if it were included in an assessment? Try to include any criteria that may be obvious to the supervisor but might not be obvious to the student.

How is the student actually performing?

The second element in effective feedback is clarifying for the student how they have actually performed. Feedback about performance can be given at different levels (Hattie and Timperley 2007), including:

- the specifics of the *task*,
- the *processes* that apply to this task but also apply to other similar tasks,
- the way in which they *manage* their learning or problem solving,
- the *person* themselves.

It is useful to take each of these levels in turn.

Feedback at the level of the *task* is feedback that is specific to the piece of work that the student has produced. Telling the student that their answer is right or wrong is an example of feedback at the level of the task (this kind of feedback is illustrated in Spotlight 5.1.A). Pointing out specific mistakes in their answer is also feedback at the level of the task. This kind of feedback can be welcomed by students; however they may find it difficult to learn a lot from this feedback because they may not see how to apply it in future exercises.

> ## SPOTLIGHT 5.1.A – TASK, PROCESS, OR THINKING?
>
> Farida* is supervising a group project in an engineering programme in which students are required to design and prototype a mobile phone app.
>
> In one session, she sees that students in one of the groups are disagreeing with each other and that students appear frustrated with each other. The students explain that they have multiple suggestions for the design of the home screen on their app, but that they can't agree which one is best.
>
> Farida looks at the various designs and suggests which one she feels is most appropriate, explaining why she thinks it is the better design.
>
> * This is a fictionalised account
of teaching experiences.

This is feedback at the level of the task, and it will help the student to solve this specific problem. The student may or may not be able to use this information to better solve future problems. Oftentimes it is not only the answer to a specific difficulty that the student has experienced that they need to know about but also why this difficulty arose. Feedback at the level of the *process* targets the general processes that are used in solving questions *of this type*. If you can start a sentence by saying, "When doing this kind of activity, it is often a good idea to ...", then this could be feedback at the level of the process. An example of process feedback to a group of students working on a design project might be,

> When you are designing something, it is often a good idea to spend some time generating lots of different possible solutions before deciding which one to pursue. In your case, you seem to be jumping too quickly to choosing your approach before really exploring the different possibilities in an open-minded way.

Rather than simply telling them that their solution is problematic, this type of feedback explains why the problem has occurred, and how it can be avoided in the future (see, for example, Spotlight 5.1.B).

> **SPOTLIGHT 5.1.B – TASK, PROCESS, OR THINKING?**
>
> Farida says to the students,
>
>> When trying to make a decision like this it is often a good idea to use one of the decision-making tools that you have seen in class. For example, in this case you could use a decision-making grid. First, you list the criteria that are important, then decide how much weight you should give each criterion. Then score each option in the criteria. This kind of approach often works when you are working on your own but also when you need to make decisions as a group.

In Spotlight 5.1.B, Farida's response is feedback at the level of the *process*. It is specifically phrased so that the student can see that it doesn't just help them with this problem but it will also help them with other similar problems. Compared to task feedback, the student has a better chance of being able to use this information to solve future problems because it is phrased in a more generalisable way.

The third level of feedback is feedback about how students are *managing* the task or the problem-solving process. Chapter 3 identified that students who can think about their thinking (metacognition) are more likely to develop transferable expertise (this issue is discussed again in Chapters 8 and 9). Sometimes students run into difficulties because they act without really defining their goal, considering what kind of strategy will help them to achieve that goal, and whether or not their current approach is working. Feedback at the level of how to manage their work or learning may help students develop their metacognitive capacities (see Spotlight 5.1.C).

> **SPOTLIGHT 5.1.C – TASK, PROCESS, OR THINKING?**
>
> Farida continues,
>
>> Remember that when you are working in industry you won't just need to be able to design mobile apps, but you will also have to

> be able to make decisions when there are lots of different criteria – cost, efficiency, effectiveness, environmental concerns, and so on. Some of these criteria might even contradict each other. When you get stuck, ask yourselves, "Is there some strategy or approach we could use to think our way out of this?" And whatever strategy you use, don't forget to wrap up by asking yourselves if you think the strategy worked well and how you could make it work better next time.

This is feedback to the student that focuses on how to solve the issue of being stuck, that is, feedback at the level of *managing* their own problem-solving or learning process. Implicit in this feedback is the message that the student has the ability to solve the problem, they just need to find the right solution strategy. Since being stuck is a common occurrence, this kind of feedback should be something that the student can apply in numerous situations.

The fourth level of feedback is feedback about the student themselves as a *person*. General statements about the student or their work such as "Great work, well done", "Good effort" (or, on the other extreme, "You just made a few stupid mistakes"), are all feedback of this type. Positive personal feedback is sometimes given by teachers who want to help students to improve their sense of self-confidence and to keep trying. Although this kind of positive feedback is often well intentioned, the research evidence suggests that it is generally not very effective (Hattie and Timperley 2007, 96). The problem with such general praise is that it often tells the student nothing about what they have done well and how they can improve. The impact of such feedback may also depend on whether or not the student believes that the teacher is simply being nice because the teacher doesn't think the student can do better. As a general rule then, this kind of general praise of the student as a person will probably not do much to help their learning or future performance. Criticism of the student as a person is likely to have a negative effect and should be avoided.

A better strategy for helping the student develop a sense of persistence is to give them positive feedback that is linked to the task or the process. Remember that feedback should be part of a process where people try, make mistakes, get feedback, and *try again*. Some students may find it hard to try again. If they already lack a belief in their own ability then seeing their mistakes listed out may simply reinforce their negative beliefs about themselves and may lead them to give up more quickly next time. At the same time, students do need to know what their errors are if they are to correct them the next time – in fact the research evidence suggests that the most effective feedback is often connected with showing a student that they got something wrong when they thought they had got it right (Hattie 2012, 139). Feedback should, therefore, contain some mixture of information about things the student has done well and things that they need to improve.

This focus on encouraging students to try again is also important if students see the task as being a *one-shot* activity rather than as a process that they will have to repeat in future. In the case study at the beginning of this chapter, for example, the student Noah could easily decide that he has completed the initial design and should now move on, rather than repeating the task in order to improve. In an ideal world, your feedback will encourage the student to go back and work through the process in order that they can develop their skill.

You can use the Case study 5.1.B and Reflection point 5.2 to apply the ideas about feedback presented so far. You can get feedback on your own understanding by comparing your answer to the sample responses at the end of the chapter.

CASE STUDY 5.1.B – DESIGNING A SOCIAL RESEARCH PROJECT

Look back on the feedback Charlotte gave to Noah on his research design in Case study 5.1.A.

What information did she give to him about (i) what he has done well and (ii) areas where he can improve?

REFLECTION POINT 5.2

Is it a good idea to give students a grade as part of giving them feedback? In thinking about this, it is worth distinguishing between three different scenarios:

a) giving feedback to students only in the form of a grade (no comments),
b) giving feedback to students only in the form of short comments (no grade),

c) giving the students short comments with a grade.

On average, which of these situations do you think will have the most positive impact on student learning? Write down your answer: (a), (b), or (c).

How can she or he improve?

It has been noted above that feedback has the potential to have a large positive impact on student learning. Unfortunately, feedback often does not have this effect, and teachers will recall situations in which they gave a student feedback on their performance only for the student to make exactly the same kind of mistake the next time.

As was highlighted in Chapter 4, students need to do the work of thinking, using, and applying the information they have received in order to learn. This is as true for feedback as it is for anything else: in order to learn from feedback, students need to actively process the information it contains. This problem is sometimes referred to as a lack of *assessment literacy*; as Berry O'Donovan and her colleagues (2016, 940) have written, "It cannot simply be assumed that when students receive feedback they will know what to do with it".

So how can a teacher get students to engage with the feedback they have received? One strategy, building on the last chapter, is the use of questions like, "Based on what I said, can you identify one or two things that will help you to solve this challenge next time you face it?" It is important to remember, however, that the purpose of such a question is not to test the student on how well they were listening, but rather to move the focus of the conversation on to how the feedback has been understood by the student and how they might use it to improve their future performance.

PUTTING IT ALL TOGETHER

A number of different dimensions of good feedback have now been identified. Effective feedback should make it clear *what good performance looks like*, it should include both positive and negative aspects about *how well the student's work has met this goal*, and, finally, it should indicate *what the student should do in order to improve*. Forward-looking feedback, that focuses on what the student can do next time they encounter a problem like this one, is most

PART II

effective for helping students develop skills that they can apply in another situation. The continuation of Case study 5.1.C provides an opportunity to see how these ideas apply in practice by revisiting Charlotte's feedback to Noah. The analysis questions ask you to revisit and question your prior assumptions or conceptions about feedback (you can check your own answers against the proposed responses to the analysis questions at the end of the chapter).

CASE STUDY 5.1.C – DESIGNING A SOCIAL RESEARCH PROJECT

Read this case study and complete the analysis questions below.

Later in the lab session, Noah has had time to think about his feedback from Charlotte and is confused. He prints a clean version of his research design and goes back to her and says "I thought I understood the corrections you gave me, but actually, I don't. Can you explain it to me again?"

She says,

> In this kind of activity you should read the task carefully. Here, you need to demonstrate that: (a) you can correctly frame an appropriate hypothesis, (b) you know about threats to validity, and (c) you know what the ethics issues are. All three of those things are mentioned in the task description. As always, you also have to present your work in the right format. That is mentioned in the course description.

"Now, here", she says, marking [1] on the page, "the hypothesis format is correct insofar as it is a testable statement, but it actually addresses if female students are integrated, not whether gender impacts on integration. The problem is there is no data from non-female students for comparison".

"Here and here", she says, marking [2], "you haven't formatted the report correctly. You need to use the Harvard referencing system, not footnotes. You should check the style guide".

"Here", she says, marking [3], "you correctly identify that you can compare the means, but given the sample size it will be a z-test

– practically speaking it is the same thing as a t-test but it is good to be precise in your language".

Now, this bit is really important. At here and here at [4], you say you will identify the student's social class, ethnicity, and gender. You will also know her faculty. This means that the person might be identifiable, even if you don't include her name in the data. Secondly you do actually have her name on a class list – that is more personal data. This is an ethics issue. In fact it is not only an ethical issue but also a data protection legal issue. You have to specify more clearly how you will treat such data.

One last important thing, here [5]. Random selection and adequate sample size are both good. This helps to ensure your claims can be valid. But to have valid findings about how gender relates to integration, you need to control for other factors, like time spent in university. This means you need additional data. You should think about what other data you could collect to address this.

H_0: There is no difference between the integration of female students in humanities courses and in science courses.

H_1: Female students are more integrated in humanities courses than in science courses.

Method: Class lists for female students in the Faculty of Arts and the Faculty of Sciences will be obtained. 100 Female students in each faculty will be selected at random.

Selected participants will be administered the Student Integration Survey [1]. Data on age, ethnicity, and social class will also be collected. The Social Integration Scores for each will be calculated. T-tests will be completed to assess if social integration is significantly higher in the arts/humanities students than in science students.

The principal ethics issues are privacy and informed consent. Surveys will be anonymous, and students will be told they don't have to take part if they don't want.

1. Dowalby et al. (1993) THE STUDENT INTEGRATION SURVEY: Development of an Early Alert Assessment and Reporting System. Research in Higher Education p. 513

Finally Charlotte says to Noah: "Ok. Based on what I've said, how does your answer compare to the criteria?"

Noah looks at the sheet and says,

> It's ok for the first one because I wrote the hypothesis correctly, but it is the wrong hypothesis. The second criterion is not ok because I forgot some threats to validity. I know we have a list of those from the lecture. I'll look at that again. And for ethics, I'm probably breaking the law on privacy. Which is not good. I need to fix that.

"Great," said Charlotte. "What will you do to fix this?" Noah responds,

> Well, I need to look at the threats to validity from the lecture and go through each one. But can you explain the anonymization thing? I thought once there was no names it was ok, but I guess that was wrong.

"There was a section in the lecture on anonymization and pseudo-anonymization as well, and a protocol to follow", says Charlotte. She continues,

> Do the same as you are planning for threats to validity. Look at the lecture notes again and come back to me if you have a problem. And don't forget to correct the referencing format. That is easy to fix.

Case analysis questions

Write down your answers to the following questions. Suggested answers can be found at the end of the chapter.

1. Charlotte explains what good performance looks like for this task. What does she say?
2. What feedback does she give Noah about the specific tasks required in this exercise?
3. What feedback does she give Noah about the processes that he can use to avoid such problems?
4. Compare the ratio of positive to negative feedback, and task to process feedback, Charlotte gave Noah. Do you think that it is a good balance to support learning?

5. How does Charlotte engage Noah in making sense of the feedback?
6. How does she help him focus on what he needs to do to perform better next time?
7. Look back at your answer to question 1 in Case study 5.1.A. How is it similar to or different from the advice you would now give to Noah based on Charlotte's second feedback? What does that tell you about the utility of Charlotte's first set of feedback?
8. Look back at your answer to question 2 in Case study 5.1.A. How do you now evaluate the advice you would have given to Charlotte before you read this chapter?

COMMUNICATING HIGH EXPECTATIONS TO EVERYONE

It is evident from Case study 5.1.C that in Charlotte's second attempt at feedback she tried to communicate to Noah what an excellent answer would look like rather than what a *good enough* answer looked like. Educational researchers have long realised that one of the causes for comparatively poor performance is that teachers sometimes implicitly communicate to some students that they actually don't expect too much from that student (e.g. Rosenthal 1994). This can happen through various mechanisms such as asking fewer questions or easier questions, or giving some students less thinking time after asking a question (these mechanisms were discussed in Chapter 4). It can also happen through teachers giving students they consider as weak more praise and less direction than other students. It appears as if teachers are often unaware that they are communicating lower expectations to some students because they are themselves unaware of the biases that are influencing their behaviour.

The effect of such implicit biases on students in university has been researched. In one study, published in 2012, Corinne Moss-Racusin and her colleagues sent a student CV to 127 faculty members. Everyone got the same CV except for one detail: for half of them the student had a masculine name (*John*), and for the other half the student had a feminine name (*Jennifer*). Teachers were asked to rate the student's suitability for a job in a lab in terms of their competence, hireability, and the salary they should receive. The results showed that, although the CVs were identical except for the name, teachers scored *John* higher than *Jennifer* on all criteria. Female faculty were just as likely to exhibit a bias in favour of *John* as were male faculty. The report's authors conclude:

> Because most students depend on feedback from their environment to calibrate their own worth, faculty's assessments of students' competence likely contribute to students' self-efficacy and goal setting ... which may influence decisions much later in their careers.
>
> (Moss-Racusin et al. 2012, 16477–8)

The bias identified in Moss-Racusin et al.'s study is probably implicit – the person holding the bias may not even be aware of it. It is unlikely that such biases are simply a generational effect of older teachers: one recent study found similar biases in third- and fourth-year male and female students in project teams, but found that students themselves were generally unaware of their own biases (Aeby et al. 2019). Implicit biases have now been widely studied and have been found, for example, to explain in part why it is that a gender gap in science and math achievement is found in some countries but not in others (Nosek et al. 2011). An online self-test for implicit biases has been developed at Harvard and can be accessed at the *Project Implicit* site (https://implicit.harvard.edu). It is probably a good idea for any teacher to take such a self-test to give themselves feedback about their potential implicit biases and to help them ensure that they communicate high expectations to all students.

HOW AND *HOW OFTEN*?

It is evident in Case study 5.1.C that when Charlotte gave better feedback to Noah she had to provide more detail and it took longer. It may be hard, therefore, to see how it would be possible to give good feedback *at scale*.

While there are definitely technological solutions that can help to give feedback at scale, the research evidence suggests a number of things that can also be done when giving *human* feedback. First, while Charlotte wrote a lot on Noah's sheet, the research evidence suggests that oral feedback can be as effective as, or more effective than, written feedback (e.g. King et al. 2008). Berry O'Donovan and her colleagues (2016), for example, suggest that *quick and dirty* feedback on lab reports delivered one-to-one by assistants during a lab session may be a more efficient use of the assistant's time than written feedback on formal lab reports handed in some time after the lab has finished.

A second useful finding from research is that oftentimes peers can give each other useful feedback. How peer feedback can work in practice is illustrated in Spotlight 5.2. Asking students to give each other feedback can be particularly effective if it is used as a way of making them more familiar with what the criteria for excellent performance look like in practice. However, it is generally not recommended that you just leave students to give feedback to each other without guidance (Hattie 2012). John Hattie recommends that if you do get peers to give each other feedback, you should use some questions or prompts to guide their feedback. Suggested prompts include:

Task level
- ☐ What knowledge/skills is the student supposed to demonstrate in this activity?
- ☐ How well was each skill demonstrated?
- ☐ Were mistakes made and if so, what were they?

Process level
- ☐ Are there things to keep in mind when working on problems or tasks like this one?
- ☐ Did the approach taken maximise the chances of being successful in the task?

Management of thinking level
- ☐ Did the student consciously chose a strategy or approach to the task or was it chosen by *intuition*?
- ☐ Were there moments of being stuck and if so what was the response?
- ☐ Were different approaches to completing the task considered before choosing one?
- ☐ Did the student evaluate their own performance, and how could they have done so?

SPOTLIGHT 5.2 – PEER FEEDBACK IN THE DANCE STUDIO

As Chapter 2 discussed, higher levels of performance in a range of artistic domains, including dance and music, have been found to be associated with learners who engage in deliberate practice. Given the focus on practice for improvement, work by Heidi Andrade and colleagues (2015, 47) has argued

> Feedback from the dance community, including peers and teachers, is important to students' growth as dancers, so formative assessment can be seen as an integral part of the creation and performance of dance. Fortunately, teachers are not the sole source of feedback in the classroom: when self- and peer assessment are carefully taught and guided ... constructive and focused feedback can come from students themselves.

In Andrade et al.'s test of the impact of peer formative feedback in the dance studio, students were provided with peer feedback sheets which specified the criteria for a given activity and which required peers to give each other positive and more critical feedback. For example, an activity which involved practising three kinds of falls from a standing position specified that there were some features shared by all three falls (e.g. falling silently, safely, and in one's own space) and some criteria which depended on the type of fall (*falling with a floating quality* for a light fall as compared to *falling with a strong quality* for a heavy fall). Peers observed each other, wrote positive feedback ("I like how ... ") and more critical feedback ("I wish ... "), then sat in pairs to discuss. In these discussions, students learned how to ascribe meaning to and take ownership of the language of the class (i.e. terms like *floating* and *strong*).

The feedback sheet also asked students to plan for improvement ("I am going to improve my light fall by ... "). Students were able here to make explicit the areas they needed to work on (such as, for a light fall, "When I fall, do it quicker and do it in sequence").

The same process of (i) clarifying the criteria, (ii) identifying positives, (iii) identifying critical points, and (iv) identifying ways of improving, was used repeatedly throughout the term.

The teacher in this case identified that the peer feedback was generally well received by students and that there were clear improvements in the groups' performances. There was also a growth in collaboration among students. In summary the researchers concluded that the process enabled the creation of "cultures of critique" in the dance classroom: "Developing such environments allowed students to comfortably provide and receive useful feedback, set goals for their work, and increase their engagement in and learning about dance and choreography" (Andrade et al. 2015, 54).

This feedback experience is valuable because it clearly describes the ways in which peer feedback was structured in order to make it as useful as possible. Although Andrade et al.'s work describes feedback at pre-university level, peer feedback is also seen in higher education. Louise Kelsey and Lise Uytterhoeven (2017), for example, describe peer feedback at a university-level choreography course. In order to enable productive feedback within the group, students used Adshead-Lansdale's Dance Analysis model which involves first describing the dance, then discerning its form, interpreting it, and then analysing. This framework was used because it was suitable for students of all ability levels and developed the analysis skills of the observer as well as providing feedback to the observed. Kelsey and Uytterhoeven conclude, "Reflection on peer, self and tutor feedback, plus on that from external visitors, helps students, as Hinett recognizes, 'develop interpersonal skills, improve confidence and sustain motivation for their studies by monitoring and taking responsibility for their own development'" (2017, 44).

TEST YOURSELF

The exercises in this section provide an opportunity for you to apply the concepts and ideas outlined in this chapter to a practical laboratory scenario. Sample answers are provided at the end of the chapter.

CASE STUDY 5.2 – HOW TO KILL BACTERIA

Read this case study and complete the analysis questions below.
Janna and Thierry* are working as lab partners on the bacterial cell viability experiment. The problem statement for the lab activity is as follows:

> Bacteria are known to be able to survive a range of conditions; however, they are not immortal. What conditions do you expect

PART II

to kill bacteria? What can bacteria survive? Please generate 1–2 testable hypotheses and design an experimental protocol that will allow you to test each hypothesis. Plan to make multiple observations to improve the measurement precisions. Use the list of materials available from the supply room to plan your experiment but keep health and safety and environmental concerns in mind, and get approval from the lab assistant for your procedure before taking anything from the supply room.

Janna and Thierry present their procedure to the lab assistant, Wei.

> ~~Alcohol~~
> ~~Salt??~~
> Detergent
> Lead
>
> Hypothesis: Does lead kill bacteria? Does detergent kill bacteria?
>
> Transfer 15 mL bacterial cell suspension solution to 4 sterile vials. Label them A,B,C + D
> Add 2 drops of detergent to 2 vial A+B. Add 0.1g lead to vials B+C.
> Place vials in a 25 deg C water bath and incubate for 8h. Swab each vial to growth medium and allow to the bacteria to grow for 12h. Measure bacterial density optically and calculate growth rates to compare the 4 different conditions.

A key goal of this exercise is for students to learn to work autonomously to develop an experimental protocol to test specific hypotheses. Wei is relieved that Janna and Thierry have finally written down their procedure, as they have been asking him questions continuously since the beginning of the session.

Case analysis questions

The analysis questions can be answered without any technical knowledge in chemistry or life sciences using the information in this case study. Write down your answers to the following questions. Suggested answers can be found at the end of the chapter.

1. Reading the problem statement and the other information contained in the case study, what are the criteria that are used to define an excellent experimental protocol in this class?

2. Wei identifies that the protocol is likely to give some interpretable results and should be able to answer the problem statement. He also identifies a few difficulties: first, the hypothesis is phrased as a question rather than as a testable statement; second the protocol has only a single observation of each condition and not multiple observations; third, the use of lead has environmental and potentially health and safety implications which are not referred to in the protocol. Using this information, what kind of feedback should he give Thierry and Janna about the *process* involved in solving a problem like this?
3. Could Wei offer students any feedback about the way in which they are *managing* their problem-solving process (hint: look back on the prompts that can be used to guide peer feedback)?
4. What positive feedback could Wei give to Thierry and Janna?
5. How much positive and negative feedback should Wei give? What factors should be taken into account in deciding this?

* This case is a fictionalised account of teaching experiences.

ACTION SUMMARY – FEEDBACK

- Clarify the criteria of assessment for the student; they may not know or understand what *good performance* looks like in practice.
- Include some positive and some critical elements in feedback.
- Feedback about the specific task is OK, but feedback that is about *problems like this one* (process feedback), or about how to manage learning and problem solving may be better.
- Feedback about the student as a person is best avoided.
- Feedback looks to the future: focus on what the student will do next time they face this problem rather than exclusively talking about what they already did.
- Consider using (well-structured) peer feedback or technological tools to generate useful feedback for students in larger groups.
- Communicate high expectations to all students, being particularly attentive to areas where implicit bias may result in unintentional messages.

CONCLUSION

As a teacher, feedback to students on work they have produced is potentially one of the most powerful tools in your armoury. Practice in labs, projects, studios, and field placements plays a very important role in higher education and, through the right kind of feedback, students can be helped to see how they can improve their performance as they practice.

It is important to note that there are a number of qualifiers in the previous paragraph: feedback is *potentially* important, and students can improve through *the right kind* of feedback. Sometimes students do not recognise feedback as feedback, especially if it is obscured by grades, if a time lag means that it arrives after they have mentally moved on to the next task, or if it refers only to the specific task in a particular problem that they will never have to face again. Feedback of this type is a recipe for frustration both for the student (who doesn't improve) and for the teacher (who has wasted their time on generating unused feedback).

But providing the right kind of feedback is feasible. It is possible to communicate high expectations to all students by clarifying the criteria for a great performance, by pointing out specific achievements as well as areas to improve, and by focusing on what students can learn from their mistakes that can be applied in other problems *like this one* in the future.

Giving feedback on work students have produced is the second tool in your armoury as a practical teacher, alongside prompting students to think for themselves by asking good questions (described in Chapter 4). The next chapter turns attention to a third teaching skill: explaining and demonstrating to students in ways that will help them learn.

FURTHER READING

This small number of sources is intended to provide further useful information for those who wish to explore the chapter topic in more detail. A full reference list for the chapter is provided below.

Methods for generating effective feedback

Petty, G. (2009). Feedback methods: Assessment for learning. In: *Evidence-Based Teaching* (pp. 245–274). Thornes: Nelson.

Stevens, D. D., and Levi, A. J. (2013). *Introduction to Rubrics: An Assessment Tool to Save Grading Time, Convey Effective Feedback, and Promote Student Learning*. Stylus Publishing, LLC.

Strategies for integrating effective feedback in teaching activities

Irons, A. (2021). *Enhancing Learning Through Formative Assessment and Feedback*, 2nd edition. London: Routledge.

Wisker, G., Exley, K., Antoniou, M., and Ridley, P. (2008). Work-based learning and keeping personal development portfolios. In: *Working One-to-One with Students: Supervising, Coaching, Mentoring, and Personal Tutoring*. London: Routledge. https://doi.org/10.4324/9780203016497.

Research evidence on using feedback

Hattie, J. (2018, September 18). John Hattie: Visible learning feedback webinar [video]. *YouTube*. https://youtu.be/RfHQAQCAqtw.

Hattie, J., and Timperley, H. (2007). The power of feedback. *Review of Educational Research*. 77(1): 81–112. https://doi.org/10.3102/003465430298487.

Petty, G. (2017). Presentation and activities based on Black + William's (1998) study at King's College. https://www.teacherstoolbox.co.uk/black-and-wiliam-1998/.

ANSWERS TO SELECTED CHAPTER ACTIVITIES

These sample answers are provided to allow you to generate some feedback for yourself. You should take time to complete the activities before comparing your answers with our ideas.

Case study 5.1.B

Charlotte appears to give Noah positive feedback about his hypothesis and method, but says that he needs to be more precise and fix some details.

Reflection point 5.2

John Hattie and Helen Timperley, in their review of the evidence, concluded that research on giving grades or comments "showed that feedback through comments alone led to learning gains, whereas marks alone or comments accompanied by marks … did not" (2007, 92). Therefore the answer to the question is (b).

Feedback is only going to be effective if the students process the information it contains. Since students often want to know first and foremost how they scored, giving them a mark or grade may satisfy their curiosity. If students get only comments and no grade it may be that they will be more motivated to read the comments carefully in order to figure out how they did. Giving comments without a grade, may, therefore, encourage student to engage more with the feedback.

Case study 5.1.C

1. Charlotte outlines what good performance on this task looks like in paragraph 2 of the case study.
2. Charlotte gives Noah positive task-related feedback in paragraph 3 and negative task-related feedback in paragraph 4.
3. Charlotte doesn't directly give Noah process-related feedback, but rather tells him to review his lecture notes to clarify what is needed, including how to ensure validity and protect participants' data.
4. Charlotte provides more negative than positive feedback, but the research design is an early draft, Noah does not seem discouraged, and since he also leaves with specific strategies to improve his research design, the result is probably that Charlotte has communicated high expectations.
5. Charlotte asks Noah to assess his own answer based on the criteria she lists. She also asks him what steps he will take to improve his research design.
6. Charlotte makes her assessment criteria explicit and also discusses with Noah the specific steps he can take to improve his design.

Case study 5.2

1. An excellent protocol in this circumstance would have the following characteristics:
    a. One to two testable hypotheses.
    b. An experimental protocol that will actually test those hypotheses.
    c. Multiple observations of each condition and a method for dealing with potential measurement errors.
    d. Avoiding the use of materials or methods that will have safety risks or a potentially negative environmental impact.
    e. Developing these hypotheses and protocol while working without significant assistance.
2. There are a number of different process elements Wei could identify:
    a. In problems like this, the criteria are made clear in the problem statement so it is important to read it carefully. Perhaps underline key words and phrases when you first read it, then, at the

end, check the protocol against the problem statement to see if you have done what you have been asked.
  b. There are often multiple possible ways of testing a hypothesis. The challenge in questions like this is to decide which one is the best one. You should weigh up the pros and cons of different possible protocols before deciding which one best meets the criteria.
3. There are a number of things Wei could give feedback on about the management of their process:
   a. Designing an experiment generally requires some creative thinking to come up with different options, and then some critical thinking to analyse the possibilities and chose the best one. It can be useful to be clear with yourself about which kind of thinking you need to do and when. Janna and Thierry have generated a number of options (creativity) but haven't necessarily evaluated them against all the required criteria (critical thinking).
   b. Janna and Thierry asked a lot of questions rather than working autonomously as required. Do they know why they ask so many questions? What do they need to do to be better able to troubleshoot this kind of lab exercise on their own?
   c. The final answer does not appear to have been checked against the criteria in the problem statement. It is useful for students to remind themselves that *the solution is not finished until it is checked*.
4. In terms of the task, the hypotheses are quite close to being testable statements and do not need much work to improve them. The protocol has included clear and appropriate control and experimental conditions. The protocol is written in a way that makes it reproducible (it is clear in terms of quantities, times, and temperatures, for example). In terms of their process, it is clear that Janna and Thierry did try to brainstorm a little before choosing some options; this strategy is generally the right one for questions of this type, they just need to improve on their analysis and decision making.
5. Wei's interaction with Janna and Thierry led him to have low expectations of them. He may be tempted therefore to over-praise them. He should certainly identify their strengths as well as weaknesses, but he should try to ensure he is clear about expecting an excellent answer from them as much as from anyone else.

PART II

REFERENCES

Aeby, P., Fong,R., Vukmirovic, M., Isaac, S., and Tormey, R. (2019). The impact of gender on engineering students' group work experiences. *International Journal of Engineering Education* 35(3): 756–765.

Andrade, H., Lui, A., Palma, M., and Hefferen, J. (2015). Formative assessment in dance education. *Journal of Dance Education* 15(2): 47–59. http://doi.org/10.1080/15290824.2015.1004408.

Beaumont, C., O'Doherty, M., and Shannon, L. (2011). Reconceptualising assessment feedback: A key to improving student learning? *Studies in Higher Education* 36(6): 671–687. https://doi.org/10.1080/03075071003731135.

Beckett, Samuel (1984). *Worstward Ho (Beckett Shorts Vol 4)*. Richmond: Calder Publications Ltd.

Hattie, J. (2009). *Visible Learning: A Synthesis of over 800 Meta-Analyses Relating to Achievement*. London: Routledge. https://doi.org/10.4324/9780203887332.

Hattie, J. (2012). *Visible Learning for Teachers, Maximising Impact on Learning*. London: Routledge.

Hattie, J., and Timperley, H. (2007). The power of feedback. *Review of Educational Research* 77(1): 81–112. https://doi.org/10.3102/003465430298487.

Kelsey, L., and Uytterhoeven, L. (2017). Scratch nights and hash-tag chats: Creative tools to enhance choreography in the higher education dance curriculum. *Research in Dance Education* 18(1): 34–47. https://doi.org/10.1080/14647893.2016.1264381.

King, D., McGugan, S., and Bunyan, N. (2008). Does it make a difference? Replacing text with audio feedback. *Practice and Evidence of Scholarship of Teaching and Learning in Higher Education* 3(2): 145–163 https://sta.rl.talis.com/link?url=http%3A%2F%2Fwww.pestlhe.org.uk%2Findex.php%2Fpestlhe%2Fartic le%2Fview%2F52%2F174&sig=71b1da58853dc9e2e1ad4524ece1880f64ef e24d40265dfe2e97d8feef8c918b.

Moss-Racusin, C. A., Dovidio, J. F., Brescoll, V. L., Graham, M. J., and Handelsman, J. (2012). Faculty's subtle gender biases favor male students. *Proceedings of the National Academy of Sciences of the United States of America* 109(41). https://doi.org/10.1073/pnas.1211286109 1647416479.

Nosek, B. A., and Smith, F. L. (2011). Implicit social cognitions predict sex differences in math engagement and achievement. *American Educational Research Journal* 48(5): 1125–1156. https://doi.org/10.3102/0002831211410683.

O'Donovan, B., Rust, C., and Price, M. (2016). A scholarly approach to solving the feedback dilemma in practice. *Assessment and Evaluation in Higher Education* 41(6): 938–949. https://doi.org/10.1080/02602938.2015.1052774.

Rosenthal, Robert (1994). Interpersonal expectancy effects: A 30-year perspective. *Current Directions in Psychological Science* 3(6): 176–179. https://doi.org/10.1111/1467-8721.ep10770698.

Chapter 6

Explaining and demonstrating to students in practical settings

CASE STUDY 6.1.A – ROCKIN' THE EXPLAINING

Read this case study and complete the analysis questions below.
  Ghali* has brought his geology class on a field trip.

> As you know the focus today is sedimentary rocks. I would like you to now take a minute to look around you and identify some characteristics that could help you determine if the rocks we are standing on have been formed by clastic, biochemical, or chemical pathways.

After allowing two full minutes for students to make their observations, Ghali invites several students to contribute an answer but avoids identifying the correct answer. As an appreciable portion of students gave an incorrect answer, he decides to give a short explanation.

> OK, so we do not all have the same answer. And I know it is easy to get overwhelmed by the different morphologies and the various influences during the long lifetime of these rocks. From your answers, I can see that everyone is clear on the mechanisms of the three pathways but having difficulty identifying relevant characteristics in the rocks themselves. Let's start by considering how these atoms, right here under my finger, came to be right here, making these specific chemical bonds with each other.

DOI: 10.4324/9781003107606-6

> Mindful that being in the field is an important opportunity for students to really engage in authentic practical learning, and of the many distractions present, Ghali keeps his explanation to one minute. Wrapping up, he says
>
>> Because coccolithophones, and their shells, are too small for us to see with our naked eyes, I have brought this clam shell as an illustration. Where did the atoms in this clamshell come from? That is to say, where were these atoms before they became part of this clamshell?
>
> **Case analysis question**
>
> Write down and keep your answer to this question; you will need it in Case study 6.1.B.
>
> 1. What are three elements of Ghali's explanation that make it effective for student learning?
>
> * This case is a fictionalised account of teaching experiences.

INTRODUCTION

This chapter addresses the quintessential teaching skill of explaining difficult material in ways that are accessible to students. Explaining is often what we think of as the primary activity of teaching. Given its visibility, explaining is often overused and frequently overvalued. This is why we start this chapter by looking at *when* to explain. Then we look at three key elements to keep in mind when explaining:

- starting where your audience is,
- keeping it short,
- supporting with illustrations.

We then present how to structure an explanation using a simple five-step template called LOAFS. From a 5-minute improvised explanation to a 45-minute lesson, either on site or online, this template is designed to help you integrate strategies shown by research to have the highest impact on learning.

Finally, we discuss some specificities of explanations in two different situations:

- modelling how experts think in oral and written explanations,
- explaining *how-to* procedures in the lab, field, or for projects.

These two situations are important opportunities for you, as a disciplinary expert, to explain and model how to think about concepts and problems in your field. For example, if you expect students to employ a problem-solving method in their work, it is essential to model the steps and results of such a method for students during these activities. Your explanations may address one or more students, and be undertaken with varying levels of formality and preparation. However intentionally applying the ideas from this chapter, even in informal moments, will both assist students' learning and allow you to become better at using them.

Case study 6.1.A provides an opportunity for you to consider the characteristics of a good explanation. The analysis questions will assist you to compare your own perspective and experience with the criteria outlined in this chapter, which will contribute significantly to your ability to apply these ideas in your own teaching. It is important, therefore, to read Case study 6.1.A and attempt the analysis question before going further.

WHEN TO EXPLAIN?

The common misconception of higher education teachers that *good teaching* means *good telling* persists in the face of enormous literature to the contrary (Herrington and Nakleh 2003; Volkmann and Zgagacz 2004). As Chapter 4 highlighted, it is not that good explanations are a hindrance to learning, but rather that receiving information without actively processing it does not result in the kind of learning targeted in practical settings such as labs, studios, and projects. Thus, before launching into an excellent explanation, you should ask yourself (i) would a question that gets students thinking for themselves be more effective?, and (ii) am I making assumptions that this student needs the additional *help* of an explanation rather using a question to guide them to figuring it out themselves? In general, it is a good idea to diagnose the level of understanding in the student or class before explaining. In Case study 6.1.A, Ghali offers us a good example by hearing from several students before deciding to explain.

It was noted in Chapter 2 that teachers generally have thousands of hours of experience as students before becoming teachers, and that the models they have internalised from this experience may be hard to displace. Explaining less may feel uncomfortable if it clashes with your own experience of *excellent* and *experienced* teachers who enabled you to acquire your current level of expertise. But, as Chapter 10 will explore, challenging your implicit ideas about good teaching and the associated teacher-ly actions is an essential step in moving to more evidence-informed strategies. Spotlight 6.1 illustrates how teaching strategies that appear good may in fact be inadequate for students to develop appropriate disciplinary thinking.

It is important to acknowledge that students might also have implicit ideas and expectations about how a good teacher is supposed to help them. In particular, they might expect you to explain even when an explanation is not the most effective way to help them. Using the techniques described in this chapter might therefore also feel uncomfortable to students. Being explicit about the reasons why you use these techniques can help, and can also be a great opportunity to discuss important principles regarding learning how to learn (Tormey and Hardebolle 2017). On the other hand, it is important to monitor students' level of frustration: while learning necessarily entails some kind of discomfort, too much anxiety can actually impair learning (Schoenfeld 1985).

SPOTLIGHT 6.1 – THE PERILS OF MAKING IT LOOK EASY

Alan Schoenfeld entitled his detailed observational study of a maths class over a semester *When Good Teaching Leads to Bad Results: The Disasters of "Well-Taught" Mathematics Courses.* In the study, Schoenfeld observed that despite the teacher's care and good intentions to help his students understand the material, they "gained at best a fragmented sense of the subject matter and understood few if any of the connections that tie together the procedures that they had studied" (1988, 145).

Schoenfeld takes care to note that the teacher did his job well, according to all standard metrics. For example, the class was well managed, there was an evident mutual respect between the teacher and the students, and students scored well on the standardised state exam. However, these metrics do not correlate with helping students learn to think mathematically.

> Two of the teaching practices that Schoenfeld identified as problematic, yet common in maths teaching, are (i) a focus on procedures as isolated skills that results in (ii) conveying the idea that problem solving is a fairly rapid and linear activity. For example, Schoenfeld observed that the teacher carefully prepared his presentations, dividing "the material in bite-sized pieces so that it would be easy for [students] to master" (1988, 161). The high number of exercises that students were expected to solve during class implicitly communicated that problem solving is a rapid activity, reinforced by the teacher's advice to memorise the procedural problem-solving steps "so you don't spend a lot of time thinking about them" (1988, 159).
>
> The teacher's actions, while potentially improving students' scores on the standardised test, did not enable students to really understand the underlying mathematics. By presenting students with pre-solved and neatly explained answers to questions, the teacher created the impression that students need to know solutions rather than conveying to them the way professional mathematicians think about or solve problems (you may recall the example of mathematician Andrew Wiles which was covered in Chapter 2).
>
> Schoenfeld concludes with the idea that teaching practices need to be informed by cognitive science, a conclusion that is in line with the approach taken throughout this book.

KEY ELEMENTS OF A GOOD EXPLANATION

The evidence on learning suggests that good explanations have three key elements:

- starting where your audience is,
- keeping it short,
- supporting with illustrations.

Starting where your audience is

A good explanation is matched to the particular needs of the student, or group of students, in terms of their prior knowledge and future needs. Thus, what makes a really good explanation is different for different students. Knowing how to pitch your explanation is difficult, but planning for two-way communication will enable you to adapt your approach to your students. Therefore, it is best to think about explanations as discussions, with questions, answers, and thinking time, rather than long one-sided speeches.

Explanations should allow students to make connections to their prior knowledge so that they can make sense of the new concepts and ideas in context, and be better able to apply their new understanding. Starting with a quick question or two to ascertain that students have the appropriate prior knowledge not only enables you to avoid talking over their heads, but also has students actively recall the information themselves. Let's take the example of an activity where students are building geometric 3D forms, which requires knowing trigonometric functions. One way of checking the background of your students would be to ask "How is the sinus function defined in a right-angled triangle?" As discussed in Chapter 4, you could prompt students to write down their answers, so that they could reuse it in their calculations.

Keeping it short

The human brain has the capacity to remember things for a long time but this long-term retention only occurs under certain conditions. One key challenge for learning is that the amount of new information we can process at any given time is limited. However, as Chapter 2 highlighted, we can store and quickly recall large quantities of information if we make connections and associations with previously acquired knowledge. This is why your explanations should not only be brief and build on a limited number of concepts/ideas, but they should also guide the student in actively connecting the ideas together, including with their prior knowledge. This can be done through questioning. For instance, the question "In which genre would you place the second movement of this symphony?" asks the student to make explicit associations between concepts and ideas, which requires an understanding of the distinctive features involved.

As our long-term memory is highly associative, providing cues (oral, visual, textual) to how different concepts relate to each other is an essential element of good explanations. Techniques for doing this include structuring your explanation using titles or sections, providing an overall *map* of the connections between ideas (see for instance *concept maps*, which are visual representations of networks of ideas [Novak 2005]), as well as highlighting (verbally or visually) the important points or key messages you want students to remember.

Supporting with illustrations

Explanations which provide students multiple ways of *seeing* the same material, by varying the nature of the representations to include theory, application, graphical representation, schematics, mathematical models, analogies, metaphors, etc., will enable students to develop a more complete understanding and to grasp aspects not immediately apparent to them (Ainsworth 2008).

Different disciplines have developed different ways of representing concepts (in particular graphically), which support the types of reasoning and problem solving commonly used in the discipline. As a teacher, it is important for you to be fluent with the representations that are commonly used in your field so that you can teach them to students. For instance, free body diagrams are essential tools in physics and engineering to reason about forces, movements, and reactions in a system. Software engineering makes extensive use of diagrams to reason about the logics of programmes, the structure of data, the architecture of systems, etc. One reason for using graphical representations in addition to oral explanations is that multimodal communication (i.e. combining speech, text, and visuals) has been shown to be more efficient for learning than unimodal communication (i.e. only text or only speech or only visuals). In addition, sketching has been shown by research to be an important tool for problem solving and is an integral part of experts' thinking processes in many disciplines (e.g. Dym et al. 2005). Prompting students to use sketches to capture their own thinking (e.g. "Have you drawn the free body diagram?") can be a useful starting point for an explanation. The teacher can then build on the representation used by the student to make reasoning steps explicit (e.g. "The free body diagram is a static view of your system. How could you visualise the evolution of the system over time?"). Finally, using representations during your own explanations to support your reasoning is an important part of modelling your thinking. This involves, in particular, making explicit the connections between reality and the model/representation (e.g. how an object is idealised as a single point mass in a free body diagram) and between different representations of the same reality (e.g. the musical note B-flat or si bémol can be represented in musical notation as "B♭" or drawn on the flat third line of the treble stave, or even as the frequency 466 Hz).

Sometimes showing students a phenomenon or procedure using a (physical or virtual) demonstration is simpler than explaining it. For instance, describing the movement of a ball when it is thrown up in the air vertically with only words can be quite lengthy and hard to grasp for students. Whereas throwing a real ball into the air clearly illustrates what happens. Think about using demonstrations to illustrate your explanations with artefacts as simple as playing cards, balls, or scarves. When teaching online, demonstrations can be turned into digital objects such as videos or online virtual simulations. The advice below applies to both physical and digital types of artefacts.

Examples are a particularly useful category of illustrations as they can play the role of a bridge between abstract and concrete, and between theory and practice. The examples you choose may impact on students' beliefs about and interest in the discipline (Perkins et al. 2006). Realistic application examples can help students to figure out the concrete use of what they are learning, which can play a motivational role, but also help students to transfer what they learn in class to concrete situations later (Perkins et al. 1994). So while your research may focus on 17th-century Korean mask dances, drawing examples from current affairs, popular culture, or the likely professional careers of students will increase the perceived relevance of your examples. Illustration examples, on the other hand, help to clarify which features of a concept are core to its definition and therefore characterise what IS, while counter-examples are crucial to help students distinguish what IS NOT. In the history of architecture, different examples of famous buildings could be used to help students understand which are characteristic of the Renaissance movement and which are not. Finally, edge cases are a category of examples which is particularly useful in science and technology, and more specifically in engineering. An edge case is the condition which occurs when one or several operating parameters reach an extreme (maximum or minimum). For instance, low-level wind shear, downdraft, and heavy rain can be considered an edge case for an airplane at landing. Working with edge cases is a highly valued skill as unforeseen edge cases can result in the failure of a system, with potential catastrophic consequences (e.g. a nuclear plant, an at-risk child, a stock-trading system, etc.). Teaching students how to identify and work with edge cases is therefore an important part of helping students develop expertise in these fields.

Finally, analogies and metaphors can be very powerful illustration tools but there are two important caveats. First, the diverse cultural community of most higher education institutions means that some students may not be familiar with particular athletic, culinary, or cultural traditions which often form the base of comparisons. Thus, an analogy or metaphor should never be the sole way a concept is presented but rather an enriching illustration. Second, if the limits of the analogy or metaphor are not explicitly discussed, students may develop problematic misconceptions. For example, describing DNA as like *a twisted ladder* implies a rigid and unchanging structure out of step with the dynamic structure that peels apart to allow access to numerous enzymes (Kapon and diSessa 2012).

CASE STUDY 6.1.B – ROCKIN' THE EXPLAINING

Case analysis questions

1. Identify where Ghali uses each of the three elements of a good explanation (starting where students are, keeping it short, and illustrating).
2. How does your answer now compare to your answer to the question in Case study 6.1.A?

CASE STUDY 6.2.A – EXPLAINING PRIORITIES AND DEADLINES FOR A PROJECT

Read this case study and complete the analysis questions below.

Ying Li* is supervising an online group of community work students who are helping to design anti-racist events for community centres. This week, she has received questions from at least five students about how to plan the deadlines for the different deliverables. Learning how to set priorities and deadlines for a project is part of the learning objectives of the module, so she starts the live online session with an explanation. "OK, I know that you have seen a lot of different tools for project management before. But for planning this project, you need to do reverse planning with a Gantt chart".

Ying Li then spends a few minutes describing the features of a Gantt chart and some online tools for collaboratively managing a chart in a team.

Getting back to our anti-racism campaigns, the first thing is to write down the final deadline. That is June 5th for us. Actually let's go back to this first week, and think about what is feasible to accomplish. It is good to have a checkpoint quite early and then they can be a little less frequent. Then when you are getting close to the end of the project, you will need to have more frequent checks in order to make sure that you are on schedule. And not falling behind.

> Ying Li continues, filling in the various tasks, deliverables, and checkpoints, and making reference to the intended events of several groups. Wrapping up, she says
>
>> Here, I can already see that you need to have all of the orders for material placed by February 15th and that the next priority will be to get feedback from the community centres who will be hosting your events. The real trick is to always use your time in the most effective way and not be waiting around.
>
> ### Case analysis questions
>
> Write down and keep your answers to the following questions. Suggested answers can be found at the end of the chapter.
>
> 1. What should Ying Li consider when deciding if she needs to give an explanation? Do you think that an explanation was necessary in this case?
> 2. What two specific pieces of advice could you give Ying Li that will help her students be more able to apply her explanations in their projects?
>
> * This case is a fictionalised account
of teaching experiences.

STRUCTURING YOUR EXPLANATIONS WITH THE LOAFS TEMPLATE

As we have seen above, structuring your explanation is important to make it effective. But what structure should you use? In this section, we present a template for structuring an explanation in which a number of evidence-informed principles for good explanations are already built-in, including the key principles we have just seen. This five-step template, called LOAFS and presented in Table 6.1, offers a versatile and reusable structure, which can be applied to 3-minute explanations and expanded to 45-minute (or more) lessons. The LOAFS structure will help you actively engage your students and promote learning from your explanation in the lab, studio, or projects.

TABLE 6.1 The five steps of the LOAFS structure for explanations

	Lead-In	Serves as your *hook* to catch students' attention and makes the connection with what your students know, value, or find interesting.
	Objectives	Makes your intentions for student learning explicit and clarifies your expectations so that students know where you want to bring them.
	Active processing	Engages your students in acquiring and processing information actively. Includes practice activities so that they structure new knowledge and start developing their skills.
	Formative assessment	Assesses the learning of your students in light of the objectives you have set for the lesson. Provides useful feedback to both you and your students about their learning (what is learned and what causes difficulties).
	Summary	Consolidates and integrates the lesson. Broadens the perspective and helps students make links to other concepts and contexts to facilitate transfer.

Icons by Freepik and Eleanor Wang on Flaticon.
Template inspired by the BOPPPS model of the Instructional Skills Workshops (Johnson 2006).

Lead-in (L----)

Because learning requires an effort, learners need to see the value in what they are going to learn. This value can take different forms depending both on the material itself but more importantly on the audience who is receiving the explanation. Knowing your audience, what they might find interesting or useful or intriguing, is therefore a key to *hook* them into your explanation. Using examples, concrete problems, or illustrations at the beginning of an explanation can help learners see the relevance and significance of what you are going to explain, which in turn can help them engage with it. For instance, you could start an explanation about managing condensation and microbial growth in the lab by asking the question: "At home, do you keep your eggs in the fridge or on the counter?"

An essential part of the lead-in is to prompt learners to recall their prior knowledge on which your explanation will build. Verbal questions, auto-corrected quizzes, or mini-problems are interesting tools to consider since they will provide you (and students) with feedback on what they remember and allow you to adapt your explanation accordingly. For instance, an exercise about the condensation of moisture onto cold surfaces could be a refresher for the lesson about microbial growth in the lab. In whole-class sessions you should consider how you and the students will get feedback on these exercises: using auto-corrected quizzes, synchronous polling questions, or simply discussing answers in plenum?

Finally, the lead-in can also assist students to see the underlying structure for the concepts you are going to explain. Presenting an overview using a structured list, a table, or a diagram will help your students build connections among concepts. In doing so you are also sharing how you, as an expert, organise knowledge in your domain, which is highly valuable for your students.

Objectives (-O---)

As Chapter 5 noted, being clear about objectives can help students understand the performance you expect them to attain so that they can direct their attention and actions, and evaluate their own achievements accordingly. Being explicit about what you expect students to learn is therefore a practice that will actually help students learn (Hattie 2009). In addition, there are two other benefits of clarifying the learning objectives of your explanation: one is to help you focus on the important points, the other is that it will actually help you design meaningful learning activities to engage students. Your learning objectives represent what you want students to be able to do after you have explained, and the learning activities that you include in your explanation (see the active learning phase just below) should typically help students to develop those abilities. Finally, it will help you and students to determine at the end of the explanation whether you – collectively – have achieved the intended objectives (see the formative assessment phase below).

Active learning (--A--)

Making an explanation accessible involves creating engagement on the part of the learner. Thus, a good explanation does not come entirely from the teacher but prompts the student to make connections, in particular to their prior knowledge and experiences, and to actively build their own understanding. The active learning phase is the core of your explanation and should probably be the longest part in your overall explanation.

One key message in this section is that giving an explanation yourself is not the only way for students to access new information. There is a wealth of active learning strategies which have students playing much more active roles than simply being attentive and taking notes (McKeachie and Svinicki 2014). Such strategies rely (i) on providing students with learning resources that they can use by themselves such as written documents, worksheets, videos, etc., and also (ii) on having students collaborate and/or teach each other, and (iii) on providing students with feedback on their learning so that they can make progress. A concrete example well suited to many practical settings is the Jigsaw activity (Aronson et al. 1978). Its main benefit is that students teach the course material to themselves and to each other, a strategy shown to promote learning (Hattie 2009).

Jigsaw is a cooperative learning activity in which students become *experts* in one part of a body of information (i.e. one piece of the jigsaw) and then cooperatively teach each other (thereby putting the pieces of the jigsaw together to get the whole picture):

1. Students are assigned to *expert groups* which are each in charge of learning a different block of the material. Students first study the learning material individually, then they discuss the material, or answer analysis questions, with their expert group, to deepen their understanding of their block.
2. *Jigsaw groups* are then formed with one expert of each of the different blocks. Each expert is in charge of teaching the group their block. The group can then collaboratively create a synthesis of the course material or work on a problem that requires integrating skills or knowledge from across all blocks. This phase should conclude with students receiving feedback on what they have learned.

A Jigsaw activity requires a sufficiently long time to be effective, which, of course, depends on the complexity of the material to learn and on the skills of the students. At minimum, it is probably not a good idea to try Jigsaw in under 30 minutes. The quality of the resources and the clarity of the instructions are key to allow students to learn autonomously. However, Jigsaw is just one example of a generic strategy which can be used in any discipline. Other types of active learning activities can also be designed around lab protocols, case studies, or project skills. When designing a learning activity, keep in mind that it should be relevant with respect to the learning objectives you have set for your explanation. Finally, consider including some collaborative tasks and provide students with feedback on their work to maximise the impact on learning of the activities you design.

SPOTLIGHT 6.2 – ARE CLASSROOM DEMONSTRATIONS MORE THAN ENTERTAINMENT?

Catherine Crouch and her colleagues at Harvard University were interested in knowing whether the demonstrations traditionally used in introductory science courses were really helping students to learn (Crouch et al. 2004). More specifically, they wanted to know if some ways of using demonstrations help students learn more than others.

In a large introductory physics class (133 students), they tested three different ways of using demonstrations. In mode A, the teachers showed the demonstration to students and provided an explanation. This mode corresponds largely to the way demonstrations are traditionally used in science classes. In mode B, the teacher first asked students to predict what the demonstration would show (e.g. "What will happen if I walk on this trolley?") and made them vote for an answer, then showed the demo and explained. In mode C, the teacher asked students to predict the outcome of the demo, to vote for their answer, were then showed the demo, and finally they discussed what they observed with their peers before hearing the teacher's explanation. A fourth group, the control group, did not see any demonstration. Seven different demonstrations were used over the semester. Each week, different sections of the class saw the week's demonstration either in one of the three modes or didn't see the demonstration at all. Students had an equal distribution of the different modes over the semester.

At the end of the semester, the researchers gave students a test that presented situations similar to those seen in the demos and asked students to state the outcome of the situation and explain why. They assessed whether students had the correct outcome or not, and whether students had the correct explanation or not.

It turned out that the students who saw the demonstration as used traditionally, i.e. in mode A, displayed no greater understanding of the underlying concepts than those who did not see the demonstration at all. Both modes B and C, in which students were engaged in predicting the outcome of the demo, showed a significantly higher rate of correct answers and correct explanations relative to both those who just saw the demo and those who didn't see the demo. The best results, both on predicting the outcome and explaining why, were obtained in mode C, when students had the chance to discuss their explanation with their peers before listening to the explanation from the teacher.

This way of using demonstrations can be found under the name *Predict – Observe – Explain* (White and Gunstone 1992). It shares a number of similarities with an approach sometimes used in lectures called *Peer Instruction* (Crouch and Mazur 2001).

Formative assessment (---F-)

A formative assessment is an evaluation of learning which is done *during* a learning activity with a view to help students to *improve*. In contrast, summative assessment comes at the end of the learning process and makes a final judgement on student learning. A final project report is a typical example of a summative assessment. A key component of formative assessment is feedback: getting feedback from students on their current understanding is useful for developing your explanations. When students get feedback it is beneficial for their learning, as you have seen in Chapter 5.

For a short explanation, the formative assessment phase can be as simple as asking a question. However, as Chapter 4 has explored, generic questions like "Is everything clear?" often solicit positive appreciative responses which are poor feedback for you and not useful for the students. It is useful therefore to pose a question which would allow the student to demonstrate that they have acquired the desired understanding. These questions are highly context and content dependant, but should ideally pose an appropriate cognitive challenge and the nature of the required response should be clear. An example of such a question presented in Chapter 4 was "What are three strategies political regimes use to exert influence on the arts community?" By asking students to respond to specific questions about the content of the session, teachers generate useful feedback for themselves and also for their students. Collecting students' answers can be done verbally, online in a quiz, by raising hands, or by using a polling system if that technology is available to you.

For more elaborate explanations, formative assessment may take the form of a longer exercise or activity. Here again you can refer back to the learning objectives you have set at the beginning of your explanation to design an exercise which will make a meaningful formative assessment. But don't forget that the principle of formative assessment is that it should be *formative* and therefore you have to think about how to give feedback to students. Will you collect students' work and share a general assessment with the class? Could you have students evaluate the work of their peers? In all cases, you should be as transparent as possible about the characteristics of an excellent performance.

Summary (----S)

The summary phase of your explanation allows students to consolidate their learning. As we have seen, long-term retention requires making connections and associating ideas together. This last phase is the right moment to look back at what has been learned and put this new learning in relation with a structure and a context which will facilitate its long-term memorisation. While it would be tempting to provide students with a well-structured review of the key points of your explanation, involving students in doing their own summary of what they have just learned (without looking at their notes, if possible) may be more beneficial for their learning.

Therefore, the summary in its simplest active form can consist in asking students to write the key ideas they retain from your explanation. You can guide them with specific questions; however, more generic questions such as "What are the three most significant things you have learned during this session?" have the advantage that they can be easily reused in a variety of contexts and disciplines. Another interesting question to ask students at the end of an explanation is whether there are elements they didn't understand. But rather than asking students to share this in front of the class, ask students to write their answer on an anonymous piece of paper and collect them. Writing answers in this way reduces the risk of a student feeling bad about highlighting their confusion, and having students write their answers will give you a more representative picture of what students did, and didn't, understand. Similarly, collecting the three key ideas as seen by students will give you rich feedback on what students have perceived (or not!) as important to learn. This technique is called the *Minute Paper*: at the end of an explanation or a lesson, ask students to write down what they have learned, collect the papers, and review them for immediate feedback on students' understanding and the nature of their difficulties. This technique scales up pretty easily for big groups, and online tools can facilitate the anonymous collection and reviewing of students' answers.

> **CASE STUDY 6.2.B – EXPLAINING PRIORITIES AND DEADLINES FOR A PROJECT**
>
> **Case analysis questions**
>
> Write down and keep your answers to the following questions. Suggested answers can be found at the end of the chapter.
>
> 1. Looking back at your answers to Case study 6.2.A, which of the concepts from the beginning of this chapter (starting where students are, keeping it short, and illustrating) are present in your answer?
> 2. How could Ying Li use the LOAFS structure to improve her explanation?

SPECIAL CASES FOR EXPLAINING IN PRACTICAL SETTINGS

So far, the principles we have seen apply to any kind of explanation in any type of situation. Here, we consider some ways to improve explanations in specific situations:

- modelling how experts think in oral and written format,
- explaining *how-to* procedures in the lab, field, or during projects.

Modelling how experts think

In Chapter 2 we noted that experts think and problem solve differently to novices. Experts tend to spend more time understanding a problem and its context than novices, and also to be more aware of errors they may be making as they work. It is important, therefore, not only to think about the content of your explanation but also the thinking process which it models to students. If you come into the lab, field, or studio with everything already all figured out, you will likely be able to run through your explanation quite rapidly without errors or uncertainty. This means that you will not model much of the thinking that students will need to do, and so even if they take detailed notes on exactly what you do, they will not be learning about the thinking process that leads to finding the solution. Further, because you have already figured out what you need to do, the initial analysis of the situation does not occur when students can observe it (this is the same problem described by Alan Schoenfeld in mathematics teaching in Spotlight 6.1). This issue is relevant even if the task you will demonstrate is not particularly complex, as students will benefit from seeing multiple examples of how to approach disciplinary tasks and will ascribe more value to the initial analysis if you model it as an integral part of practical work. Additionally, it can often be difficult for students to identify which theories or concepts to apply in practice, so this is a particularly useful step for novices.

In practice, this means not jumping right into performing the procedure or solving the problem, but showing students how you would assess the situation, and modelling how you would determine what the outcome should be and what equipment will be necessary. Taking the time to consider multiple approaches and to discuss the characteristics of the situation which prompt you to favour a specific approach is valuable for students, as it makes the source of expert intuition visible. The time you devote to analysing the situation, the pauses you take to think, and side notes to yourself all become characteristics of your students' conception of expert problem solving. Remember that realistic responses to encountering cognitive difficulty include pauses, reviewing or rereading information available, proceeding slowly, and reversing course. If none of these feature in your demonstrations of problem solving in your discipline, you may be giving students an unrealistic sense of how experts in your discipline work.

Another important aspect of modelling your thinking is demonstrating not only how to reason and problem solve, but also how to evaluate the result. While reviewing and checking our thinking should be the final step of problem solving, it is frequently omitted from explanations. Making explicit how you, as an expert, evaluate your thinking is an important way to enable students to acquire appropriate disciplinary habits for knowledge justification (Isaac, forthcoming). Many students enter university with the idea that answers are either right or wrong, and that true experts are never uncertain (Baxter-Magolda 1992). These perceptions are completely different from those of professionals, who regularly encounter situations where the best answer remains subjective and tentative (e.g. Gainsburg 2007). Beliefs in absolute correct answers and the authority of experts have been shown to be stronger or to persist longer for students in programmes that result in professional qualification (Wise et al. 2004), such as engineering or nursing. These findings should stimulate us to be more explicit in modelling our thinking in practical settings. The continuation of Case study 6.2.A provides an opportunity to consider how the advice presented above translates into a fieldwork setting.

The words you employ during your explanations can serve as a model that challenges students' self-limiting beliefs, such as a belief in the existence of fixed academic ability (an idea we return to in Chapter 9). Acknowledging that you have not always had your current level of proficiency, and may have in fact struggled at times is useful modelling. Instead of "I always use a 5 mL vials for …", try "I've found that using a 5 mL is easier when …" or "It took me a while to figure out how to organise myself for interviewing …"

EXPLAINING *HOW-TO* PROCEDURES IN THE LAB, THE FIELD, STUDIOS, OR DURING PROJECTS

Hands-on activities provide students with the opportunity to learn practical skills such as the use of specific equipment or software. For example, you may need to demonstrate how to clean and import a data set, how to store a biological sample, or how to use the laser cutter in the workshop. It happens frequently that students struggle to reproduce a procedure, even just after a demonstration of the procedure. Kate Exley and her colleagues (2019) have identified a useful strategy for demonstrating procedures that allow groups of students to see what expert performance looks like, as well as decomposing it in a way that allows them to learn the process and understand what kinds of practice would be necessary for them to become proficient.

> *Step 1: introduce the skill and contextualise it.* It can be useful to ask students questions which activate any prior knowledge which they may have and may need in this setting. At this stage, the teacher can explain what the procedure is and, importantly, *why* this procedure is important or appropriate. Teachers can also explain how much practice students will need to become fluent with the skill or procedure.
> *Step 2: demonstrate expert performance.* The teacher demonstrates the skill, in real time without verbal commentary.
> *Step 3: demonstrate decomposed performance.* The teacher repeats the demonstration but this time breaks it down into steps and explains what is

happening at each step. The teacher engages the students by asking them questions about what is going on and encourages students to ask questions. The teacher draws students' attention to things that they may not easily perceive. For example, when demonstrating using cutting tools, students' attention may be drawn to the cutting edge and not to the way in which the teacher's stance gives them stability.

Step 4: learners describe the process. The teacher (or one of the students) may demonstrate the process again, but this time with learners guiding the demonstrator through the process. The teacher may provide hints and guidance for learners by using questions.

Step 5: students practice the process themselves. Students practice the skills themselves with feedback from the facilitator or from peers.

Although it may look quite different from other kinds of presentation, you may note that Exley's structure for demonstrating a procedure follows closely the five phases of LOAFS, described above (if you wish to take a few minutes to map the five steps onto the LOAFS framework, you may find this to be a productive learning activity).

MODELLING THINKING IN DOCUMENT FORMAT – WHAT YOU THINK VS. WHAT YOU WRITE DOWN

It may be that many of the explanations you provide to students are in written format. Lab protocols are often written in advance and, in field practice settings, students may rarely be all together in a class and your primary means of communication may be in writing. Text-based resources that you prepare for your students should incorporate many of the elements discussed above. A good written resource includes not only how to perform a procedure but also explains the underlying expert thinking of how to figure out that this is an appropriate procedure for a given situation. Structuring your written explanations to explicitly include both the procedural steps and the thinking that accompanies the gestures will help students recognise the thinking processes that are required of them.

CASE STUDY 6.1.C – ROCKIN' THE EXPLAINING

Read this case study and complete the analysis questions below.

Ghali, on the geology field trip with his students, explains *how to perform the acid test*.

Okay, can everyone hear me? I'm going to demonstrate how to do the acid test. You should be ready to perform the acid test on a sample yourself when I'm done explaining. This is a really simple test that you will use frequently in your field work, starting today and continuing throughout your career, so please ask me if there is anything unclear.

Ghali picks up a fist-sized rock. "Looking at this rock, what possible types of rock could it be?" Students call out a few suggestions. "Good, I heard several different kinds of carbonate minerals. And the acid test is a good first step to figuring out which kind, based on the degree or vigour of the reaction with hydrochloric acid".

Ghali first completes the acid test procedure once in real time. He then directs students to page 6 of their field guide and repeats the procedure, providing a detailed, step-by-step commentary to accompany his actions of applying a drop of acid to the surface of the rock. "OK, looking at the table on page 7 of your field guide, how would you characterise the reaction that we just saw?" A few students make suggestions.

For a *very weak* reaction, you would typically need a magnifying glass to see the CO_2 produced. So *weak* is a better characterisation. Then you consult the second table on page 7 to see what kinds of rocks have a *weak* reaction. What are our options?

Again, students make a few suggestions.

These are good ideas. Let's do the reaction again, to see if we can get more detailed observations. I'll just break the rock to get a clean surface. Ok, just call it out, what is the first step I need to do to repeat the acid test?

The students call out the procedural steps, which Ghali performs or questions if appropriate. This time however the acid produces a vigorous bubbling reaction.

Wow. That doesn't look like the reaction from the first time at all. Make a quick pair with a neighbour and together review the steps

I took for each of the trials. I'll give you two minutes to discuss
– what was different?

Ghali intentionally looks down at his notes to signal to students that
he is done talking and that they should start discussing with a neighbour. Despite keeping his eyes down, Ghali remains attentive to the
discussions around him and after about 1.5 minutes there is a lull in
the discussions. "OK, great. Let's come back together again. We will go
through the procedure step-by-step, and you let me know when anything
was different". Ghali has students call out the steps in order, again, but
this time he does not need to make any corrections. "Excellent, you have
all the steps. But what was different? Which test would you trust more,
the first test or the one after I broke the rock open?" Monique's hand
shoots up, "The second one! You broke the rock open and used a fresh
surface that hadn't been exposed to weathering!" Ghali smiles, "Right,
so now you are ready to go and do the acid test yourself. And don't forget to use a fresh surface to get reliable results!"

Case analysis questions

Write down and keep your answers to the following questions.
Suggested answers can be found at the end of the chapter.

1. What are the different actions that Ghali asks students to do during his demonstration?
2. Ghali uses some of the elements of the LOAFS structure. Can you identify which elements? In which order does he use them?

*This case is a fictionalised account of teaching experiences.

TEST YOURSELF

The activities in this section provide an opportunity for you to review and apply the ideas from this chapter. We highly recommend doing these activities before continuing to the chapter conclusion. You can use the sample answers to these activities provided at the end of the chapter to give yourself feedback.

REFLECTION POINT 6.1

Write a summary of the key points you have learned about explanations from this chapter, before comparing it to the Action summary at the end of the chapter.

CASE STUDY 6.3 – EXPLAINING HOW TO GIVE FEEDBACK TO PHYSIOTHERAPY CLIENTS

Read this case study and complete the analysis questions below.

Vivek's* physiotherapy students give a one-day free clinic at a local community centre each year. Vivek has noticed that his students often fail to consider the precarious living conditions of the clients, many of whom live in shelters or on the street, and consequently make inappropriate recommendations (e.g. recommending daily hot baths). Another recurrent issue is not giving clients adequate feedback to enable them to keep working on their exercises independently, since they are unlikely to have another opportunity to see a physiotherapist. These concerns have prompted Vivek to create a few extra resources to help his students prepare, including a short online video about giving effective feedback. Table 6.2 presents some of his ideas for the video on feedback.

> * This case is a fictionalised account of teaching experiences.

Case analysis questions

Write down and keep your answers to the following questions. Suggested answers can be found at the end of the chapter.

1. Review the two options for each phase of LOAFS presented in Table 6.2, noting the strong and weak points in terms of what students can learn from the explanation.
2. How could you improve Vivek's outline so that it better models expert thinking?

PART II

TABLE 6.2 LOAFS structure for a video on giving effective feedback

Phase	Option 1	Option 2
Lead-in	"I love being a physio. But do you know what I hate? When clients don't do their exercises between sessions with me. So it was a light bulb moment for me when I realised that how I gave them feedback during a session could have a big impact on my clients actually doing their exercises. I now see giving good feedback to clients as an important professional skill".	"It is great that so many of you volunteer for this clinic each year. It is a great way to give back to some really disadvantaged people in our community. This video will help you make a bigger impact from your time and therefore on the health of these people who live in difficult conditions".
Objective	"I want you to 1. be aware of clients' situations, to see them as people in their environments, and not simply muscles and tendons. 2. give clients process-focused feedback that is structured to increase retention by people who have experienced trauma".	Show slide: at the end of this video, you should be better able to 1. Target the level of difficulty to motivate clients to invest effort that will help them heal. 2. Provide monitoring skills that enable clients to recognise when they are doing an exercise correctly and to continue to improve independently.
Active processing	"Pause this video and make a list of five or more key ideas about feedback, recalling concepts from class. Restart the video when you are done". Vivek briefly reviews the key ideas about feedback, using cases from last year's clinic to illustrate. "Now that you've heard from me, pause the video again and review your list above. Complete or revise as necessary in order to create a good memo about feedback for yourself".	"As you watch this video of an interaction between a physio and a client, make notes about what you notice about the client (both physical and emotional states). Pause whenever you need. Then write some feedback as you would say it to the client, before starting the video again". Vivek reruns the video of the interaction, pausing when necessary, to describe what he sees and how he would give the client feedback.

Feedback	Online quiz – five cases with background about the person and a video of them doing a physio exercise. Students choose the best feedback (multiple choice) to give the client in each case.	Video of an interaction between a physio and a client – students revise the script to improve the feedback given to the client and submit to Vivek.
Summary	Vivek reviews key points, making connections to other concepts like deliberate practice.	Return to objective slide. Tell students to pause and write their own summary.

REFLECTION POINT 6.2

1. Write out a *how-to* procedure that you have previously explained to your students.
2. Where did you start? How does this connect with what your students already know? Did you keep it short? Did you use any illustrations?
3. Revise your explanation above to include each element of the LOAFS format, taking particular care to explain your expert thinking and to integrate opportunities for students to practice.

ACTION SUMMARY – EXPLAINING

- Is it really necessary to explain it? Is there another strategy you could use that would involve your students more?
- If an explanation is really needed, be sure to find a starting point adapted to your students, keep your explanation short, and support it with illustrations.
- Whether for 5 or 45 minutes, use the LOAFS template to structure your explanations and involve students throughout your explanations.
- When using physical or digital artefacts to improve your explanation, make sure to engage students using questions.
- When modelling your thinking for an audience, be sure to include all the steps that inform how you, as an expert, analyse the situation.
- Provide written solutions that model how you expect students to approach the task.
- Enable students to learn from the process of hands-on activities by encouraging awareness of the thinking strategies underling the procedures.

CONCLUSION

While delivering clear information is frequently taken as equivalent to good teaching, this chapter has sought to illustrate that good explanations involve being attentive to students' prior knowledge, and proposing activities that stimulate cognitive engagement and promote structure, and conclude with feedback on what has been understood. This feedback from students is a key tool in fighting your *curse of knowledge*, i.e. your inability as an expert to understand or remember the difficulties encountered by novices when learning in your discipline. Throughout this chapter, we have tried to make explicit that interactivity is essential to good explanations, so the advice on questions in Chapter 4 and on managing interactions with the class in Chapter 7 is complementary to this chapter. Another important tool is understanding how students' brains (and your own!) work. This chapter has been designed to help you incorporate what we know from neuroscience into how you structure and prepare your explanations. The next chapter, on managing interactions with a class, considers both logistical and emotional aspects of establishing a productive relationship with students.

FURTHER READING

This small number of sources provide further practical guidance for structuring explanations and methods for sharing information that are most effective for learning. A full reference list for the chapter is provided below.

Structuring explanations

Davis, B. G. (2009). Chapter 16. Explaining clearly. In: *Tools for Teaching*, 2nd edition. (pp.148–161). San Francisco: Wiley.
Le Duc, I. (2018). Structuring explanations with LOAFS [Video]. *SwitchTube*. https://tube.switch.ch/download/video/af20b0a8.
Quigley, A. (2013, May 11). Explanations: Top, vol. 10. Teaching tips [Blog]. *The Confident Teacher*. https://www.theconfidentteacher.com/2013/05/explanations-top-ten-teaching-tips/.
Tormey, R. (2018). Explaining using a board (STEM focus) [Video]. *SwitchTube*. https://tube.switch.ch/download/video/8f6448b2.

Methods for communicating information

Davis, B. G. (2009). Chapter 15. Delivering a lecture. In: *Tools for Teaching*, 2nd edition. (pp.148–161). San Francisco: Wiley.
Exley, K., and Dennick, R. (2009). *Giving a Lecture: From Presenting to Teaching*, 2nd edition. Key Guides for Effective Teaching in Higher Education. London: Routledge. https://doi.org/10.4324/9780203879924.
Exley, K., Dennick, R., and Fisher, A. (2019). Chapter 9. Hands-on, practical teaching in small groups. In: *Small Group Teaching: Tutorials, Seminars and*

Workshops, 2nd edition. (pp. 153–161). London: Routledge. https://doi.org/10.4324/9780429490897.

McKeachie, W., and Svinicki, M. (2014). Chapter 6. How to make lectures more effective. In: *McKeachie's Teaching Tips*, 14th edition. Belmont, CA: Cengage Learning.

ANSWERS TO SELECTED CHAPTER ACTIVITIES

These sample answers are provided to allow you to generate some feedback for yourself. You should take time to complete the activities before comparing your answers with our ideas.

Case study 6.1.B

1. Ghali uses several effective strategies, starting with situating his explanation in terms of why it is relevant to students and stimulating some curiosity. He asks students questions to find out what they already know and is therefore able to start his explanation in an appropriate place, rather than guessing what they already know or may need to be reminded of. He also finishes with a question that gives him feedback on what students have understood from his explanations. Finally, he keeps his explanation short and uses the larger shell as an illustration.

Case study 6.2.A

1. Some students have asked questions which suggests there may be a need for an explanation. But Ying Li doesn't have much information about what her students already know. If she isn't sure, she should ask them questions to avoid repeating unnecessary details.
2. The lack of structure in Ying Li's explanation, as she jumps back and forth in time, will make it hard for her students to apply her explanation. She also starts right in with what they need to do, without explaining *why* this is what they need to do – this means that her students will be less likely to recognise the next situation when a Gantt chart is appropriate. Her failure to model the key features of her expert thinking also shows up when she says "the trick is ..." and "here I can see ..." but doesn't tell her students what details she is basing her assessment on. Finally, Ying Li doesn't involve

EXPLAINING AND DEMONSTRATING IN PRACTICAL SETTINGS

her students at all and therefore has no feedback on what they have understood or not from her explanations.

Case study 6.2.B

2. Ying Li jumps directly into her explanation, when it would be helpful for students if she formulated a lead-in to contextualise her explanation and to hook students' attention. Ying Li does not tell her students the learning objective, so they do not know what they should be attentive to. Ying Li does all the talking, so her students are passive rather than active during the live online session. Ying Li concludes with a clear statement about good planning but she does not ask for any feedback from students on what they have understood.

Case study 6.1.C

1. Ghali gets students to recollect what they already know, to watch him perform the procedure fluently, to follow the written procedure while he demonstrates the stepwise process, and then he asks students to tell him how to do the procedure twice. He also has students discuss with a neighbour.
2. L – Ghali stimulates interest by telling students that they will use this procedure today and throughout their careers. Although the different test results observed later probably do more to stimulate students' curiosity.
O – he states that students should be able to perform the acid test themselves.
A – Ghali's students are actively involved when they tell him what steps to do and when discussing with a peer. Students are also called on to answer questions at the beginning and end of his explanation.
F – Ghali has students tell him twice how to do the procedure, allowing him to see what students have understood.
S – Ghali doesn't do a summary. Overall, the order of his phases is OLAFL.

TABLE 6.3 Evaluating the LOAFS structure for a video on effective feedback

Phase	Option 1	Option 2
Lead-in	Strong points – teacher's character and experience are present, clear focus on the topic (feedback). Weak points – doesn't address the other part of Vivek's goals, not related to the context of the one-day clinic, doesn't connect to prior knowledge.	Strong points – context of the one-day clinic, connects to motivation of students. Weak points – doesn't introduce the topic of feedback or connect to prior knowledge.
Objective	Strong points – relates to the context of the clinic, includes both emotional and cognitive goals. Weak points – teacher-focused ("I want ..."), the meaning of the term "process feedback" may be clear to Vivek but not to his students.	Strong points – formulated in terms of students learning skills, written down so that students get the message in audio and visual. Weak points – context of the one-day clinic absent.
Active processing	Strong points – students are actively processing (minute paper strategy), recalling concepts from class, uses illustrations. Weak points – focus is mostly on concepts and Vivek doesn't model his expert thinking.	Strong points – modelling expert thinking. Weak points – no review of key concepts means a high cognitive load for students.
Feedback	Strong points – multiple opportunities to practice, immediate feedback for students. Weak points – task is not very authentic since students are choosing best feedback, not creating their own.	Strong points – focus on thinking skills, watching and responding to a client. Weak points – no immediate feedback on their learning for the students.
Summary	Strong points – clear what students should remember. Weak points – students are passive, introduces ideas not previously seen in this video.	Strong points – focused on students' learning of skills, active processing for students. Weak points – students do not get a clear summary at the end.

Case study 6.3

1. The options for each LOAFS phase have both strong and weaker points, as illustrated by the analysis presented in Table 6.3.
2. The most relevant activity for modelling expert thinking occurs in active processing, option 2. An improved outline could be created by tweaking the activities above to combine the most successful aspects of the two options.

REFERENCES

Ainsworth, S. (2008). The educational value of multiple-representations when learning complex scientific concepts. In: J. K. Gilbert, M. Reiner & M. Nakhleh (eds.), *Visualization: Theory and Practice in Science Education* (pp. 191–208). Basel: Springer. https://doi.org/10.1007/978-1-4020-5267-5_9.

Aronson, E., Blaney, N., Stephin, C., Sikes, J., and Snapp, M. (1978). *The Jigsaw Classroom*. Beverly Hills, CA: Sage Publishing Company.

Baxter Magolda, M. B. (1992). *Knowing and Reasoning in College: Gender-Related Patterns in Students' Intellectual Development*. San Francisco: Jossey Bass

Crouch, C. H., and Mazur, E. (2001). Peer Instruction: Ten years of experience and results. *American Journal of Physics* 69(9): 970–977. https://doi.org/10.1119/1.1374249.

Crouch, C., Fagen, A. P., Callan, J. P., and Mazur, E. (2004). Classroom demonstrations: Learning tools or entertainment? *American Journal of Physics* 72(6): 835–838. https://doi.org/10.1119/1.1707018.

Dym, C. L., Agogino, A. M., Eris, O., Frey, D. D., and Leifer, L. J. (2005). Engineering design thinking, teaching, and learning. *Journal of Engineering Education* 94(1): 103–120. https://doi.org/10.1002/j.2168-9830.2005.tb00832.x.

Gainsburg, J. (2007). The mathematical disposition of structural engineers. *Journal for Research in Mathematics Education* 38(5): 477–506. https://doi.org/10.2307/30034962.

Hattie, J. (2009). *Visible Learning: A Synthesis of over 800 Meta-Analyses Relating to Achievement*. London: Routledge. https://doi.org/10.4324/9780203887332

Herrington, D. G., and Nakhleh, M. B. (2003). What defines effective chemistry laboratory instruction? Teaching assistant and student perspectives. *Journal of Chemical Education* 80(10): 1197–1205. https://doi.org/10.1021/ed080p1197.

Isaac, S. (forthcoming). *Epistemic Practices: a framework for characterising engineering students' epistemic cognition*. Lancaster, UK: Lancaster University.

Johnson, J. B. (2006). *Instructional Skills Workshop Handbook for Participants*. Vancouver, BC: The Instructional Skills Workshop International Advisory Committee. http://www.iswnetwork.ca/.

Kapon, S., and diSessa, A. A. (2012). Reasoning through instructional analogies. *Cognition and Instruction* 30(3): 261–310. https://doi.org/10.1080/073700 08.2012.689385.

McKeachie, W., and Svinicki, M. (2014). *McKeachie's Teaching Tips, 14th edition*. Belmont, CA: Cengage Learning.

Novak, J. D. (2005). Results and implications of a 12-year longitudinal study of science concept learning. *Research in Science Education* 35(1): 23–40. https://doi.org/10.1007/s11165-004-3431-4.

Perkins, D. N., and Salomon, G. (1994). Transfer of learning. In: T. Husen & T. N. Postelwhite (eds.), *International Handbook of Educational Research, 2nd edition*, Vol. 11. (pp. 6452–6457). Oxford: Pergamon Press.

Perkins, K. K., Gratny, M. M., Adams, W. K., Finkelstein, N. D., and Wieman, C. E. (2006). Towards characterizing the relationship between students' interest in and their beliefs about physics. *AIP Conference Proceedings* 818(1): 137–140. https://doi.org/10.1063/1.2177042.

Schoenfeld, A. H. (1985). *Mathematical Problem Solving*. Orlando: Academic Press Inc.

Schoenfeld, A. H. (1988). When good teaching leads to bad results: The disasters of "well-taught" mathematics courses. *Educational Psychologist* 23(2): 145–166. https://doi.org/10.1207/s15326985ep2302_5.

Tormey, R., and Hardebolle, C. (2017). Apprendre à étudier en sciences et ingénierie [MOOC]. *EPFL Etudier*. https://go.epfl.ch/mooc-etudier.

Volkmann, M. J., and Zgagacz, M. (2004). Learning to teach physics through inquiry: The lived experience of a graduate teaching assistant. *Journal of Research in Science Teaching* 41(6): 584–602. https://doi.org/10.1002/tea.20017.

White, R. T., and Gunstone, R. F. (1992). *Probing Understanding*. London: Routledge (Falmer). https://doi.org/10.4324/9780203761342.

Wise, J. C., Lee, S. H., Litzinger, T., Marra, R. M., and Palmer, B. (2004). A report on a four-year longitudinal study of intellectual development of engineering undergraduates. *Journal of Adult Development* 11(2): 103–110. https://doi.org/10.1023/B:JADE.0000024543.83578.59.

Chapter 7

Managing relationships with a class

CASE STUDY 7.1.A – DISRUPTIONS THREATEN LAB SAFETY

Read this case study and complete the analysis questions below.

Today is Valentina's* first day in the lab with this semester's students. She has heard people say that the first encounter with students sets the tone for the semester, and this matches her own experience. She wants the lab to run smoothly and efficiently, so Valentina immediately starts by presenting the safety regulations related to today's lab, saying "Please pay attention, this information is very important for you and your peers' safety". She then takes three minutes to explain the health and safety issues, and while she speaks, she walks around the class handing out a printed page with the university regulations.

As she finishes, she notices seven students entering the room who have missed the presentation on safety regulations. As they take their seats, Valentina hands them the printed information and makes no comment. The students take the paper and sit down, and Valentina continues with her introduction of the experiment.

The following week, Valentina notices at least ten students arriving after the safety review. She decides that this needs to be addressed before a pattern develops and so she takes the names of the late students and informs them that a half-point will be taken off their lab report. This information causes quite a few students to react: they say that taking off points is unfair because they weren't warned. Valentina is surprised at their vehemence, and senses most of the class looking at her with surprise as well.

Case analysis questions

Write down and keep your answers to the analysis questions. Suggested answers can be found at the end of the chapter.

1. Which of Valentina's actions contribute to establishing a relationship with the class? For each, is the effect of the action positive or negative?
2. Identify what actions Valentina took to manage the class and prevent disruptions.
3. Is there anything she did which you think was unhelpful to manage the class?
4. What should Valentina do next to avoid future disruptions?

* This case is a fictionalised account of teaching experiences.

INTRODUCTION

If the goal of practical work is for students to engage in the desired activities, how should teachers interact with students to maintain the focus on learning? This final chapter of Part II explains how teachers and teaching assistants can manage their interactions with students to minimise disruptions and maximise learning. We discuss the interplay of three social dimensions of how students see their teachers (warmth, trust, and competence), and consider how implicit biases can influence the mutual perceptions of teachers and students. We propose an approach combining preventative strategies with a progressive escalation of corrective strategies to reduce the occurrence of problematic behaviours that do not support learning in practical settings. Before continuing, take a moment to do the analysis questions for Case study 7.1.A. Doing the Reflection point activities throughout the chapter will increase your ability to apply the strategies presented here in your own teaching.

Class management has often been identified as a key concern of teachers during their early years of teaching (Conway and Clark 2003). Indeed,

Andrea Reupert and Stuart Woodcock (2010) identify that class management is the most significant cause for concern for those in teacher-training programmes. Roland Tormey's (2019) survey of higher education graduate teaching assistants found that class management was the area where they felt least confident; more than half of teaching assistants said that they were not confident managing a class and over 20% said they were not confident in their ability to handle disruptions. This means that Valentina's difficulty in establishing a constructive relationship with her class in Case study 7.1.A represents a common concern of teachers.

This is not surprising because, while many of us get into teaching because we love our discipline, our actual teaching work is fundamentally about interacting with other people. This has been emphasised by Kathleen Quinlan's (2016) work on the fundamentally relational nature of education, including higher education:

> When students perceive that their teachers listen and show immediacy through behaviours that generate a sense of closeness, they experience the class more positively, feel emotionally supported, and can express their own emotions more authentically.
>
> (2016, 104)

While Quinlan notes that these emotional relationships are often neglected in the literature on higher education teaching and learning, research at other levels of education shows that student–teacher relationships are an important contributor to learning (see Chapter 9).

If class management and relationships are an issue in any higher education class, it is particularly important in experiential learning settings. While student behavioural norms are easily identifiable in traditional lectures (sit down, pay attention, take notes, don't disturb the teacher or other students), in *learning by doing* settings a frequent, yet often implicit, expectation is that students will learn how to manage and direct their own work. Consequently, students have more autonomy and flexibility in their movements to allow them to develop the ability to structure and guide their own work. This can be at odds with health and safety issues in labs, fieldwork, and studios. In chemistry labs, for example, students are regularly exposed to corrosive, explosive, easily oxidising, flammable, irritating, toxic, and polluting materials. In this context, it is imperative that students behave in ways that minimise risk to themselves, others, and the environment, while still allowing them to learn. In disciplines like dance, injury is a recurrent risk even among experienced dancers, and one study on university dance students found an overall injury rate of between 67% and 77% over two semesters (Weigert 2005). Careful management of the environment in practical settings is, therefore, of paramount importance.

The good news about class management is that it is a skill that can be learned. Linda Darling-Hammond and colleagues (2002) carried out a study of nearly 3,000 novice teachers' self-perception of their readiness to teach. They found that novice teachers who had followed a training programme were significantly more confident in their ability to develop the class environment when compared to those who relied only on their own experiences.

Class disruptions are often considered in terms of student behaviours that are annoying or problematic to teachers. However, these individual behaviours are part of the broader context of the civility or incivility of the interactions between the teacher and the students. Focusing on the patterns of these interactions helps us, as teachers, to see how our relationship with students contributes to positive class environments. So while disruptions are a worrying issue for teachers, our approach starts with proactive strategies related to developing constructive relationships that will serve to decrease instances of incivility and therefore disruptions.

This chapter explains how teachers can approach class management and relationships with a view to maximising learning and to minimising disruptive behaviour. It starts by looking into perceptions of teachers and students as to what kinds of behaviour are and are not appropriate in class. It then explores three dimensions of class relationships that play a role both in class behaviour and in learning. Building on this, it identifies a number of preventative and corrective strategies that teachers can use to manage class relationships and behaviour.

Central to Case study 7.1.A is the fact that Valentina and her students appear to have a different understanding of what was expected in the lab and what sanctions were reasonable. This chapter starts, therefore, with an exploration of the similarities and differences in the behaviours seen as a problem by teachers and by students.

CLASS DISRUPTIONS: IS IT THEM OR IS IT ME?

What kinds of behaviour in a higher education class are problematic? Complete Reflection point 7.1 to reflect on your own perspective, then read on to compare with studies of incivilities in higher education.

REFLECTION POINT 7.1

Placing yourself in a practical setting where you teach, identify the student behaviours on the list below that you think you would notice and the ones where you would usually intervene.

	I would usually notice	I would usually intervene as soon as I saw it	I would usually intervene later
Starting to pack up, or tune out, before the end of the session.			
Making fun of and/or not listening to classmates' contributions.			
Raising a topic unrelated to the current discussion or presentation.			
Challenging the teacher's authority verbally or non-verbally with body language or posture.			
Arriving late or leaving early (online – connecting late or disconnecting early).			
Working on something else during a session.			
Making sarcastic comments.			
Having side conversations, either via online chat or in person, that continue even after being asked to stop.			
Taking class time to complain about feedback or grades they received.			
Dismissing or undermining the contributions of peers from underrepresented groups.			
One or two students dominate class discussions and leave little space for others to participate.			

One of the early landmark studies on disruptions in university classes was carried out by Bob Boice in the 1990s. Boice had noted when observing classes for new faculty that class incivilities "emerged as a major factor, frequently dominating classes, often making or breaking novice teachers" (1996, 454). He explored the area of class disturbance through in-class observations and hundreds of interviews with teachers and students in 16 different courses through a full semester at a large New York state university.

Boice noted that students and teachers agreed that certain types of behaviour in the class were disturbing:

- students talking to each other so loudly that teachers and other students could regularly not be heard,
- students confronting teachers either with sarcasm or with conspicuous noises such as groaning, sniggering, or slamming of books,
- students complaining to, or disagreeing with, the teacher in an aggressive or insulting fashion.

Thereafter teacher and student perceptions as to problematic behaviour diverged. For teachers, the following types of behaviour were identified as causing problems:

- students not participating in class, not answering questions, or not displaying interest,
- students being unprepared for class,
- students who demanded accommodations from teachers such as make-up exams or extensions to deadlines,
- students who came to class late or left early in a disruptive fashion.

While teachers identified the preceding list of behaviours as problematic, students were generally less likely to do so. On the other hand, there were also behaviours perceived as problematic by students but not perceived as problematic by teachers:

- teachers who appeared cold, distant, or uncaring,
- teachers who surprised the class with unanticipated tests,
- teachers who arrived more than five minutes late, or who cancelled classes without warning,
- students who taunted or belittled other class members.

These patterns are summarised in Figure 7.1.

A few things are evident from Boice's work. First, although there is some overlap, teachers and students often had different impressions about

MANAGING RELATIONSHIPS WITH A CLASS

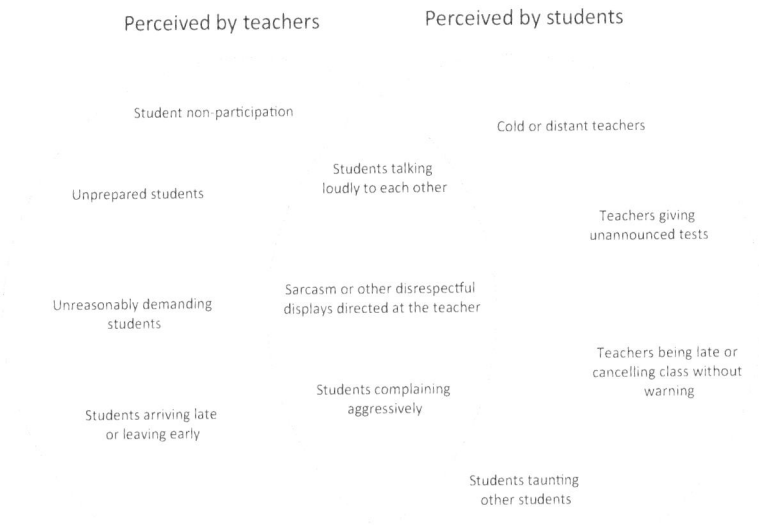

FIGURE 7.1 Teachers' and students' perceptions of class incivility
(Graphical representation of patterns described in Boice 1996)

what kinds of behaviour were problematic. Some of the student–student interactions which were seen as problematic by students were not visible to teachers, so that many of the behaviours regarded as problematic by one group were not seen as an issue by the other. This is important, because Boice found that it was not until teachers became aware of what others saw as problematic in their classes that "there was evidence of understanding that translated into reliably changed practices in classrooms" (1996, 465). Second, it is evident that students did not see the problems as being a case of *us* (students) against *them* (the teacher). Rather many students saw the behaviours of some of their classmates as a problem and saw themselves as being on the *same side* as the teacher, but at the same time they expected the teacher to manage the situation. In interviews with Boice students said things like, "I put the responsibility on him. He's not a good teacher if he doesn't take the effort to be heard", and (about a different class) "I don't understand this. Why doesn't she just tell some of those guys to shut up? Who's in charge?"

A third key finding in Boice's work is that the levels of students' disruptive behaviours in class were related to specific types of teacher behaviour – where teachers (perhaps unintentionally) communicated that they didn't care about the class or the students, levels of problematic behaviour were higher. And once these patterns were established in a class, they were very hard to break. However the same teacher could achieve better class behaviour if they established good relationships with new classes by doing things like: arriving early and informally chatting to students; trying to communicate warmth and openness to the class; avoiding showing impatience or frustration with students; ensuring an appropriate pace, and checking students' understanding of the material before moving on (1996, 479).

Although Boice's data is interesting, his data collection is not systematic and so it is not clear that his findings are representative. It is also clear that a lot has changed in student life since the early 1990s. Wendy Bjorklund and Diana Rehling (2009) carried out a large study of uncivil behaviour by students in which they asked over 3,600 students to rate a list of problematic behaviours. The most problematic behaviours according to students were those which were actively disruptive, including *continuing to talk after being asked to stop*, *allowing a cell phone to ring*, and *conversing loudly with others*. These all scored above four on a five-point scale. Mid-ranked problematic behaviours included those that might be termed distracting disengagement, like *arriving late / leaving early*, *text messaging*, and *packing up before the class is over*. These all scored above three on the five-point scale. Other disengaged activities like *eating and drinking*, or *yawning* were seen as even less problematic by students, scoring two out of five points. Students were also asked about what disruptive behaviours they encountered most frequently. The most commonly cited were *text messaging*, *packing up books before class is over*, *yawning*, and *eating and drinking*.

Boice's work and his focus on putting relationships at the centre of class management have been very influential, and more recent research on class incivilities has built on and extended this work (e.g. Braxton and Bayer 2004; Alt and Itzkovic 2015). The involvement of both teachers and students in the teaching and learning relationship is illustrated in Spotlight 7.1, which discusses Cynthia Clark's work on how the emotions of teachers and learners in practical settings influence problematic behaviour. In the next section, we present a three-dimensional model for thinking about class relationships between teachers and students, and explore how this can help make sense of how teachers can approach class management in face-to-face teaching but also when teaching online. But before continuing, you should complete analysis questions for Case study 7.1.B.

SPOTLIGHT 7.1 – INCIVILITY IN CLINICAL PRACTICE SETTINGS

> Incivility is like a dance – one dancer leads and the other follows – and sometimes the dancers do both. The steps ebb and flow, and often, the dancers are swept away – moving and gyrating to a frenzied, raucous rhythm, while a sense of defiance seems to take over – and from there, anything can happen.
>
> (Clark 2008, E37)

In a study on incivility in nursing education, Cynthia Clark gathered responses from 194 faculty members and 306 students from 41 states. She notes that clinical practice is identified as one of the most anxiety-producing components of nursing education. Students are stressed both by the fear of making a mistake that could have terrible consequences for a patient and, at the same time, by their interaction with clinical instructors. This stress, in turn, led to an increased risk of incivility, irrational anger, and even violence.

Faculty members identified both faculty stress and a feeling of superiority as contributing to incidents of faculty incivility. Students on the other hand seemed unaware of the stress faculty were under, and perceived only the feeling of superiority as the cause of faculty incivility. One representative student description of faculty incivility was:

> Faculty is frequently late, constantly making changes to the schedule, authoritarian, and inflexible. They provide no chance for us to explain why we did whatever we did and questions are looked upon as challenging their authority. Grading is extremely subjective and varies from instructor to instructor.
>
> (2008, E46–E47)

Incivility was seen by respondents to be important in nursing education because *care* is at the heart of the nursing identity, and because the stress which arises from such incivility can negatively affect patient outcomes. As one faculty member put it: "If nursing is a caring profession, what does uncivil behaviour among students and faculty say about us? What does it say about future generations of nurses?"

(2008, E47). The types of student incivility noted by both students and faculty were quite similar to those identified by Boice (1996).

While the stakes involved in clinical practice courses in nursing may well be higher than in practice placements in some other disciplines, the importance of *care* to the profession and the emotions experienced are comparable. Roisin Corcoran and Roland Tormey (2012) found student teachers on practice placements felt stress, sorrow, joy, fear, care, anxiety, anger, and annoyance. Some student-teachers described being so fixated on teaching that they were unaware of their own emotions until they were overcome by them. As was noted in Chapter 2, the multiple roles of practice placement, as being a time to learn and also a time where their *performance* is judged, contributed to the heightened emotional energy surrounding it. More than that, the stakes involved in practice placement courses were higher for students than in other courses because practice placement related centrally to their chosen professional identity; in other courses they learned about learning, but in practice placement they were *being* a teacher. Hence experiencing failure or difficulties here was felt more personally than was the case in other courses.

In her nursing study, Clark concluded:

> The findings show that incivility in the student-faculty relationship is a dynamic process and almost never a one-sided experience. Both groups are involved in the *dance*; thus, blaming one group or the other for the problem is not a useful solution. When faculty and students work together to build a respectful learning environment, trust is fostered and civility prevails.
>
> (2008, E52)

CASE STUDY 7.1.B – DISRUPTIONS THREATEN LAB SAFETY

Case analysis questions

Look back at the case study at the beginning of this chapter and answer the following questions:

1. Bob Boice identified that students and teachers often do not perceive the same behaviours as problematic. What behaviours were problematic to Valentina but which were likely not seen as problematic by the students? What behaviours seemed appropriate to Valentina but were likely perceived as problematic by the students? How could these mutual misunderstandings be addressed?
2. Boice identified that once a semester started it was hard to change the established class dynamics, but that a better dynamic could be established if the teacher began the term using specific management strategies. What strategies did Boice recommend? Drawing on this, what specific advice would you give Valentina?
3. How is your answer to question 2 above different from your answer to question 2 in Reflection point 7.1?

THREE DIMENSIONS OF TEACHER–STUDENT RELATIONSHIPS IN HIGHER EDUCATION

It is evident in the last section that the warmth, care, and authority that a teacher communicates affect both learning and class management. But how are warmth, care, and authority related to each other?

Roland Tormey (2021), building on work by the psychologist of emotion Jennifer Jenkins, has proposed that teacher–student emotional responses can be understood in terms of three social goals (see for example Oatley 2004, 81):

- affiliation or warmth towards each other (which commits us to friendly cooperation),
- attachment or a sense of safety with others (which helps to identify when we are safe from danger),
- assertion or sense of status (which provides us with a sense of our position with respect to others in a social hierarchy).

Thinking of class relationships in terms of these three emotional dimensions can be very useful.

Warmth

Bob Boice argued that the teacher's contribution to the dance of incivility is what he called *teacher immediacy*, that is "the extent to which the teacher gives off verbal and nonverbal signals of warmth, friendliness, and liking" (1996, 458). His evidence suggested that when the teacher displayed this kind of warmth to their class, student inclinations to behave in an uncivil way dropped off dramatically. Indeed, a lack of teacher immediacy was itself seen by students as a kind of teacher disruptive behaviour in the class.

Psychologists of emotion identify that the sense of warmth or affection plays an important social role in giving us a sense of being connected to a group of people with whom we can cooperate (Oatley 2004). A sense of warmth is associated with emotions like happiness. As an emotion, happiness encourages people to continue what they are doing while its opposite (sadness) gives rise to withdrawal and disconnection. As Keith Oatley puts it, "happiness is the emotion of cooperation" (2004, 90). It is not surprising then that teacher warmth and immediacy are associated with positive outcomes for students in higher education courses. When teachers show immediacy, students are more likely to enjoy the class and to experience an increased sense of hope and pride (Titsworth et al. 2010; Titsworth et al. 2013).

Of course, *friendliness* needs to be balanced with *professionalism* (see the section on power and status, below). The teacher's role is not to be the student's friend but it is possible to be both professional and warm or friendly. Indeed, evidence about class relationships and class management suggests that displaying warmth should be a goal. It is also important to note that *friendliness* is not a personality trait which is fixed and unchangeable – there is lots of evidence that teachers can change the extent to which students see them as warm (see Reflection point 7.2).

Trust

In Boice's study it was not just the teacher's warmth or coldness that was at issue but also the extent to which they were seen as dependable or trustworthy: teachers imposing unannounced tests, for example, was seen as an uncivil behaviour. Similar things can be seen in Cynthia Clark's study on nursing programmes: for the student quoted in Spotlight 7.1, problematic teacher behaviour included "constantly making changes to the schedule, and [grading which is] extremely subjective and [which] varies from instructor to instructor" (2008, E46–E47).

The second dimension of social relations identified by psychologist Jennifer Jenkins is attachment or a sense of trust. Since learning requires the student to push themselves to try things that they currently cannot do, trust is extremely important. Nobody succeeds at everything the first time every time, and so making mistakes and learning from them is (as Chapter 5 explores) a normal and important part of the learning process. Students will be less likely to do this, however, if they do not feel safe to try things, to make mistakes, and to try better. As Keith Oatley describes it, when people feel a sense of security and a sense of trust, it provides them with a "home base" of the teacher's presence from which they feel the "courage to explore the world" (2004, 87–88).

Power and status

It is evident in the work of Bob Boice that the perception that there is one set of rules for the students (who must, for example, be on time) and another for the teacher (who can be late or cancel classes without notice) is seen as a problematic type of teacher incivility. Likewise, in Cynthia Clark's work, it is seen to be a problem if teachers are, in the student's words, "authoritarian". On the other hand, if students do not show appropriate respect for the teacher (through, for example, being sarcastic or rolling their eyes) this is also seen by both students and teachers as a problem. Furthermore, as Boice made clear, students expected and wanted the teacher to take control of the situation and to manage problematic behaviour. The students in Clark's study expected the teacher to be authoritative (but not authoritarian).

If warmth (and cooperation) is a facet of social life, so too are questions of power and social status. When someone feels anger, it is often a sign that they feel under attack in some way. Aristotle described anger as a response to "a conspicuous slight directed without justification towards what concerns oneself or toward what concerns one's friends" (quoted in Haidt 2003, 856). The *conspicuous slight* is often a perceived attack on the person's social status: if a student or teacher does not get the respect they feel they deserve, they may respond with annoyance or anger. This kind of response can evidently impact on classroom behaviour; however, it is worth noting that it also impacts on learning (Thiel et al. 2011).

In a learning context, however, questions of status are not all about feeling slighted or annoyed. When students see a teacher as impressive or highly competent, they will feel positive emotions towards the person including a sense of being inspired or even in awe. Indeed, Roland Tormey's study (2021) on the emotional relationships in university classes found that it was this *status* (or *perception of competence*) dimension of the relationship which had the strongest relationship with students' overall evaluation of the quality of the course.

Implication of the three-dimensional approach for improving class relationships

Class management advice for teachers often feels contradictory: "Be friendly, but you are not there to be their friend". It is not unusual to hear novice teachers being told by other teachers that they shouldn't smile too much for the first few weeks in order to make sure students respect them, yet this idea seems to be incompatible with the importance of warmth and teacher immediacy. It is not surprising that class management can seem like an impossible and forbidding task.

The three-dimensional approach to thinking about class relationships can help to clarify some of these challenges. Using the approach presented in this chapter, it is possible to see that smiling and displaying warmth are actually independent of seeming competent and professional. The evidence suggests it is possible to do either, both, or neither. From a class management and relationship perspective, it seems likely that it is better to do both.

We noted above that whether or not a teacher seems warm or outgoing to students may depend in part on their personality. However, it *is* possible for a teacher to adopt behaviours which communicate warmth (see Reflection point 7.2 – Developing warmth and non-verbal immediacy). At the same time, it is not easy for everyone to act warm or friendly towards students. The multidimensional model presented here suggests that even if someone does not find it easy to convey warmth, it may also be acceptable to focus attention on eliciting trust (the safety dimension) and on eliciting admiration (the status dimension). Indeed, it is notable that Tormey found that the status and trust dimensions had the most predictable effect on student evaluation of courses. As such it may be that warmth has been somewhat overemphasised in the literature thus far.

REFLECTION POINT 7.2 – DEVELOPING WARMTH AND NON-VERBAL IMMEDIACY

Many of the studies of immediacy rely on measures of *teacher non-verbal immediacy* – that is the ways in which teachers behave and the warmth they communicate. Teachers can use this measure themselves to reflect upon the messages their body language sends to students, and to change their own behaviours accordingly.

Video your class (or ask a colleague to observe) and use the statements below to assess your teaching.

Use the following rating scale: never = 0; rarely = 1; occasionally = 2; often = 3; very often = 4.

1. Gestures while talking to the class.
2. Uses monotone/dull voice when talking to the class*.
3. Looks at the class while talking.
4. Smiles at the class while talking.
5. Has a very tense body position while talking to the class*.
6. Moves around the classroom while teaching.
7. Looks at the board or notes while talking to the class*.
8. Has a very relaxed body position while talking to the class.
9. Frowns at the class while talking*.
10. Uses a variety of vocal expressions when talking to the class.

Once you have finished scoring your video [note – items which are marked with an asterisk (*) are reverse scored (i.e. 0 instead of 4, 1 instead of 3, etc.], identify (i) behaviour where you score lowest and consider how you could incorporate it more often during your teaching and (ii) behaviour that feels easier for you and therefore may represent an accessible way to communicate warmth to your students.

This scale comes from work by James McCroskey and colleagues (1995). These kinds of measures can be criticised on the basis that emotional displays may differ from culture to culture and may not be equally applicable in all cultures. Qin Zhang and John Oetzel (2005) have created a Chinese Teacher Immediacy Scale.

PERCEPTIONS OF GENDER, ETHNICITY, AND AGE IN CLASS MANAGEMENT AND RELATIONSHIPS

Relationships involve two parties, and the way in which people experience class relationships depends, not only on the behaviours of one side, but also on the interpretation of the other. Thus far we have focused largely on the way in which the teacher (or student) acts. In this section, we turn our attention to the way in which we are interpreted and seen by others.

The different dimensions of relationships described above are not only a result of the teacher's (or student's) behaviour. They also result, in part, from the rapid and often implicit judgements which people make about other people. We have explored in Chapter 5 how many people hold implicit or unconscious assumptions about, for example, women in science disciplines, and that these implicit biases can impact upon their judgements (including perhaps the feedback that is given to female and male students) (Moss-Racusin et al. 2012).

These rapid and implicit appraisals can also impact upon the dimensions of class relationships, such as on the perception of others as being either warm or competent. Research on stereotypes held by undergraduate students in the US, for example, has found that women are often stereotyped as being warmer but less competent than men (Fiske et al. 2002). The same study (with a majority White population) found that White people were stereotyped as warmer and more competent than Black people, who in turn were seen as warmer and more competent than Hispanic people. It is important to be clear that these stereotypes do not reflect the actual warmth or competence of members of these groups – they are simply implicit prejudices that can impact on people's behaviours. One way this can be seen is by looking at how the stereotypes change from place to place in line with cultural biases. For example, while a US sample found that Irish people were stereotyped as being both warm and competent (Cuddy et al. 2007), similar research in a number of European countries found the Irish to be stereotyped as moderate in warmth but low on competence (Cuddy et al. 2009). Another study on business undergraduate students in Switzerland found that people above 50 years old are perceived as warmer but less competent than younger ones and are thus, less likely to get called for a job interview (Krings et al. 2011).

These stereotypes can shape the rapid implicit appraisals which people make of each other and are likely to implicitly impact upon students' and teachers' judgements of each other, and consequently to impact upon their relationships with each other. As such, it is possible that some students may implicitly judge a female teacher to be less competent than a male teacher, or (in the UK or Europe) an Irish teacher to be less competent than a British teacher. A student who holds these stereotypes may then implicitly find it harder to accept the authority of the teacher. There is some evidence, for example, that while outright hostile behaviours are rare in higher education classes, they are directed significantly more often towards women, minorities, and foreign instructors (Alberts et al. 2010). Hostilities described ranged from informal treatment (calling teachers by their first name rather than title) to overt sarcasm and disrespectful comments. Likewise, there is evidence that students also respond to each other in ways consistent with implicit biases (see Spotlight 7.2).

It may not be enough, therefore, for a teacher to communicate warmth, competence, and trust. Students, and teachers, may also need to be provided with opportunities to examine their prior implicit beliefs about themselves and each other. And it may also be necessary for departments and department heads to be able and willing to support teachers where implicit (or indeed, explicit) biases are impacting upon student behaviour.

SPOTLIGHT 7.2 – IMPLICIT BIAS IN INTERGROUP INTERACTIONS AND LEARNING THROUGH GROUP PROJECTS

Group projects are a common part of student life, and are often seen as providing an excellent opportunity for students to learn the professional skills of managing projects and working in teams alongside learning the ability to apply technical knowledge in specific contexts. However what happens inside the student group is often something of a *black box* for teachers: a task is assigned, a group is formed, and the teacher often has little idea about the internal dynamics of the group until the group's work emerges at the end of the project.

There is, however, a growing body of evidence that implicit biases impact upon the relationships within and, as a consequence, the learning within, many student groups. When male and female students work together, for example, there is evidence that women are less likely to be assigned technical tasks and are more likely to be assigned secretarial tasks (e.g. organising meetings) and communicating tasks (e.g. report writing) (Natishan et al. 2000; Meadows and Sekaquaptewa 2011). Other studies have found that in small groups, men, on average, talk more and more assertively than women (Leaper and Ayres 2007; Karpowitz et al. 2012). Even among high-performing students there is some evidence of gendered patterns of expectations and behaviours – Prisca Aeby and colleagues (2019) found that both male and female high-performing students in group projects were primed to anticipate difficulties arising more often for female students than for male students. They also found that male students were more likely than female students to report that they were confident that their opinions and suggestions would be valued by other group members.

PART II

> To address this, Siara Isaac (Ramachandran & Isaac, 2021) has developed a workshop that provides opportunities for students to role-play addressing incivilities related to bias and stereotyping which may arise within during teamwork. The activities appear to (i) assist students to be more aware of their own implicit biases about others and (ii) to be ready to speak up when they hear or see discriminatory things.

HOW TO CREATE CONSTRUCTIVE RELATIONSHIPS WITH THE CLASS

Up to this point, the chapter has explained the characteristics of class incivilities or disruptions. We now turn to ways that teachers can avoid and react to class disruptions and student incivilities. It is important to recall that Boice (1996) found that students expect their teachers to address and resolve problematic behaviours. So, what should teachers do?

Effective class management has two parts. The first part is prevention through strategies that anticipate and avoid disruptive behaviour (Woodcock and Reupert 2012). The second part is addressing misbehaviours when they occur (Sorcinelli 1994; Reupert and Woodcock 2015; 2010). The following section presents several practical preventive and corrective strategies.

Preventive strategies

Many would agree that it's easier to prevent problems than to repair things afterward. Preventive class management strategies are ways in which a teacher promotes a positive class climate that favours learning and discourages disruptions (Sorcinelli 1994). These strategies can be a written set of rules distributed to students, developed collaboratively with the class, or specific expectations for student behaviour communicated by the teacher at relevant moments.

Written rules, such as codes of conduct, set boundaries and make explicit the teacher's definition of acceptable and unacceptable behaviour in class. Students are more likely to respect rules when they understand their benefit for their learning, i.e. a quiet class will help them concentrate. Indeed, students will be less likely to arrive late or to leave early once they become aware that this is annoying to the rest of the class. You may notice that your expectations vary from those of your colleagues, given the high mobility and internationalisation in education; it's a good idea to discuss, and potentially adjust, your expectations with each class. In the first class, clearly communicating your expectations will set the tone for your course (Sorcinellli 1994; Nilson 2010). Do not forget to explain the rationale for your rules, as this will make them seem less harsh and subjective. This issue will be taken up in Spotlight 7.3 which looks at student incivilities in online courses.

Prevention requires listening and making adjustments. Listening to your students' perspective will help you adjust imperfect rules and shows tolerance (Sorcinelli 1994). Higher education students will typically share their ideas about improving the conditions for learning (Nilson 2010). As explained previously in this chapter, an open discussion of your expectations on student behaviour would set the right balance between authority and trust. Listen to what students have to say, they may share points worth considering. For example, in Case study 7.1.A, Valentina's lack of communication about her expectation on punctuality damaged her relationship with the class when she punished late arrivals. Instead, if she had discussed this rule with students, she might have learned why they arrived late (it is possible that, for instance, their previous class was located on the opposite side of campus). This would have provided her with useful information while simultaneously developing a positive relationship with the class.

Decreasing student anonymity is also an efficient preventive strategy. The more a teacher is seen as a person, and the more students know about each other, the higher the likelihood for them to act responsibly. Learning students' names and asking them about their studies or career plans are strategies that help to reduce student anonymity. However, different strategies may apply for large and small classes. Teachers of large classes could use nametags or practice mnemonic techniques to memorise student names (Alberts et al. 2010), whereas in smaller groups teachers can easily recall students by sketching students' sitting places and asking them to keep the same seats. Bluntly, one teacher explained: "Once they know that I know who they are, there's enhanced interaction and little [nonsense]" (Alberts et al. 2010, 452).

Although it has been shown that teachers' biggest worries about incivilities rarely occur (Reupert and Woodcock 2010; Alberts et al. 2010), putting preventive strategies in place can reduce stress. Violent or inappropriate behaviour from students such as attending class under the effect of substances, criticising the teacher's competence, and disagreements about grades are the most feared disruptions mentioned by teachers (Alberts et al.

2010). While they happen rarely, it is a good idea to have some corrective strategies on hand to manage them.

> ## SPOTLIGHT 7.3 – STUDENT INCIVILITIES IN ONLINE COURSES
>
> Teachers report that it is particularly hard to manage incivilities in online courses (Baker 2008; Galbraith and Jones 2010; Prescott 2012). Online environments deprive us of much visual and physical information that helps to regulate interaction between people and assist us to understand another person's intention. Further, the disembodied interaction between students, and between students and the teacher, impedes teachers from using moderating tools such as body language, eye contact, and tone of voice. These constraints leave teachers feeling uncertain about how to react to unpleasant, provocative, offensive, or inappropriate comments.
>
> Students participating in online courses also have difficulty moderating the tone of their interactions and receive reduced information about the reactions to their behaviour. Renate Prescott explains that the
>
>> causes of incivility are largely fostered through online students' sense of relative anonymity. Students are not as visible in the online classroom as they are in the physical classroom, and they are therefore emboldened, believing they can be anonymous behind the computer, to say whatever they wish with little or no action being taken against their incivility.
>>
>> (2012, 91)
>
> It is therefore important to have some strategies to deal with incivilities in online courses because they quickly change the tone of a course, and situations may escalate faster than in face-to-face teaching.
>
> Two case studies of online student incivilities reported by Kent State University in Ohio both occurred in discussion forums, but interventions from the teachers led to different outcomes. The first case occurred in the context of the analysis of a text in a literature

course, when a student posted a comment that was broadly perceived as anti-religious. Many students openly complained and asked the student to apologise and the teacher to react. The teacher emailed the student in question, who posted an apology but didn't retract the comment. The teacher decided to delete this student's postings and associated threads. While the student in question passed the course, her end-of-term course evaluation expressed her dissatisfaction with the teacher for having deleted her postings. Nevertheless, the rest of the class ended on a good note. The second case study evolved quite differently. In a history course, a student posted openly racist and offensive comments in the discussion thread. When confronted by other students and the teacher, she offered neither an apology nor a retraction. Unlike the teacher in the previous example, this teacher left the posts online and let the students manage their peer who had caused offence. The negative climate escalated into a *cyber war* of comments. The teacher justified her reaction as a lesson for students to learn to confront prejudice, but the teacher's own testimony shows her disempowerment: "This was a brutal class. I got to where I hated to turn on the computer" (Prescott 2012, 96). The void created by a lack of clear regulations for such cases at this university has since been addressed but these experiences suggest that teachers should react promptly and directly to show support for students who feel targeted by incivility in discussion forums.

Undesirable corrections

There are two approaches to responding to disruptive or uncivil behaviour: *direct corrections* and *later corrections*. Knowing the difference between *direct* and *later corrections* will help you determine how to respond to disruptions in ways that maintain a positive class climate. *Direct corrections* are in-the-moment firm reactions that stop a disruption immediately. They are more likely to be perceived by students as abrupt, subjective, and unfair. Confiscating a student's phone or calling everyone's attention to late arrivals are examples of *direct corrections*.

While *later corrections* are also firm, they are more discreet. Catching a student after the lab to ask them not to use their phone or wrapping up a session with a general reminder to be on time next week are *later corrections*. In their study of geography teachers in the US, Heike Alberts and colleagues concluded "that the more personal the response [of the teacher], the more effective it was" (2010, 451) in curbing problematic behaviour. It is easier to establish a constructive, personal tone with *later corrections* than *direct corrections*.

In general, *later corrections* are the most appropriate first response to correcting problematic behaviour. Escalating to *direct corrections* is more effective and appropriate only after *later corrections* have been disregarded by students. An example related by a teacher in a study by Alberts et al. (2010, 450) was to take proactive action: The next time we meet I will usually go up to the cluster before class and gently say: "You aren't going to give me any trouble today ... are you?" I always get a prompt, "No Sir". A more forceful example of a series of escalating steps (spread over several minutes) is an initial general reminder of your *no texting* rule, followed by looking directly at a student who is continuing to use her phone with a short, silent pause and finally, directly asking the student to stop using her phone.

Escalating *later corrections* with *direct corrections* may help to manage the class in the moment but may also have a negative effect on the class climate by harming your trust relationship with the class. When escalating your reaction, it is important that your message reaches the appropriate students and does not give other students the impression that you do not see their good behaviour. For example, loudly complaining at the beginning of a class that half the class has not yet arrived inconveniences only those students who *are* there and does not reach the students who are late. Alberts and colleagues (2010) confirmed that mixing strategies works best. Consequently, a better approach would be to first establish a constructive class climate using preventive strategies and then safeguard it by applying *later corrections* and only escalating to *direct corrections* if necessary.

This means that there is no one-size-fits-all solution to problematic behaviour in class, and that you should anticipate combining corrections with preventive strategies throughout the lab, project, or studio time with students. Case study 7.2 provides an opportunity for you to apply these ideas.

CASE STUDY 7.2 – CREATE A HABIT OR WAIT FOR IT TO HAPPEN?

Read this case study and complete the analysis questions below.

Petra* is the faculty supervisor for the weekly seminar in clinical psychology which aims to develop students' ability to critically analyse and participate in scholarly discussions of clinical interventions by reading reports of therapeutic treatments and patient outcomes. All students are expected to prepare by reading an assigned article. Petra begins today's session by providing students with a series of questions about the reading. Sam, a student sitting at the front of the room, promptly volunteers to answer the first question. Petra asks the second question and when nobody raises a hand, Sam volunteers to answer again. Petra moves on to the third question, and without hesitation, Sam starts talking while the other students listen.

Petra faces a dilemma: should she just keep going or should she tell Sam to stay quiet? She knows that students won't develop their own critical thinking skills by just listening to Sam, but she also doesn't want to create a confrontation or an awkward situation.

What could Petra have done to avoid Sam monopolising the conversation and to stimulate participation from more students?

Two alternative scenarios are outlined below.

Scenario 1

When nobody volunteers an answer to question 2, Petra reminds students about the seminar's rules:

- Everyone should speak at least once each week.
- Keep each contribution to under two minutes.
- If you have just spoken, do not speak again until at least one other student has spoken.

After this reminder, Petra asks question 2 again and this time two students answer. When Sam raises their hand to participate again, Petra thanks them for their interest. Later Petra again reminds everyone that they are expected to speak at least once and, looking at Sam, to take turns. This seemed to help and Sam spoke again only after other students had a chance to participate. Every time a student spoke, Petra kept an eye on the time and made eye contact with students who were approaching the two minutes mark. By the end of the session, the dynamics of participation had settled in and continued naturally for the rest of the term.

Scenario 2

When nobody volunteers an answer to question 2, Petra reminds students that they need to be active in order to develop their critical thinking skills. She says that without volunteers, she will be obliged to call students at random to answer the questions and make sure that people are participating. Her admonitions fail to stimulate students and she is indeed obliged to call on students at random. Petra moves to stand beside Sam, but Sam stops raising their hand. Finally, Petra turns to Sam and asks them the last question directly. From then on the habit of only answering when their name was called was established and Petra kept a list to keep track of participation.

Case analysis questions

Write down and keep your answers to the following questions. Suggested answers can be found at the end of the chapter.

1. Which scenario describes a *preventive* approach and which *direct correction*? Which scenario is more likely to be more effective in terms of meeting Petra's goals?
2. How could you adapt Petra's approach if you were to apply it yourself?

* This case is a fictionalised account of teaching experiences.

TEST YOURSELF

The activities in this section provide an opportunity to review and apply the ideas from this chapter. We highly recommend doing these activities before continuing to the chapter conclusion. You can use the sample answers to these activities provided at the end of the chapter to give yourself feedback.

CASE STUDY 7.3 – BUILDING PRODUCTIVE RELATIONSHIPS IN A STUDIO

Read this case study and complete the analysis questions below.

Sasha* will teach a new project course on rehabilitation architecture entitled *Approaches to vulnerability* for 12 students from a diverse range of backgrounds. Each student will produce a *reconstruction protocol* for rehabilitating towns hit by natural disasters. As his field of expertise is in reconstruction after natural disasters such as earthquakes, he is overjoyed to introduce architectural vulnerability in this new course.

The course has two parts – Phase I takes place in the studio and provides students with the core material about architectural vulnerability and concludes with the first deliverable. Phase II is a one-week field trip to an affected village, followed by work on the projects in the studio. Phase II has a second intermediate deliverable and then the final submission.

As in most project courses in architecture, the interaction between students is constant and intense, while interaction in the presence of the teacher is intermittent. Students share a working space daily, and will share accommodation during the field trip. Sasha, on the other hand, is busy with many projects so can only be present one and a half days per week in the studio. He plans to have a more intensive presence during the field trip.

On the first day in the studio, Sasha sees two students, Laura and Katarina, rolling their eyes, quietly snorting with laughter, and doodling on their notepads while he speaks. He looks away and continues presenting. At the end of his talk, he looks at them and asks them a direct question about their understanding of the course. They reply that they understood the material, and he leaves it at that.

Their distracting gestures and chatting become more obvious in the following sessions, and the other students take notice. During a break, Sasha hears Laura and Katarina having a loud argument with James, a student who sits close to them in the studio. He can't quite hear what they are saying but he asks them to return to their seats. He has the impression that the argument had a cultural or sexist implication that he does not feel prepared to deal with. He decides to report it directly to Student Affairs, who suggests that he is not required to take further action if no one has reported anything to him.

The first set of, deliverables for Phase I are good: two groups submit excellent work and nine are satisfactory, including Laura and Katarina's. Sasha has the impression that the project is running well.

While Sasha spends most of each day during the field trip with students, he avoids socialising as much as possible. He also takes a backstage position during the site visit, and lets the guest expert lead. Laura and Katarina behave disrespectfully to the expert guide, but he only learns this afterwards when the expert complains about Laura repeatedly turning her back and Katarina wandering away.

The second deliverables are less promising: two are good, five are satisfactory, and five (including Laura and Katarina) are surprisingly poor. He is particularly concerned that Laura and Katarina do not seem to be integrating his feedback. He decides to repeat the same feedback a second time, and they agree to work harder.

The final protocols are submitted: two are exemplary, the majority are good and everyone passes the course even though a couple are quite weak. He is disappointed that the students have not done more with the resources and effort he invested in the studio.

The course leaves him with a bitter taste. Despite two of the student projects being really high quality, the disengaged and disrespectful behaviour is what he remembers most. The results of the teaching evaluation reflect his feeling. The most frequent theme in student feedback was poor class management: "the teacher should've intervened when the argument happened" and "the studio environment was just awful". One comment says "I worked very little and passed this course".

Case analysis questions

Write down and keep your answers to the following questions. Suggested answers can be found at the end of the chapter.

1. What connection exists between the class management and the quality of deliverables?
2. When should Sasha have reacted to student disruptions, and how? What was his gut reaction to the gestures and chatting while he was speaking?
3. Do you have a hypothesis as to what James, Laura, and Katarina were arguing about? Should Sasha have engaged with them further about the argument?
4. What combination of *later* and *direct corrections* could he have employed when James, Laura, and Katarina were arguing?
5. Was discussing the case with Student Affairs an appropriate reaction?

6. What are some preventive strategies and corrections Sasha might employ for future courses?

*This case is based on a real-life teacher experience.

ACTION SUMMARY – MANAGING RELATIONSHIPS WITH A CLASS

- A balance of warmth, trust, and authority in teacher–student interactions will help maintain respect and promote learning.
- Be attentive to how your implicit ideas about gender, ethnicity, and age affect your reactions to students (and how their implicit ideas may affect their interactions with you).
- Use preventive strategies to establish good habits and patterns of interaction that support learning – communicate warmth, be clear on your expectations of them, and on your reasoning.
- If you perceive something as misbehaviour, try to understand how the students in question see it. Try to ask students, if possible, rather than making assumptions.
- Use corrective strategies when necessary. If possible start with later corrections, and use direct corrections sparingly. In doing so, try to ensure you communicate warmth and authority, and that you are perceived as being reasonable and consistent.

CONCLUSION

This chapter presents class management as fundamentally relational by emphasising the student–teacher relationship as an important contributing factor for learning. When teachers are attentive to their own perceptions, and those of students, class management can be handled mostly in a proactive and preventative way. Being attentive to issues of bias and discrimination, and maintaining a positive class climate help eliminate potential obstacles to learning.

Establishing a good relationship with the class involves balancing the three social dimensions of the teacher role: warmth, trust, and authority. Considering these three dimensions will help teachers present themselves to students, to choose class management strategies, and to establish respect and trust.

Good class managements results from the combination of preventive strategies and corrections. This chapter aims to provide a set of tools and insights to help teachers manage the class. Experienced teachers typically feel confident in escalating preventive strategies with well-targeted corrections, but their approach is that "rather than becoming more controlling *per se* ... [they] employ less intrusive corrective strategies" (Woodcock and Reupert 2012, 16). Remember that there is no one-size-fits-all class management rule book. It is possible that a combination of strategies that worked with one class will not give your desired outcome for another. Overall, good class management results from iterative experimentation and reflection (see Chapter 10) in order to figure out the right balance for your own teaching context.

FURTHER READING

This small number of sources provides further guidance on creating effective learning environments, promoting equity, and reducing disruptions. A full reference list for the chapter is provided below.

Davis, B.G. (2009). Chapter 5. Diversity and Inclusion in the Classroom. In: *Tools for Teaching*, 2nd edition (pp.57–72). San Francisco: Wiley.

Exley, K., Dennick, R., and Fisher, A. (2019). Chapter 3. The Physical, Psychological and Social Conditions for Successful Small Group Teaching. In: *Small Group Teaching: Tutorials, Seminars and Workshops* (pp. 23–42). London: Routledge. https://doi.org/10.4324/9780429490897.

Fisher, A., Exley, K., and Ciobanu, D. (2014). Chapter 4. Technology for Interaction. In: *Using Technology to Support Learning and Teaching* (pp. 72–103). London: Routledge. https://doi.org/10.4324/9780203074497.

Petty, G. (2009). Chapter 26. Evidence Based Classroom Management and Discipline. In: *Evidence-Based Teaching*. Cheltenham: Nelson Thornes. Note: This chapter is not in the book but can be downloaded from http://geoffpetty.com/geoffs-books/evidence-based-teaching-ebt/.

Answers to selected chapter activities

These sample answers are provided to allow you to generate some feedback for yourself. You should take time to complete the activities before comparing your answers with our ideas.

Case study 7.1.A

1. Valentina sets a negative tone for her relationship with the class by not introducing herself or the lab, and also when she surprises students by deducting points. She does not appear to do much to establish a positive relationship with the class.
2. Valentina manages the disruption by noting down the late students' names and saying that she will deduct points from their lab reports.

3. Valentina's lack of reaction the first week and then deducting points without prior warning make her unpredictable to students. Further, she did not explain why being late is an issue for safety and does not appear ready to accommodate any issues that students may have (medical appointments, cancelled trains, etc.).
4. Valentina could explain about the importance of being present for the introductory safety information each week. She could also provide students with a policy about how she will react to lateness and what a student should do if they anticipate that they will be late one day. Before finalising that, however, she may wish to find out why the students are consistently late – it may be that there is some good reason that she is unaware of.

Reflection point 7.1

Wendy Bjorklund and Diana Rehling (2009) have characterised student behaviours as being either immediate disruptions, or minor disruptions with an escalating effect. Compare your responses to this activity to their classification below. When teachers react suddenly to these escalating minor disruptions they run the risk of being perceived as arbitrary or unfair (after all, if it was OK for the first students to chat to their neighbours earlier in the class, why is suddenly not ok for the sixth person to do the same?).

Minor disruptions with an escalating effect	Immediate disruptions
Reading unrelated documents during class or studying for another class.	One or a few students dominate classroom discussions.
Packing up before the end of the class.	Making fun of or not listening to a classmate's contributions.
Arriving late/leaving early.	Speaking on a topic not related to the discussion or content.
Answering the phone or texting.	Making sarcastic comments.
Having conversations or chit-chats and continuing when being asked to stop.	Challenging the teacher's or assistants' knowledge (verbally or non-verbally with body posture).
	Taking class time to complain about grades or the marking.

Case study 7.1.B

1. Students arriving late was problematic to Valentina, but probably not to the students. Valentina's sudden decision to deduct points was problematic to students. Valentina appeared to be a little distant or cold in her interaction with students. This may also have been seen as problematic by them.
2. Boice suggests establishing good relationships by chatting informally chatting with students, communicating warmth, and avoiding showing impatience or frustration. Based on this, Valentina should spend time on the first day of class getting to know a bit about her students, telling them a little about herself professionally, and clearly communicating what she expects from them in terms of behaviour to avoid mutual misunderstandings.

Case study 7.2

1. Scenario 1 presents a preventative approach and scenario 2 a direct correction. Petra's goal of developing students' ability to participate in discussions is likely best met by scenario 1, as the guidelines create a situation similar to the implicit expectations in professional settings.
2. Some ideas: Petra's rules are quite specific and are told to students, rather than being developed collaboratively with students to increase ownership. Periodic reminders and perhaps encouragement of less participative members would likely be necessary over the term.

> Note: Sam's gender was intentionally communicated as non-binary through the use of the pronouns "they" and "them".

Case study 7.3

1. Good class management is about setting and maintaining a safe learning environment in the class. This studio is no exception. Students were engaged for the first deliverable, but Sasha's absence from the studio may have created a perception of a lack of interest. It is also not clear that students assimilated the feedback and understood how to advance their projects after receiving it. Again, this may create the impression that Sasha is being somewhat arbitrary in his grading.

After initial high investment, some students seemed to lose trust in the teacher. The student comment "I worked little and passed the course" suggests that some students did not perceive the teacher as setting high standards for them.
2. Sasha should perhaps have reacted the first time when he saw Laura and Katarina laughing, gesturing, and doodling. He could have spoken to them in private about their behaviour.
3. When faced with part of a story, people generally implicitly use their prior knowledge and beliefs to fill in the blanks (this is a well-researched cognitive bias). What details, what story did your brain fill in to *explain* the argument? This is a useful way to make your own implicit biases more visible to yourself. When you are more aware of your own biases, you are better able to reduce their effect on your reactions. While it may be natural to not want to get sucked into someone else's arguments, learning to work constructively in a group, to manage disagreements, and to respond to prejudiced or discriminatory speech are all important professional skills. Sasha probably needed to take responsibility for ensuring that these transversal or professional learning goals were met.
4. A first *later* correction would be to call them back to the class and to remind them that loud arguments are inappropriate behaviour in a professional environment like the studio. A second and necessary *later* correction is to speak to each one of them to better understand what happened and how he should respond. While the content of the argument might not be related to the course, it appears it did affect the interpersonal relationships in the studio. Depending on the nature of the argument, he may want to introduce some sessions looking at how to respond to disagreements or discriminatory behaviour in professional settings.
5. Going directly to Student Affairs may seem quite an extreme step to students, particularly when he doesn't have much information about the argument. Sasha could have started by having a discussion with the students involved in order to decide what was a reasonable and appropriate way to address the issue.
6. A useful preventive strategy would be to have ground rules for interpersonal behaviour in the studio. These could be written and explained to the students, or developed in discussion with them. Since the studio is a workplace-like environment, these ground rules can be seen as learning the skills of *acting like a professional*. Being explicit about the need to productively challenge interpersonal bias

and prejudice could well be appropriate as part of these ground rules. Instruction about how to make the most of the field trip may also be helpful in making clear his expectations of how they should learn. Sasha may also want to pay attention to making sure students see him as being present and active in the course and in the field trip. Arriving early for the first few sessions, chatting to students, and getting to know them a little may be helpful. If issues arose in future classes, Sasha should consider starting by using later corrections and only moving to direct corrections during class if necessary.

REFERENCES

Aeby, P., Fong, R., Vukmirovic, M., Isaac, S., and Tormey, R. (2019). The Impact of Gender on Engineering Students' Group Work Experiences, *International Journal of Engineering Education* 35(3): 756–765.

Alberts, H.C., Hazen, H.D., and Theobald, R.B. (2010). Classroom Incivilities: The Challenge of Interactions between College Students and Instructors in the US, *Journal of Geography in Higher Education* 34(3): 439–462. https://doi.org/10.1080/03098260903502679.

Alt, D., and Itzkovic, Y. (2015). Assessing the Connection Between Students' Justice Experience and Perceptions of Faculty Incivility in Higher Education, *Journal of Academic Ethics* 13(2): 121–134. https://doi.org/10.1007/s10805-015-9232-8.

Baker, S.D., Comer, D.R., and Martinak, M.L. (2008, juin 1). All I'm Askin' Is for a Little Respect 1: How Can We Promote Civility in Our Classrooms? *Organization Management Journal* 5(2): 65–80. https://doi.org/10.1057/omj.2008.8.

Bjorklund, W.L., and Rehling, D.L. (2009). Student Perceptions of Classroom Incivility, *College Teaching* 58(1): 15–18. https://doi.org/10.1080/87567550903252801.

Boice, Bob (1996). Classroom Incivilities, *Research in Higher Education* 37(4): 453–486.

Braxton, J.M., and Bayer, A.E. (2004). Introduction: Faculty and Student Classroom Improprieties, *New Directions for Teaching and Learning* 99(99): 3–7. https://doi.org/10.1002/tl.153.

Clark, C.M. (2008). The Dance of Incivility in Nursing Education as Described by Nursing Faculty and Students, *ANS. Advances in Nursing Science* 31(4): E37–E54. https://doi.org/10.1097/01.ans.0000341419.96338.a3.

Conway, P.F., and Clark, C.M. (2003). The Journey Inward and Outward: A Re-Examination of Fuller's Concerns-Based Model of Teacher Development, *Teaching and Teacher Education* 19(5): 465–482. https://doi.org/10.1016/S0742-051X(03)00046-5.

Corcoran, R.P., and Tormey, R. (2012) *Developing Emotionally Competent Teachers; Emotional Intelligence and Pre-Service Teacher Education*. Oxford: Petra Lang.

Cuddy, A.J.C., Fiske, S.T., and Glick, P. (2007). The BIAS Map: Behaviours From Intergroup Affect and Stereotypes, *Journal of Personality and Social Psychology* 92(4): 631–648. https://doi.org/10.1037/0022-3514.92.4.631.

Cuddy, A.J.C., Fiske, S.T., Kwan, V.S.Y., Glick, P., Demoulin, S., Leyens, J.-P., Harris, B., Croizet, J.-C., Ellemers, N., Sleebos, E., Htun, T.T., Kim, H.J., Maio, G., Perry, J., Petkova, K., Todorov, V., Rodríguez-Bailón, R., Morales, E., Moya, M., Palacios, M., Smith, V., Perez, R., Vala, J., and Ziegler, R. (2009). Stereotype Content Model across Cultures: Towards Universal Similarities and Some Differences, *British Journal of Social Psychology* 48(1): 1–33. https://doi.org/10.1348/014466608x 314935.

Darling-Hammond, L., Chung, R., and Frelow, F. (2002). Variation in Teacher Preparation: How Well Do Different Pathways Prepare Teachers to Teach?, *Journal of Teacher Education* 53(4): 286–302. https://doi.org/10.1177/0022487102053004002.

Fiske, S.T., Cuddy, A.J.C., Glick, P., and Xu, J. (2002). A Model of (Often Mixed) Stereotype Content: Competence and Warmth Respectively Follow from Perceived Status and Competition, *Journal of Personality and Social Psychology* 82(6): 878–902. https://doi.org/10.1037/0022-3514.82.6.878.

Galbraith, M.W., and Jones, M.S. (2010). Understanding Incivility in Online Teaching, *Journal of Adult Education* 39(2): 1–10. https://files.eric.ed.gov/fulltext/EJ930240.pdf.

Haidt, J. (2003). The Moral Emotions. In: R.J. Davidson, Scherer, K.R., and Goldsmith, H.H. (eds.), *Handbook of Affective Sciences* (pp. 852–870). Oxford: Oxford University Press.

Karpowitz, C., Mendelberg, T., and Shaker, L. (2012). Gender Inequality in Deliberative Participation, *American Political Science Review* 106(3): 533–547. https://doi.org/10.1017/s0003055412000329.

Krings, F., Sczesny, S., and Kluge, A. (2011). Stereotypical Inferences as Mediators of Age Discrimination: The Role of Competence and Warmth, *British Journal of Management* 22(2): 187–201. https://doi.org/10.1111/j.1467-8551.2010.00721.x.

Leaper, C., and Ayres, M.M. (2007). A Meta-Analytic Review of Gender Variations in Adults' Language Use: Talkativeness, Affiliative Speech, and Assertive Speech, *Personality and Social Psychology Review* 11(4): 328–363. https://doi.org/10.1177/1088868307302221.

McCroskey, J.C., Richmond, V.P., Sallinen, A., Fayer, J.M., and Barraclough, R.A. (1995). A Cross Cultural and Multi-Behavioural Analysis of the Relationship between Nonverbal Immediacy and Teacher Evaluation, *Communication Education* 44(4): 281–291. https://doi.org/10.1080/03634529509379019.

Meadows, L.A., and Sekaquaptewa, D. (2011). The Effect of Skewed Gender Composition on Student Participation in Undergraduate Engineering Project Teams. In: 2011 American Society for Engineering Education Annual Conference & Exposition, Vancouver, BC, 26–29 June, pp. 22.1449.1–22.1449.13. https://peer.asee.org/18957.

Moss-Racusin, C.A., Dovidio, J.F., Brescoll, V.L., Graham, M.J., and Handelsman, J. (2012). Faculty's Subtle Gender Biases Favor Male Students. *Proceedings of the National Academy of Sciences* 109(41): 16474–16479. https://doi.org/10.1073/pnas.1211286109.

Natishan, M.E., Schmidt, L.C., and Mead, P. (2000). Student Focus Group Results on Student Team Performance Issues, *Journal of Engineering Education* 89(3): 269–272. https://doi.org/10.1002/j.2168-9830.2000.tb00524.x.

Oatley, K. (2004) *Emotions: A Brief History*. Oxford: Blackwell.

Nilson, L. (2010). *Teaching at Its Best: A Research-Based Resource for College Instructors*, 3rd edition. San Francisco: Jossey-Bass.

Prescott, R.W. (2012). Online Student Incivility: What It Is and How to Manage It. In: R. Hogan (ed.), *Transnational Distance Learning and Building New Markets for Universities* (pp. 87–105). Hershey, PA: IGI Global.

Quinlan, K.M. (2016). How Emotion Matters in Four Key Relationships in Teaching and Learning in Higher Education, *College Teaching* 64(3): 101–111. https://doi.org/10.1080/87567555.2015.1088818.

Ramachandran, V., and Isaac, S. (2021, May 19–20). *Make It Awkward: Strategies to Tackle On-Campus Discrimination* [conference session], Graduate Students in Teaching Conference, University of British Colombia, Vancouver, Canada.

Reupert, A., and Woodcock, S. (2010). Success and near Misses: Pre-Service Teachers' Use, Confidence and Success in Various Classroom Management Strategies, *Teaching and Teacher Education* 26(6): 1261–1268. https://doi.org/10.1016/j.tate.2010.03.003.

Reupert, A., and Woodcock, S. (2015). Does a Year Make a Difference? The Classroom Management Practices of Primary Student Teachers before and after a One-Year Teacher Education Programme, *Emotional and Behavioural Difficulties* 20(3): 265–276. https://doi.org/10.1080/13632752.2014.949986.

Sorcinelli, M.D. (1994). Dealing with Troublesome Behaviours in the Classroom. In: K.W. Prichard, and Sawyer, R.M. (eds.), *Handbook of College Teaching: Theory and Applications* (pp. 365–373). Westport, CT: Greenwood Press. Reprinted with Permission of Greenwood Publishing Group, Inc. Westport, CT.

Thiel, C.E., Connelly, S., and Griffith, J.A. (2011). The Influence of Anger on Ethical Decision Making: Comparison of a Primary and Secondary Appraisal, *Ethics and Behavior* 21(5): 380–403. https://doi.org/10.1080/10508422.2011.604295.

Titsworth, S., Quinlan, M.M., and Mazer, J.P. (2010). Emotion in Teaching and Learning: Development and Validation of the Classroom Emotions Scale. *Communication Education* 59(4): 431–452.

Titsworth, S., McKenna, T.P., Mazer, J.P., and Quinlan, M.M. (2013). The Bright Side of Emotion in the Classroom: Do Teachers' Behaviors Predict Students' Enjoyment, Hope, and Pride? *Communication Education* 62(2): 191–209.

Tormey, R. (2019). *EPFL Doctoral Survey III*. Lausanne. Ecole polytechnique fédérale de Lausanne. https://www.epfl.ch/education/phd/wp-content/uploads/2019/05/EPFL-Doctoral-III-Survey-2019-questionnaire-included.pdf, accessed 11.05.2020.

Tormey, R. (2021). Rethinking Student-Teacher Relationships in Higher Education: A Multidimensional Approach. *Higher Education*. https://doi.org/10.1007/s10734-021-00711-w.

Weigert, B.J. (2005). Does Prior Training Affect Risk of Injury in University Dance Programs?, *Medical Problems of Performing Artists* 20(3): 115.

Woodcock, S., and Reupert, A. (2012). A Cross-Sectional Study of Student Teachers' Behaviour Management Strategies throughout Their Training Years. *Faculty of Education: Papers (Archive)* 1: 159–172. https://doi.org/10.1007/s13384-012-0056-x.

Zhang, Q., and Oetzl, J.G. (2005). Constructing and Validating a Teacher Immediacy Scale: A Chinese Perspective. *Communication Education* 55(2): 218–241. https://doi.org/10.1080/03634520600566231.

Part III

Chapter 8

Research findings about the thinking that gives rise to learning

> Learning results from what the student does and thinks and only from what the student does and thinks. The teacher can advance learning only by influencing what the student does to learn.
>
> (Simon quoted in Ambrose et al. 2010, 1)

INTRODUCTION

A key argument in this book is that teaching should be informed by the evidence available about learning.

Over the last 20 years, numerous reviews of research evidence about learning have been published, drawing on different sorts of data. Three of the most important sets of reviews are:

- the American Psychological Association's review of evidence about learning and its implications for school reform (Lambert and McCombs 1997),
- the US National Academies' multiple reviews of evidence about how people learn (Bransford et al. 2000; Kober 2015; National Academies of Sciences, Engineering, and Medicine 2018),
- a number of reviews of quantitative studies of learning (notably Hattie, 2009; Hattie and Donoghue, 2016; Fiorella and Mayer 2015; Dunlosky et al. 2013).

Each of these reviews has a different focus and draws on different types of evidence. Yet what is interesting is the extent to which a common set of ideas emerges from them. This chapter and the next will briefly explain some of the key findings from these reviews of research evidence about how people learn which can and should inform how we design and support projects, labs, studios, and fieldwork in higher education.

The key ideas addressed in this chapter and the next are:

- Learning is an effortful process that requires student work.
- Students learn best when complexity is introduced progressively.
- Learning involves storing information and ensuring it can be retrieved when appropriate.
- What and how people learn depend on their prior knowledge (and on their prior misconceptions).
- To put in the effort required, learners have to see the value in accomplishing what is being asked of them.
- Learning is affected by the learner's social identity, and by their interaction with others.
- Students learn more when they develop the ability to be independent and goal-directed.
- Learning involves the mind, the emotions, and the body of the learner.

It is clearly impossible to capture all of the research findings about learning in a few short chapters. Those interested in more detailed accounts of the evidence about learning might be interested in:

- National Academies of Sciences, Engineering, and Medicine (2018) *How People Learn II: Learners, Contexts, and Cultures*, which summarises in a very readable form the key findings from learning research in neuroscience, psychology, and social psychology,
- Susan Ambrose et al. (2010) *How Learning Works, 7 Research-Based Principles for Smart Teaching* which also summarises the research evidence but also describes how it might be applied to higher education teaching.

Many studies of learning see the learner as a bit like Robinson Crusoe – working alone, dependent solely upon their own mental resources and processes, as if they are cut off from the world. Humans do not, usually, learn alone on a desert island – they learn in contexts in which there are other people and in which those other people matter for learning. The mental processes that take place in people's brains are also dependent upon the body in which those brains are encased. To fully understand learning, it is necessary to pay attention to these social and biological systems and the way they interact with the cognitive processes of learning. These social and biological processes are dealt with in the next chapter.

If the importance of these social and biological factors should not be understated, as the quote at the beginning of this chapter implies, they are not in themselves sufficient to explain learning: learning is, ultimately, dependent upon what the learner does. This chapter therefore starts with the evidence from studies which look at learning from a more individualistic perspective. The key ideas from such individualistic studies of learning are captured in the first four of the eight bullet points above. This chapter will treat these four ideas, starting with the finding that most of the learning required of students in university will involve mental effort.

LEARNING IS AN EFFORTFUL PROCESS THAT REQUIRES STUDENT WORK

One of the key findings of research on learning over the last few decades is that learning is largely an effortful process that requires work on behalf of the learner – the learner has to be active in the process. This section will clarify what is meant by *active learning* and how this focus on students actively working with information can be seen in real-life learning situations.

Much of the learning that a student will have to do will involve expending energy through paying attention to things, organising thoughts and ideas, going back over them, thinking about how they relate to other thoughts and ideas, and so on. It is important to note that when learning researchers talk about *active learning* they are not using the term *active* to refer to students moving about or talking (even if that it sometimes part of active learning). Instead they are referring to *cognitive* activity:

> "Active learning" is typically defined by educational researchers as learning that requires students to engage cognitively and meaningfully with the materials, to get "involved with the information presented, really thinking about it (analyzing, synthesizing, evaluating) rather than just passively receiving it".
>
> (Chi and Wylie 2014, 219)

When reviewing the evidence on learning, the American Psychological Association concluded: "The acquisition of complex knowledge and skills demands the investment of considerable learner energy and strategic effort" (Lambert and McCombs 1997, 19). This link between cognitive effort and learning in science and engineering is explored in Spotlight 8.1.

SPOTLIGHT 8.1 – FROM PASSIVE TO INTERACTIVE LEARNING

Michelene Chi and her colleagues* from University of Pittsburgh, MIT, and Arizona State University hypothesised that students would learn more if their engagement with scientific content became more active. Specifically, they wished to compare student learning under four conditions:

- *Passive engagement* referred to receiving information such as by reading a text or listening to a lecture (P in ICAP).
- *Active engagement* referred to some manipulation of the information such as by taking verbatim notes in a lecture, or underlining in a text (A in ICAP).
- *Constructive engagement* meant generating new ideas using the information, such as by creating diagrammatic representations or taking notes in one's own words (C in ICAP).
- *Interactive engagement* meant discussing the ideas with others, such as by debating with peers (I in ICAP).

They carried out a study with 120 undergraduate engineering students. All participants read a short text to re-familiarise themselves with the key ideas in a particular domain in material science (chemical bonding). Then they assigned students at random to one of four conditions:

- reading a longer text passage out loud (passive engagement),
- reading the same text while highlighting the most important sentences (active engagement),
- completing graphs and an activity sheet on the same content, but without reading the longer text (constructive engagement),
- working in pairs to complete the graphs and activity sheet, again without reading the longer text (interactive engagement).

Students took both a pre-test and a post-test in each of the four conditions, represented by the four letters of ICAP.

The average score of students on the pre-test in each of the four groups ranged from 50.6% to 53.1%, indicating no notable differences between the groups.

The average scores on the post-test are presented in Figure 8.1.

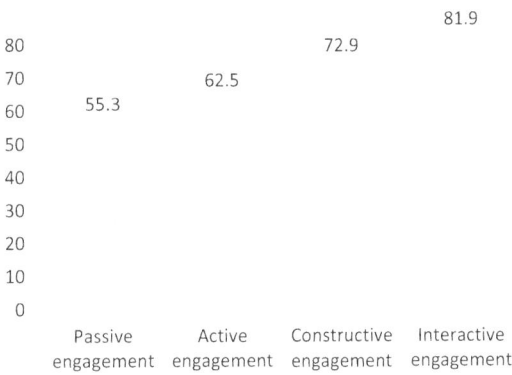

FIGURE 8.1 Posttest scores on ICAP experiment
(Reported by Menekse et al. 2013, 363)

> Menekse, Stump, Krause, and Chi concluded
>
> student gain scores increased steadily from the passive to the active to the constructive and to the interactive conditions ... Although the materials for the passive and active conditions clearly provided the normative information for each concept, students did significantly better in the constructive and the interactive conditions even without such information being directly stated, by constructing their own knowledge and understanding from the guided inquiry-oriented activity sheet that contained only question prompts.
>
> (2013, 364)
>
> * The study was first reported in Menekse, Stump, Krause, and Chi (2013). A more detailed explanation of their *ICAP Hypothesis* is found in Chi and Wylie (2014).

As Spotlight 8.1 suggests, most learning seems to involve working with and processing information in one form or another. While it is possible for students to do this in lectures and when reading, practical learning settings don't just allow students to process information but actively encourage and require it. Students may well find this mental work harder to do than more passive approaches to learning. For example, research on note taking by hand found that it was harder for students to do because they have to synthesise and summarise more than they would if using a laptop — but that, on average, they learn more (Muller and Oppenheimer 2014). Where students have to work even harder, such as by figuring things out, generating new ideas, and discussing them with others, the evidence suggests they typically learn more again.

Students may prefer to listen passively rather than having to figure out for themselves and may prefer to follow recipe-like instructions rather than to make decisions for themselves. However the research evidence suggests that the more students actively process information, the more they learn. In this book the chapter on asking questions (Chapter 4) comes before the chapter on explaining (Chapter 6) precisely to emphasise that when planning for learning we should focus first on asking questions and encouraging students to process information themselves, with teacher explanations being a secondary activity: the first thing that any teacher should think about in planning for an activity is how they will encourage and enable students to actively process information.

> **REFLECTION POINT 8.1**
>
> When you interact with your students in your practical course, do you focus primarily on asking questions and posing thinking tasks for students, or on supplying explanations that allow students to adopt a more passive *listening* approach to learning?
>
> If you apply the ICAP classification to the activities that students undertook during your last session with them, what percentage of time was spent in constructive or interactive activities?

STUDENTS LEARN WHEN COMPLEXITY IS INTRODUCED PROGRESSIVELY

One of the key mental attributes that is used in learning is *attention*. This section will highlight the role of attention in intentional learning and identify issues that arise from the fact that human attention is a limited resource.

Students learn what they pay attention to, or to put it differently, they do not learn facts and ideas that they do not pay attention to. To get a better understanding of the way in which the human attentional system works, complete the Reflection point 8.2 and then continue reading.

> **REFLECTION POINT 8.2 – THE ALLOCATION OF ATTENTION***
>
> For the sentences below, read each one and then cover it with a sheet of paper.
>
> As you read each sentence: (i) decide whether the statement is true or false, and (ii) at the same time, remember the final word in each sentence. Further instructions will be provided when you have worked through all the sentences.
>
> > *Dogs have ears.*
> > *Cats read philosophy.*
> > *Sausages grow on trees.*
> > *Milk comes from cows.*
> > *Wood floats on water.*
> > *Vampires crave tea.*
> > *Airplanes are lighter than air.*
> > *Arms have knees.*
> > *Butter is made from iron.*
>
> After you have read and hidden the final sentence in the list, write down all of the (final) words that you can remember. Then go back and check how you performed.
>
> Many people doing this activity will notice that it becomes harder to remember the final word in each sentence as the activity progresses. When they are already remembering five words, it can be challenging to remember the sixth while also evaluating the truth of each new statement.
>
> > * This activity is based on an experiment described by the neuroscientist Torkel Klingberg in his (2009) book *The Overflowing Brain: Information Overload and the Limits of Working Memory*.

The task outlined in Reflection point 8.2 requires you to focus attention on two different things at the same time. As one might expect, it is relatively easy to do this for a small number of sentences, but as the number of sentences and words to remember grows, the task becomes harder to complete successfully. Attention is a limited resource – humans can only pay attention to a limited number of things at a given time. Over the last few decades it has become commonplace to say that, on average, people can pay attention to between five and nine discrete pieces of information at any given time. More recent evidence suggests that the number of distinct pieces of information we can process at the same time may in fact be even fewer (Shell et al. 2010, 19). The range of different things a person is paying attention to at any given time is called the *cognitive load*. When a person is unable to hold in mind all of the information they require at a given time, then they have breached the limits of cognitive load.

It is worth considering how it is that higher education teachers can struggle to remember six simple words, but can at the same time store, recall, and apply all that they need to know about thermodynamics, critical social theory, or art history. Part of the answer is that the limits of cognitive load are most evident when people work with new information. Since higher education teachers have had extensive practice in working with and manipulating information in their domain, they have, as a result, stored it in their long-term memory in ways that ensure it can be rapidly recalled and used (Ambrose et al. 2010, 104) without generating a heavy cognitive load.

SPOTLIGHT 8.2 – COGNITIVE LOAD IN THE BALLET STUDIO

Learning to dance obviously involves repetition of precise physical movements until they can be performed fluently. But learning to dance also involves significant cognitive activity. Learners need to concentrate their attention on body positioning, timing, centring, and moving of weight and balance, coordinating movements, remembering and organising chunks of choreographic phrasing, as well as focusing on the quality of any given movement (that is, does the movement feel like it is explosive, gliding, floating, collapsing, pressing, and so on). Although experienced dancers may well find it easy to rapidly learn new sets of choreographic phrases, excellent performance typically requires a great deal of attention and deliberate practice to capture the required quality of the movements.

One way of reducing the load of learning complex new choreographies is what is called *marking*, which is to say enacting the choreography at low intensity levels and with much reduced movements. Marking allows the dancer to focus on specific aspects of the phrasing and its qualities without having to also contend at the same time with managing other aspects of the performance (such as balance and coordination). Marking plays a role in managing the physical effort of the dancer, but researchers have recently recognised that it also reduces the cognitive load on the dancer as it allows them focus on specific aspects of their performance without having to attend to everything else at the same time.

A study carried out with the Department of Dance at the University of California, Irvine split 38 experienced dance students into 2 groups. Each group was asked to learn two cognitively challenging choreographies of equivalent difficulty. Group 1 learned Routine A at full effort and Routine B by marking, while Group 2 learned Routine A while marking and Routine B at full effort. The performances were then evaluated by a combination of two experienced judges who did not know which techniques each student had used when learning their routines.

For both pieces, the students who had learned by *marking* statistically significantly outperformed those who had practiced at full intensity. The researchers concluded that although many dancers adopt marking as a strategy because they believe it conserves physical effort, a hidden side effect is that it also allows them to focus attention where it is most needed. Edward Warburton and colleagues (2013, p.1737) note that dancers have "evolved a strategy that benefits them by relieving cognitive load and supporting more efficient encoding and consolidation [of learning]".

Much of the research on cognitive load difficulties has actually been carried out in domains like mathematics. However it is evident that one of the things that makes experiential learning situations so useful and important is that they typically are more complex and unpredictable than lecture- and library-based learning. As such, we can expect that when students work in studios, labs, and on projects, they are likely to be faced with cognitive load challenges (see Spotlight 8.2). This problem can be exacerbated if the teacher, who can readily do in an automated way things which still require the students' full attention, underestimates how difficult a student will find sorting through many sources of information at a given time. Indeed, the teacher may even conclude that the difficulty lies with the cognitive ability of the student rather than with the framing of the task. In addition to making it difficult for a student to solve a particular problem, unnecessary cognitive load can also hinder learning by making it difficult for students to pay attention to the features of the problem that the teacher wants them to recognise (Sweller 1988).

This is not to suggest that students should not face complex tasks. Many practical tasks are intrinsically complex, and it may not be possible to make them less challenging. When introducing new ideas or techniques, however, it is often possible to reduce unnecessary complexity by modelling how a task can be completed (as was explored in Chapter 6), by formatting the task in an accessible way, or by removing unnecessary details or information. Simulations can provide a way to reduce the cognitive load of practical situations by eliminating details that are not central to developing fluency in a specific task, and then progressively introducing complexity that makes the context more similar to real-life application. Questions and prompts, as illustrated in Chapter 4, can also be used to draw the student's attention to the salient features of a task in the early stages of skill development. This can give students an opportunity to build fluency in using new strategies and approaches before the teacher or teaching assistant introduces greater complexity in problems.

REFLECTION POINT 8.3

Are the tasks that you assign to students structured in such a way that they can build some fluency with the sub-skills before they have to perform the entire task?

Are tasks more complex than is necessary to learn the particular skill or competence you want them to learn?

Are students expected to focus on different things at the same time (for example, being asked to pay attention to the specifics of a project task while at the same time learning techniques of project management)?

LEARNING INVOLVES STORING INFORMATION SO THAT PEOPLE CAN RETRIEVE IT WHEN APPROPRIATE

Thus far, this chapter has identified that learning requires students to work, and that some of that work involves paying attention to facts, ideas, actions, and to their own body (noting that attention is a limited resource). People do not, however, simply store and perfectly recall all of the things to which they pay attention. Instead, people forget and additional work is required to prevent forgetting. This section looks at what is known about forgetting, and at how practice, repetition, and context can enable retrieval when the information is needed. It also looks at a number of practice strategies which have been found to be particularly effective, namely deliberate practice (which was introduced in Chapter 3), but also spaced practice, interleaved practice, and retrieval practice.

People forget most of what they have initially paid attention to and they forget it relatively quickly. In one well-known study, for example, students who had learned a list of Spanish words remembered, on average, only 53% of them when tested later the same day, 39% when tested 7 days later, and only 21% when tested 30 days later (Bahrick 1979). This finding is quite consistent with other studies of forgetting going all the way back to the origins of modern psychology in the 1880s. It should not, therefore, be a surprise that students who have passed a probabilities and statistics course in which they learned about binomial distributions can struggle to remember how to proceed when they have to test a hypothesis in a lab or a social research project some months or years later. In order to be able to store and recall this information when required, students need to do something more than just pay attention to an idea when it is first introduced to them.

Normally, the term *learning* is applied to things that people remember, which is to say, things they can store and recall over time. Central to the process of storing information is work in the form of *practice* and *repetition*. This idea is so fundamental to learning research that Duane Shell and his colleagues have elevated it to the status of a rule: "Information that is attended to repeatedly is stored in long-term memory" (2010, 24). The term *attended to repeatedly* includes rote learning through repetition of a given idea or phrase. The term *information* applies equally to facts and ideas (called *semantic memories*) and particular ways of thinking or doing (called *procedural memories*). Many people used repetition as a strategy when learning multiplication tables in primary school, and it remains a strategy that may well be appropriate for some more complex information that needs to be memorised in higher education. There are, however, other and perhaps more interesting strategies that could be used.

If learning requires practice and repetition, what kinds of practice or repetition are most effective for long-term learning?

First, in order to develop a skill or to retain knowledge, there is no point in repeating something (an idea or a movement) which is wrong. Rather the knowledge and procedures that the learner repeats need to be right (as noted in Chapter 3, "practice doesn't make perfect – perfect practice makes perfect"). This is a particular challenge in higher education where students often work more or less alone and as a consequence can find it difficult to discover that the procedure they are repeating is in some way flawed (Laurillard 2002, 102). Practice is, therefore, most effective when it involves (i) completing activities that require using a new skill, (ii) getting feedback on how well the skill is being performed, and (iii) then getting an opportunity to try again. In Chapter 3 this kind of practice was referred to as *deliberate practice* (Ericsson et al. 1993), and there have been multiple studies which demonstrate that it is particularly valuable in developing skills in areas as diverse as playing music and playing chess (Hambrick et al. 2014). In studies on academic learning, the right kinds of feedback have also been found to be particularly important (Hattie 2009; this is described in detail in Chapter 5).

Second, *spacing practice* over time tends to be more effective than cramming practice all into a short time period. This finding is also well established in the research literature. Nicholas Cepeda and colleagues, for example, reviewed over 250 studies involving over 14,000 participants and found that spacing out practice over time had a large positive effect on long-term learning. They concluded that "every study examined here with a retention interval longer than 1 month demonstrated a benefit from distribution of learning across weeks or months" (2006, 370). John Hattie (2009) also reports that spreading the repetition over longer periods appears to be particularly beneficial for more complex tasks. Structuring tasks so that students can return to the same idea a few times during a semester will increase the likelihood of spaced practice taking place.

Although students typically learn material in blocks (i.e. they learn about linear kinematics, then do some exercises and a lab on the topic, then they have lectures on friction followed by exercises and a lab on that topic and so on), they are often assessed on this knowledge in a way that requires them to figure out which concepts and tools are applicable in different situations without the aid of chapter headings. A third profitable practice strategy, therefore, is what is referred to as *interleaved practice*, which is to say, mixing different topics together when studying. Studies on interleaved practice have found that while students often do less well on interleaved practice exercises during the practice sessions, they typically perform better in the final assessment. It seems likely that this is because interleaved practice helps students to mentally differentiate between the different kinds of problems and situations during practice, and thereby helps to ensure that they are more likely to use the correct solution method for each one under test conditions (Rohrer and Taylor 2007). Practical sessions can provide excellent opportunities for interleaved practice because real-world problems often require drawing from different parts of a course. Because students can struggle on *interleaved* problems when learning, they may react more negatively to them than to blocked practice. Ultimately students may need to be convinced that the additional challenge is a productive one that will help their long-term learning.

Deliberate, spaced, and interleaved practice are all more or less concerned with the process of storing facts and ideas in a person's long-term memory. However, the term *learning* does not simply mean storing information in one's memory – it is also important that the information can be retrieved when it is required. There is good evidence that such retrieval can be improved through *retrieval practice*. Henry Roediger and Jeffrey Karpicke (2006), for example, examined the impact of having students take tests on material as compared to having students repeatedly study the same material. In one such experiment, they had a control group of students who studied the same material four times and an experimental group whose four sessions involved studying the material once and being tested on it three times. Although the testing group had far fewer opportunities to review the material, their practice in retrieving it led them to score notably higher on the final test one week later. The retrieval practice effect is now quite well established by learning researchers.

Interestingly, Henry Roediger and Jeffrey Karpicke noted that students who re-studied the material were generally more confident in their ability to recall the material than those who experienced retrieval practice (2006, 254). This is despite the fact that these students actually scored on average worse than those who experienced retrieval practice. This probably matches the experience of many teachers who find that a lot of students would prefer if something is re-explained to them, but would probably learn it better if they were encouraged to dig into their own memory to find the answer for themselves. The idea of encouraging learning through asking students to practice recall rather than explaining was explored in Chapter 4.

The final idea in this section is that learning activities should develop students' ability to recall information when they need it. This is related to an important facet of experts' thinking (introduced in Chapter 2): the ability to easily retrieve information relevant to the current situation (*conditionalisation of knowledge*). One of the key benefits of experiential learning is providing environments that support students to develop these aspects; while we typically think of experiential learning occurring in the physical world, it can also occur with computer-based simulations.

The kind of simulations used for experiential learning are called *operational models* and typically include both cognitive and non-cognitive tasks (De Jong and Van Joolingen 1998). These simulations are often created around a scenario, such a launching a fictional product, caring for a patient, or managing a supply chain, and are used extensively in business and health sciences education. In addition to the advantages for cognitive load discussed earlier, the capacity to provide students with immediate, specific feedback is an important advantage. Simulations can also provide opportunities for students to practice tasks that require considerable resources or high expenditure, occur over extended times, or pose risk to themselves or the public. De Jong and Van Joolingen (1998) caution that there is "no clear and univocal outcome in favor of simulations" and it appears that careful attention is required to obtain a successful balance of cognitive effort, cognitive load, contextualisation of tasks, and attention to the thinking process itself.

REFLECTION POINT 8.4

Do your students have an opportunity to practice working with an idea or a process repeatedly over time? Do they receive feedback that could help them improve?

Are labs, exercises, or field experiences *blocked* together or are they spread over time (in a way that promotes learning through spaced and interleaved practice)?

Are explanations from books or lectures typically repeated in the hands-on session, or are students required to practice retrieving knowledge themselves?

WHAT AND HOW PEOPLE LEARN DEPEND ON THEIR PRIOR KNOWLEDGE (AND ON THEIR PRIOR MISCONCEPTIONS)

The kind of learning that arises from repetition is sometimes seen as superficial learning (indeed, as Chapter 3 discussed, it is sometimes called taking a *surface approach* to learning). A student who has learned in a sociology lecture how social class is defined may find it hard to remember or use this information when they have to identify how to classify the occupation of a survey respondent. In everyday language, this is often referred to as the difference between *knowing* something and *understanding* it. While repetition and rehearsal can build *knowing*, further work by the student is needed to build understanding. This section looks at the way in which the further work of elaboration and organisation of ideas contributes to learning. It also highlights a significant issue in learning in higher education – the problem of students' prior misconceptions.

The work that is required of the student in moving beyond *knowing* and towards *understanding* is the work of making connections between new knowledge and what they already know, often referred to as the elaboration and organisation of ideas. As the American Psychological Association's review of evidence on learning noted:

> Unless new knowledge becomes integrated with the learner's prior knowledge and understanding, this new knowledge remains isolated, cannot be used most effectively in new tasks, and does not transfer readily into new situations.
>
> (Lambert and McCombs 1997, 17)

Prior knowledge in this situation might mean knowledge from earlier in the same course or from previous courses. When a student first comes to study rotational movement in physics, for example, they will often find it easier to remember rotational concepts if they make connections with what they already know about linear movement (torque is the rotational analogue of force, inertia is the rotational analogue of mass and so on). They may also make wider connections or analogies (power is to energy as velocity is to distance, for example). Making such connections and distinctions between ideas is referred to as *organisation*. Making such connections will help them understand what ideas apply in what situations and why. Encouraging students to remember what they already know about a topic before studying new material may well help them to prepare to make the connections and distinctions they will need to make in order to understand material.

Looked at from the perspective of practical learning, it is evident that the kinds of experiential knowledge which students derive from hands-on learning can also provide *prior knowledge* into which students can integrate new knowledge. For example, students who learn about the ideal gas law might make a connection between the calculations they do on paper and what happens when a balloon rises into the sky or is submerged in water. Making this kind of connection which helps to make information meaningful is often referred to as *elaboration*. Indeed, making this kind of connection with what students can see, hear, smell, touch, or taste is very often the principal goal of experiential learning in labs, projects, and in the field. Making connections between ideas, and between ideas and memories, and interrogating these connections to clarify misunderstandings, is known as *deep processing* of information (Craik 2002).

REFLECTION POINT 8.5 – ENERGY AND MASS*

Answer the following question:
  Jared lost a lot of weight eating a low-calorie diet. Where did the fat/mass go?

a. The mass was released as CO_2 and H_2O.
b. The mass was converted to energy and used up.
c. The mass was converted to ATP molecules.
d. The mass was broken down to amino acids and eliminated from the body.

The correct answer is provided in the text below.

* This question comes from a paper by Charlene D'Avanzo (2008) which looked at ways that instructors in biology could identify and track changes in student misconceptions.

One of the challenges for learning in higher education is that sometimes a learner's prior knowledge may be incorrect. This is because learners come to higher education having lived in the world for many years and so have developed, by experience, a set of common-sense ideas about how it works. These ideas are often implicit (in the sense that student may find it hard to articulate them out loud) and are often flawed. These problematic understandings of the world are often evident in social and human sciences because many of the technical terms used in such disciplines (terms like social class, power, culture, democracy, or representation) are widely used in fuzzy and poorly articulated ways in everyday speech. Even when they are easy to spot, however, it is nonetheless a challenge to discourage students from falling back on implicit *folk* understandings of such concepts during their studies.

Although the phenomenon may be less visible in natural sciences, it is nonetheless a factor. One such example is that many students' *common-sense* ideas about force and movement are incompatible with the Newtonian mechanics that form the basis of introductory physics courses (Hestenes 1992). Andrea diSessa's study illustrated this by having students carry out a lab task which involved changing the trajectory of a moving ball (1982). Students, typically, first acted as if the ball would move exactly in the direction of their push, thereby neglecting the important fact that the ball was already moving. This inability to take into account the actual relationship between force and velocity was true even of those who had studied physics in school and who had been exposed to Newton's laws of motion (diSessa 1982).

Indeed, researchers also established that lectures and exercises typically had little impact on these false beliefs, in part because the courses tended to be assessed in such a way that students could learn the methods and algorithms necessary to pass end of semester exams without actually thinking about how these ideas applied in real-world situations (Crouch and Mazur 2001). Subsequent research found that the problem of students' prior misconceptions was not isolated to the classical mechanics class: students' implicit prior misconceptions have been identified in a wide range of scientific disciplines including chemistry, biology, astronomy, geoscience, materials science, and mathematics. The question presented in Reflection point 8.5, for example, has been used in biology to identify a *common-sense* confusion between matter and energy which leads students to think that the fat is directly turned into energy (answer b) rather than the correct response of being broken up into smaller molecules (answer a; D'Avanzo 2008).

Practical learning can often provide opportunities for students to be confronted with their own misconceptions in a way in which lecture, exercise, and reading activities cannot. This does not simply happen when students have an experience but rather when students are challenged to confront their own misconceptions. Catherine Crouch and colleagues (2004) found that when students observed physics demonstrations, their understanding of the underlying concepts was typically no better than that of students who learned the concepts without any demonstration at all. However, when students were required to predict the outcome before seeing the physics demonstration, they showed significantly greater understanding of the underlying concepts (see Spotlight 6.2). In Chapter 3, the idea of the investigation techniques of a discipline was introduced. In science, this approach is frequently called *inquiry* and highlights that scientific thinking is based on making hypotheses, making observations or measurements, comparing these with the initial hypotheses, and trying to make sense of what emerges. As the work of Catherine Crouch and colleagues makes clear, inquiry approaches to thinking about labs or fieldwork are not only integral to the *representative tasks* of their disciplines (see Chapter 2) – they also appear to improve conceptual learning in those disciplines.

Indeed, the evidence suggests that unless students' misconceptions are explicitly addressed, students may integrate new knowledge into flawed prior models without changing their underlying misconception. To address this, teachers need to be aware of the kinds of misconceptions that students hold and explicitly address them. A range of *concept inventories* have been developed which include questions like the one in Reflection point 8.5 that are designed to make these prior misconceptions explicit and to give feedback to students. As Chapter 5 identified, the most effective feedback is often connected with showing a student that they got something wrong when they thought they had got it right (Hattie 2012, 139). Therefore posing students conceptual questions of this type can be a very powerful learning strategy.

> **REFLECTION POINT 8.6**
>
> Are your labs, exercises, studios, or field experiences used as opportunities to confront people with the gap between their prior knowledge or implicit assumptions and more disciplinary-specific understandings?
>
> Are your students engaged in investigative thinking techniques of your discipline, such as making hypotheses, observing, and interpreting their findings? Can an inquiry approach be used to help students make connections between their disciplinary learning and its applications in *real-life* settings?

CONCLUSION

This chapter has summarised the research evidence about how people learn which focuses on the thinking processes involved in learning in higher education with a particular focus on how they are applicable to practical settings. It highlights that the students learn through paying attention to things and that, because attention is a limited resource, getting them to pay attention to the right thing (such as through gradually introducing complexity) is important. It further highlights that, having paid attention, students then need to

THE THINKING THAT GIVES RISE TO LEARNING

actively process this information through practice and repetition, ideally with feedback and over time. In order to understand and use the ideas they are learning, students need to organise and elaborate new ideas and to challenge their own misconceptions.

These findings have a number of implications which have influenced the structure and organisation of this book. Some of the most important of these ideas are:

- Where possible, students should be actively thinking for themselves rather than passively listening to a teacher think.
- As Chapter 6 explored, when explaining things:
  - activating students' prior knowledge can make it easier for them to integrate new ideas with what they already know,
  - being clear with students about learning objectives can help students direct their attention appropriately,
  - concluding with a summary can help students organise ideas.
- As Chapter 4 explored, questions are an important strategy which can play a number of roles:
  - directing students' attention and reducing any non-productive complexity in learning tasks,
  - prompting students to engage in retrieval practice,
  - prompting students to engage in elaborating and challenging ideas.
- As Chapter 5 explored, feedback plays an important role:
  - ensuring that practice becomes deliberate practice,
  - helping students to identify and challenge their own misconceptions.

At the outset of this chapter, it was noted that learning is often seen as an individual phenomenon. At the end of a course students are frequently assessed as individuals, and at the end of a degree programme it is an individual who takes away the diploma. This chapter has, so far, reflected this *individualistic* bias in that it has described cognitive processes of *paying attention*, *repetition*, *elaboration*, and *organisation* which could well be completed by a learner who is alone on a desert island.

But humans are social animals and learning is a social as well as an individual phenomenon. Furthermore, the learning brain is subject to emotions and encased in a body that also influences how learning happens. In order to tell the full story of learning, then, it is necessary to stretch beyond the individualistic and cognitive focus of this chapter. These social and biological dimensions of learning will be summarised in the next chapter.

FURTHER READING

These three books and two videos provide an excellent way to further explore the conditions and activities that best support learning. A full reference list for the chapter is provided below.

Ambrose, S.A., Bridges, M.W., Di Pietro, M., Lovett, M.C., and Norman, M.K. (2010). *How Learning Works, 7 Research-Based Principles for Smart Teaching*. San Francisco: Jossey Bass.

Bransford, J.D., Brown, A.L., and Cocking, R. (eds.) (2000). *How People Learn; Brain, Mind, Experience, and School*. Washington, DC: National Academy Press. https://doi.org/10.17226/9853.

Ericsson, K.A. (2020, February). Skill Mastery & Peak Performance *via* Deliberate Practice with Psychologist Anders Ericsson [Video]. *Youtube*. https://youtu.be/qiBne5EGBQ8.

Hattie, J., and Yates, G.C.R. (2013). *Visible Learning and the Science of How We Learn*. Abingdon: Routledge. https://doi.org/10.4324/9781315885025.

Tormey, R. (2018). Evidence about Learning (Part II) [Video]. *SwitchTube*. https://tube.switch.ch/download/video/63ce553e.

REFERENCES

Ambrose, S.A., Bridges, M.W., Di Pietro, M., Lovett, M.C., and Norman, M.K. (2010). *How Learning Works, 7 Research-Based Principles for Smart Teaching*. San Francisco: Jossey Bass.

Bahrick, H.P. (1979). Maintenance of Knowledge: Questions about Memory We Forgot to Ask. *Journal of Experimental Psychology: General* 108(3): 296–308.

Bransford, J.D., Brown, A.L., and Cocking, R. eds. (2000). *How People Learn; Brain, Mind, Experience, and School*. Washington, DC: National Academy Press.

Cepeda, N.J., Pashler, H., Vul, E., Wixted, J.T., and Rohrer, D. (2006). Distributed Practice in Verbal Recall Tasks: A Review and Quantitative Synthesis. *Psychological Bulletin* 132(3): 354–380. https://doi.org/10.1037/0033-2909.132.3.354. PMID: 16719566.

Chi, M.T.H., and Wylie, R. (2014). The ICAP Framework: Linking Cognitive Engagement to Active Learning Outcomes. *Educational Psychologist* 49(4): 219–243. https://doi.org/10.1080/00461520.2014.965823.

Craik, F.I.M. (2002). Levels of Processing: Past, Present … and Future? *Memory* 10(5–6): 305–318. https://doi.org/10.1080/09658210244000135.

Crouch, C., Fagen, A.P., Callan, J.P., and Mazur, E. (2004). Classroom Demonstrations: Learning Tools or Entertainment? *American Journal of Physics* 72(6): 835–838. https://doi.org/10.1119/1.1707018.

Crouch, C.H., and Mazur, E. (2001). Peer Instruction: Ten Years of Experience and Results. *American Journal of Physics* 69(9): 970–977.

D'Avanzo, C. (2008). Biology Concept Inventories: Overview, Status, and Next Steps. *BioScience* 58(11): 1079–1085. https://doi.org/10.1641/B581111.

De Jong, T., and Van Joolingen, W.R. (1998). Scientific Discovery Learning with Computer Simulations of Conceptual Domains. *Review of Educational Research* 68(2): 179–201. https://doi.org/10.3102/00346543068002179.

DiSessa, A.A. (1982). Unlearning Aristotelian Physics: A Study of Knowledge-Based Learning. *Cognitive Science* 6(1): 37–75.

Dunlosky, J., Rawson, K.A., Marsh, E.J., Nathan, M.J., and Willingham, D.T. (2013). Improving Students' Learning With Effective Learning Techniques: Promising Directions From Cognitive and Educational Psychology. *Psychological Science in the Public Interest* 14(1): 4–58. https://doi.org/10.1177/1529100612453266.

Ericsson, K.A., Krampe, R.Th., and Tesch-Römer, C. (1993). The Role of Deliberate Practice in the Acquisition of Expert Performance. *Psychological Review* 100(3): 363–406. https://doi.org/10.1037/0033-295x.100.3.363.

Fiorella, L., and Mayer, R.E. (2015). *Learning as a Generative Activity: Eight Learning Strategies That Promote Understanding.* Cambridge: Cambridge University Press.

Hambrick, D.Z., Oswald, F.L., Altmann, E.M., Meinz, E.J., Gobet, F., and Campitelli, G. (2014). Deliberate Practice: Is That All It Takes to Become an Expert? *Intelligence* 45: 34–45. https://doi.org/10.1016/j.intell.2013.04.001.

Hattie, J. (2009). *Visible Learning, A Synthesis of Over 800. Meta-Analyses Relating to Achievement.* London: Routledge.

Hattie, J. (2012). *Visible Learning for Teachers: Maximizing Impact on Learning.* Routledge/Taylor & Francis Group.

Hattie, J., and Donoghue, G. (2016). Learning Strategies: A Synthesis and Conceptual Model. *npj Science of Learning* 1: 16013. https://doi.org/10.1038/npjscilearn.2016.13.

Hestenee, D., Wells, M., and Gregg Swackhamer, G. (1992). The Force Concept Inventory. *Physics Teacher* 30(3): 141–158. https://doi.org/10.1119/1.2343497.

Klingberg, T. (2009). *The Overflowing Brain; Information Overload and the Limits of Working Memory.* Oxford: Oxford University Press.

Kober, N. (2015). *Reaching Students: What Research Says About Effective Instruction in Undergraduate Science and Engineering.* Washington, DC: National Academies Press. http://www.nap.edu/catalog/18687.

Lambert, N.M., and McCombs, B.L. (eds.) (1997). *How Students Learn: Reforming Schools through Learner-Centered Education.* American Psychological Association. https://doi.org/10.1037/10258-000.

Laurillard, D. (2002). *Rethinking University Teaching: A Framework for the Effective Use of Learning Technologies*, 2nd edition. London: Routledge Falmer. https://doi.org/10.4324/9780203160329.

Menekse, M., Stump, G.S., Krause, S., and Chi, M.T.H. (2013). Differentiated Overt Learning Activities for Effective Instruction in Engineering Classrooms. *Journal of Engineering Education* 102(3): 346–374. https://doi.org/10.1002/jee.20021.

Mueller, P.A., and Oppenheimer, D.M. (2014). The Pen Is Mightier than the Keyboard: Advantages of Longhand over Laptop Note Taking. *Psychological Science* 25(6): 1159–1168. https://doi.org/10.1177/0956797614524581.

National Academies of Sciences, Engineering, and Medicine (2018). *How People Learn II: Learners, Contexts, and Cultures.* Washington, DC: National Academy Press. https://doi.org/10.17226/24783.

Roediger, H.L., and Karpicke, J.D. (2006). Test-Enhanced Learning: Taking Memory Tests Improves Long-Term Retention. *Psychological Science* 17(3): 249–255. https://doi.org/10.1111/j.1467-9280.2006.01693.x. PMID: 16507066.

Rohrer, D., and Taylor, K. (2007). The Shuffling of Mathematics Problems Improves Learning. *Instructional Science* 35(6): 481–498. https://doi.org/10.1007/s11251-007-9015-8.

Shell, D.F., Brooks, David W., Trainin, G., Wilson, K.M., Kauffman, D.F., and Herr, L.M. (2010). *The Unified Learning Model, How Motivational, Cognitive, and Neurobiological Sciences Inform Best Teaching Practices.* Dordrecht: Springer. https://doi.org/10.1007/978-90-481-3215-7_2.

Sweller, J. (1988). Cognitive Load During Learning: Effects on Learning. *Cognitive Science* 12(2): 257–285. https://doi.org/10.1207/s15516709cog1202_4.

Warburton, E.C., Wilson, M., Lynch, M., and Cuykendall, S. (2013). The Cognitive Benefits of Movement Reduction: Evidence from Dance Marking. *Psychological Science* 24(9): 1732–1739. https://doi.org/10.1177/0956797613478824.

Chapter 9

Research findings about the contexts of learning

In the previous chapter it was identified that learning involves the student engaging in cognitive work which includes paying attention, repeating and practicing, and elaborating and organising ideas and experiences. At its most basic, then, learning requires cognitive effort from the learner. In practical settings, the obvious effort and activity may be physical – learners may be moving, talking, and touching and manipulating things – but they also need to be cognitively active if they are to learn.

The introduction to the previous chapter also identified that, in addition to these cognitive processes, learning also involves social, emotional, biological, and metacognitive processes. Specifically learning sciences research has identified that:

- To put in the effort required, learners have to see the value in accomplishing what is being asked of them.
- Learning is affected by the learner's social identity, and by their interaction with others.
- Students learn more when they develop the ability to be independent and goal-directed.
- Learning involves the mind, the emotions, and the body of the learner.

This chapter will summarise the research findings under each of these headings, starting with the question of learner motivation.

LEARNERS MUST SEE THE VALUE IN ACCOMPLISHING WHAT IS BEING ASKED OF THEM

The kinds of work identified in the previous chapter require effort and time. In order to learn something, students will often need to stick with it,

DOI: 10.4324/9781003107606-9

PART III

sometimes when there are other distractions, often when learning seems a bit dull, and frequently when they are frustrated and feeling like they are not making progress. In Chapter 2, it was noted that one of the characteristics of deliberate practice is that it is *not* play. Indeed it is often not enjoyable in itself. Managing the motivation required to continue to complete and improve performance on practice tasks is, therefore, crucial to learning. This perhaps helps to explain the phrase associated with the inventor Thomas Edison, "Genius is 1% inspiration and 99% perspiration".

Before a learner will invest that much time and effort in something, they will need to be appropriately motivated. Writing about university learning, Susan Ambrose and colleagues (2010, 69) argued, "The importance of motivation, in the context of learning, cannot be overstated". This section begins by looking at the different kinds of value a student may see in a project, a lab, a studio, or in a field experience, including intrinsic value and utility value. It then looks at the importance of the goals that students set for themselves, distinguishing between performance goals and mastery goals. It identifies the ways in which interaction with teachers and teaching assistants can help influence the kinds of goals students set for themselves.

When thinking about motivation, many people focus on the issue of quantity, that is, "Does this student have enough motivation to put in the work required?" It is important to note that rather than seeing motivation as a given quantity that the student brings with them to the course, it is more appropriate to see motivation as an emergent phenomenon, something which develops and changes as the student experiences learning (National Academies of Sciences, Engineering, and Medicine 2018, 111). Finding something interesting, finding it challenging, and experiencing success all affect students' motivation.

A second key issue to consider in thinking about motivation is *motivated to do what?* Students in fieldwork or labs are often confronted by novelty, which is itself inherently interesting. Debby Cotton, for example, described the experience of geographic novelty for students on a field trip:

> We went for a look round, saw a strange rodenty creature with green eyes which was pretty cool, a locust, and an owl and some other things which I'm not quite sure what they are or they might have been a figment of my imagination. Doesn't matter, it was still very exciting.
>
> (this was previously cited in Chapter 1; 2009, 171)

For learning to take place, however, it is generally not enough to be interested in having an experience. A student also needs to be motivated to follow through on thinking about and making sense of that experience. As Cotton notes, "memorability *per se* is not necessarily of educational benefit. Indeed, the exciting aspects of this trip were rarely linked to students attaining an enhanced understanding of the local ecosystem". This issue equally applies to other kinds of practical experience where the wonder of the new or the excitement of *chemistry magic* may well captivate attention but does not, in itself, necessarily mean students will learn.

One obvious predictor of a student's motivation to do the cognitive and physical work required for learning is the value they see in the material covered in the course. *Value* can be understood in terms of the intrinsic value of the material (e.g. seeing the material as interesting or the learning as enjoyable) or in terms of its utility value (e.g. seeing that a particular lab course will be helpful when they will need to operationalise the concept of lab hygiene in later courses and in their working life). There is some suggestion from the research evidence that perceived utility may be particularly important in giving rise to successful performance (Hulleman et al. 2008). Susan Ambrose and colleagues (2010, 83–84) therefore suggest that higher education teachers should focus on showing students the relevance of what they will learn in their practical class to their future courses and to their future professional lives. This can often be readily done in practical learning settings where students are performing *representative tasks* of their discipline or profession and which allow students to see the relevance of material that might seem abstract and dry when presented in lectures, tutorials, and exercises.

Motivation is not only influenced by the perceived value of the content material but also by the learners' goals with respect to that material. John Hattie's review of quantitative studies of learning, for example, highlights the existence of challenging goals as being critical for enhancing student learning (2009, 163–164). In particular, he distinguishes between setting the goal as *do your best* (which typically does not do much to help learning) and setting the goal as *strive to the highest* (which usually does have a positive impact on learning): "Goals have a self-energising effect if they are appropriately challenging for the student, as they can motivate students to exert effort in line with the difficulty or demands of the goal" (2009, 164). It may well be hard for students to make the decision to invest in learning if they are not all that clear about what success looks like – hence being clear with students about what success looks like (something which was also discussed in Chapter 5 as being integral to effective feedback) may also play a role in motivating students (clarifying objectives was also identified as important in Chapter 6 on explaining).

If having a goal can be important for motivation, the specific type of goal that a learner sets for themselves is also important. Researchers distinguish between those who are motivated by the desire to perform well or to outperform others (*performance goals*) and those who are motivated by the desire to increase their competence, skill, or understanding of the material (*mastery goals*) (Pintrich 2000). While learners in both of these situations may be highly motivated to do well, the evidence suggests that they will often approach learning differently and with a different result. In particular, those who are motivated by a desire to improve their knowledge or skill (*mastery goals*) tend to enjoy challenging tasks, to be more willing to exert effort, to be more persistent in the face of setbacks, and to view failure as an opportunity to learn and improve (National Academies of Sciences, Engineering, and Medicine 2018, 119). Given this impressive set of characteristics, it is worth considering how to promote *mastery goals*.

The kind of goals a student sets (*mastery*, *performance*, or, in a worst-case scenario, *avoiding failure*) is not simply something they carry with them into the course, but is often influenced by the way the course or the teaching is organised. For example, if errors and mistakes during the course are seen as a normal and valuable part of the learning process, then this communicates that *getting better* is what is valued. On the other hand if students get the feedback that mistakes are embarrassing, then they may focus more on performance. The issue of class climate and its role in learning was explored in Chapter 7. Likewise feedback (see Chapter 5) which ranks students with respect to others is likely to encourage performance goals, while feedback that identifies what excellence looks like and how it can be achieved may orient students more towards *mastery goals*. Table 9.1 summarises some of the ways in which the classroom climate can orient students towards *mastery* or *performance goals*.

REFLECTION POINT 9.1

What motivates students in your practical course? The novelty of the experience? How inherently interesting it is? The utility of the knowledge and skills they can learn?

What are students motivated to do in your practical class? To experience fun or novel experiences? To do the cognitive or physical work required to learn the skills and develop the required understanding?

Is the class climate in your practical course focused on students showing you what they can do, or on improving what they can do?

TABLE 9.1 Achievement goals and class climate

Climate dimension	Mastery goal	Performance goal
Success defined as ...	Improvement, progress	High grades, better performance than others
Value placed on ...	Effort/learning	High ability
Reasons for satisfaction ...	Working hard, challenge	Doing better than others
Teacher oriented towards ...	How students are improving	How students are performing
View of errors/mistakes ...	Part of learning	Anxiety eliciting
Focus of attention ...	Process of learning	Own performance relative to others
Reasons for effort ...	Learning something new	High grades, winning, performing better than others
Evaluation criteria	Absolute, progress	Normative

Source: Adapted from National Academies of Sciences, Engineering, and Medicine (2018, 121)

LEARNING IS AFFECTED BY INTERACTION WITH OTHERS AND BY THE LEARNER'S SOCIAL IDENTITY

As the previous chapter noted, thus far learning has been largely described as if it is something that can be done by a person who is isolated and without social contact. At the same time, the social context has not been entirely absent from the story about learning which has unfolded across these chapters. When discussing the *work* of learning, the strong positive impact of *interactive* learning strategies was identified (see Spotlight 8.1). Teachers have been identified as important both in framing learning tasks to minimise the negative impact of cognitive load as well as in helping students recognise implicit prior misconceptions. In discussing motivation, the role of class culture in influencing students to adopt achievement goals has also been identified. This section looks in more detail at this idea of social context, focusing on the role of the student's peer group in supporting their learning, on the way they can model themselves on an expert, and on the way in which learning can be affected by a learner's image of themselves, which in turn can be influenced by their social context.

One recurring theme in this book has been that sometimes working with peers can significantly increase how much a student learns. In Spotlight 8.1, for example, it was identified that students who worked *interactively* scored on average 9% higher than students who worked *constructively*, and 19% more than those who worked *actively* on the same material (Menekse et al. 2013). Likewise, the Harvard physicist Eric Mazur found that when students discussed their misconceptions with each other, their learning was greater than when the teacher re-explained the content (Mazur 1997). Students working together like this may have a positive impact on learning for a number of reasons. For example, it seems likely that students will elaborate and organise their ideas during the interaction with each other. One consequence of this elaboration and organisation effect is that interaction has a positive effect for both students involved, that is, for the student doing the explaining as well as for the one receiving the explanation. John Hattie and Gregory Donoghue (2016, 8), for example, report on a review of 839 studies involving more than 160,000 participants which found that, on average, being a peer teacher increased a student's attainment by half a standard deviation. As we noted in Chapter 2, this kind of interactivity is very common in practical settings such as labs (where multiple students frequently collaborate around a single bench), team projects, and in studios.

Groups can also help to solve difficulties which arise due to cognitive load limits. Femke Kirschner and colleagues (2011), for example, have carried out experiments which required students to work on complex problems either in groups or alone, and then tested them on their ability to use this problem-solving knowledge and skills. When attempting to learn by completing a complex problem, students in groups can reduce the cognitive load difficulty by relying on each other to each remember some of what is required to solve the problem – a kind of *group memory*. This in turn may free up some of their attention to focus on actually learning how to solve the problem. Hence, the researchers found that, in the final performance test, those who studied by completing complex problems in groups performed, on average, better than those who studied by completing the same complex problems alone. Working in groups is not a magic bullet, however. Working in groups is actually in itself a kind of work since interacting with others requires attention and effort (Dillenbourg and Bétrancourt 2006). When the learning tasks were simpler and imposed a smaller cognitive load, students did not need the *group memory* and, in that situation, the group can become a complicating factor which may even inhibit performance.

One other reason why students' explanations to each other may be particularly effective is perhaps evident from the discussion in the previous chapter about the organisation and elaboration of knowledge, and indeed, from the discussion of expertise in Chapter 2. While undergraduate students in a course are meeting a given idea for the first time, experts (higher education teachers or work-placement supervisors) have, over a period of years, revisited, rehearsed, explained, discussed, elaborated, and organised that same idea. In short, research on expertise has identified that experts have a large repertoire of knowledge in their discipline, that they have organised this knowledge around core concepts or big ideas, and as a consequence they can fluently recall what they know at the right time (Bransford et al. 2000, 31–44). One of the downsides of this is that experts will frequently find it hard to see what it is that a novice does not know, and will overestimate the ability of students to understand what it is the expert is telling them. This bias is referred to as the *curse of knowledge* (Wieman 2007). One reason why peer discussion and peer tutoring can be effective, then, is that a peer who has recently learned something is often better able to understand what it is that another student does not know and can, consequently, often provide a more appropriate explanation.

While the general pattern of the data presented so far seems to suggest that working in groups is of benefit to students when they work on tasks which are complex to them, it should be noted that not all groups are made the same. Pierre Dillenbourg and Bertrand Schneider (1995), for example, highlight that most of the benefits that have been identified above are evident in relatively small groups. Larger groups are more likely to have *free riders*; students who are nominally group members and take credit for the group's outputs without contributing much to the group's activity. They also note that heterogeneous groups seem to perform better than homogeneous groups, within certain limits: "Results indicate there exists some *optimal heterogeneity*, i.e. some difference of viewpoints is required to trigger interactions, but within the boundaries of mutual interest and intelligibility" (1995, 133). Pierre Dillenbourg and Bertrand Schneider also note that the nature of the task provided plays a key role in enabling learning. If students can work in parallel without requiring interaction then the group is unlikely to contribute much to their learning. If the students are asked to perceive information or to rapidly complete motor tasks without time for reflection and discussion, then, once more, doing so in a group is unlikely to help them learn. This suggests that, for learning to happen, a person needs to be confronted by an inconsistency between what they believe and some contrary evidence, and the person needs to do some work to resolve that inconsistency. Groups can help this happen when there are at least two members who have clearly divergent ideas and who are forced to confront this divergence and to then build a shared understanding. Ideally then, group activities are organised to ensure students are interacting with each other, articulating differing ideas, and working to resolve those differences.

> ## REFLECTION POINT 9.2
>
> Are students organised in groups in your practical learning settings? Are the groups large or small? What strategies do you have in place to manage the *free-rider* problem?
>
> Are group tasks organised so that students are required to collaborate with each other, or could students simply work in parallel?
>
> Is the group task one which will give rise to divergent ideas which the students will need to work on in order to resolve?

If there are times when student-to-student communication is the most appropriate way of ensuring learning, communication between teachers and students can also be extremely valuable because one of the ways that students can develop competence is by watching experts at work. While most of the discussion of learning in the previous chapter implied that learning always requires practice and feedback to improve (what might be called trial-and-error), humans have also a capacity for *one trial* or *no trial* learning through observation of others. Early studies of learning through observation and modelling in the 1960s found that when something was learned through observation, the learners did not simply mimic the behaviour but they also understood the intention of the modelled behaviour and were therefore able to adapt it. The corollary is that if someone cannot understand the implicit intention or structure of a behaviour that is being modelled then they may focus on irrelevant features of the action being modelled (National Academies of Sciences, Engineering, and Medicine 2018, 41). One way in which this idea of observational learning has influenced teaching and learning is through the idea of *cognitive apprenticeship* (e.g. Collins et al. 1989). Allan Collins and colleagues identified that in traditional apprenticeships, the apprentice watched the master at work before trying to replicate what the master had done, while the master offered coaching, before fading into the background as the apprentice developed the ability to smoothly perform the skill. Allan Collins and colleagues applied the same idea to teaching a range of different academic disciplines. They used the term *cognitive apprenticeship* to describe the way in which teachers can model to students the processes that experts use to handle complex tasks (such as solving a complex and changing problem in a workplace situation, or in designing and interpreting empirical investigations). Jean-Philippe Rivière and colleagues (2018), for example, have studied how expert contemporary dancers learn new routines. They note that all of the dancers they interviewed reported observation as the first action in the learning process. They describe observation not as a once off but as an iterative process. As one of the dancers they interviewed said:

> I'm looking at it from different angles. You are brought to see it [the movement] several times. The first look is a global look. I look at the energy, the situation in space, the most important ones. My second look will focus on the details.
>
> (2018, 3–4)

A key feature of the modelling in cognitive apprenticeship approaches is that the teacher often *talks aloud* about the kinds of strategies and heuristics that are required to perform complex cognitive tasks but which are typically left implicit (this idea has been explored in Chapter 6 on explaining to students).

Peers and teachers do more than explain and model knowledge and thinking to the student: they also give the students feedback about themselves. The previous section identified that motivation is an important determinant of a student's learning and that the perceived value of the material being taught as well as the nature of the student's goals (mastery or performance) impacted upon their motivation. Another factor which impacts upon a student's motivation is the way in which the student thinks about themselves and their relationship with the discipline. Put simply, when students believe that they are capable of succeeding at a task, they are more likely to put in the effort and to demonstrate the persistence required to perform well, and they are less likely to feel anxious, stressed, or depressed. This belief in their own ability in a given area is called *self-efficacy* (Bandura 1977). An important feature of self-efficacy is that it is distinct from self-esteem or confidence more generally – self-efficacy describes how good a person thinks they will be at doing something in specific rather than how they feel about themselves in general. Barry Zimmerman (2000) identifies that self-efficacy beliefs could be enhanced by getting learners to set goals which were in the form of *small-steps towards excellence* as these kinds of goals allowed learners to see their improvement. Providing feedback on goals and how students can make progress towards them was also associated with enhanced self-efficacy. Barry Zimmerman (2000) also reports that seeing someone model a particular cognitive strategy also had a more positive impact on self-efficacy than simply telling students how to use the strategy.

> ## SPOTLIGHT 9.1 – DIGITAL TOOLS CAN BUILD COMMUNITY FOR STUDENTS ON PRACTICE PLACEMENTS
>
> Learning in professional disciplines like teaching, nursing, engineering, or law will often involve students being involved in practice placements or internships. While in some disciplines and countries, there are well-developed systems for ensuring that students focus on the desired learning goals of the practice placement, it is not unusual for the student to feel more or less isolated from their peers and from their university when on practice placement. This isolation can exacerbate perceptions of a theory-practice gap, and can lead the student to separate their experiential learning from the reflection and theorisations that are necessary to develop deep understanding and genuinely expert practice. As Beat Schwendimann and colleagues put it (2015): "The dual context approach often leads to disconnected, inert and fragmented knowledge that cannot be applied to solve problems".
>
> Bridging the gap between the classroom and the field can be done in two directions: experiences which students have in practice placements and internships can be brought back to the educational institution and used as a basis for reflective activities which link experiences to conceptual knowledge gained within the university's walls. Equally, students can be asked to work with and apply what they have learned in their traditional courses during their practice placements. But making these connections is not obvious or spontaneous. In some cases, it may be actively hampered by an *anti-intellectual* culture in workplaces where students are told, in effect, to "forget all that theory, now you will see how it is really done". While students are often required to engage in reflections while on practice placements, when these reflections happen on paper they are typically only accessible to higher education staff during brief placement visits and may not be of much interest to on-site supervisors. Digital tools can play a role in bridging this *theory/practice, university/workplace* divide.

> For example, electronic portfolios can be used to allow students to collect digital traces of their work (e.g. photographs or images of something which they have been working on), to augment them (tagging them with concepts, organising them as related to specific ideas, and commenting on them, etc.), and to discuss these with peers (in a different workplace), with supervisors (in their own workplace), and with higher education staff (again, at distance). This kind of digital space has been referred to using the German language term *Erfahrraum* which translates as *experience reflection room* (Dillenbourg and Jermann 2010).
>
> Beat Schwendimann and colleagues (2015) describe multiple uses of such electronic *Erfahrraum* to support making theory-practice connections in internships and practice placements. In one example, student health care workers (dental assistants) used a web-based collaborative writing environment (e.g. a wiki) to reflect on things which went wrong during the workplace placement. They first collected artefacts which represented things which went wrong (e.g. a defective radiography). These were collected and organised by the teacher and uploaded to a shared environment. Each student had to comment on a different artefact, under a range of headings. The teacher then managed a whole-class discussion on the activity, and finally each entry was revised in light of the discussion. In this way, students' experiences went from being something which happened when they were away from university and isolated, into being something which was a basis for building their understanding in interaction with peers and teachers.

Students' self-efficacy beliefs are not simply linked to themselves but also linked to their ideas about *people like me*. As the National Academies of Sciences, Engineering, and Medicine (2018, 126) have noted, people tend to engage in activities that connect them to their social identities because this can aid their self-esteem and their sense of belonging, and can reduce a sense of isolation. Depending on the prevailing culture within which the student finds themselves, this social identification can have both positive and negative impacts on learning. Numerous studies in the US have shown that where students from 'racial' or ethnic minorities hold positive attitudes towards their own ethnic group, this is associated with greater interest and engagement in formal education. However, where there are negative stereotypes about particular ethic groups, this can also impact on learning and performance. Numerous studies have identified that where negative academic stereotypes exist about particular social groups, this can negatively impact on students from that social group when they are being examined. This phenomenon is called *stereotype threat* (Steele et al. 2002). For example, in one study male and female university students, who had been selected as being high performing in mathematics, were given a difficult mathematics test. In an experimental group, students were explicitly told that on this test women normally scored as well as men. A control group were given no specific information (and so the researchers believed that the prevailing stereotype that women were less competent than men at mathematics would apply). The results were dramatic: women in the experimental group (who had been told that the dominant stereotype did not apply) performed as well as the men, while women in the control group (where the prevailing stereotype had not been challenged) performed less well than both the men in the control group and the women in the experimental group (Steele et al. 2002, 381). Stereotype threat has been found to negatively impact on the performance of a wide range of negatively stereotyped identity groups. Drawing on data from the National Longitudinal Study of Freshmen, for example, Maya Beasley and Mary Fischer (2012) looked at attrition from science and technology degree programmes and concluded that,

> the experiences of stereotype threat among Black men and women as well as White and Hispanic women have a significant influence on STEM attrition ... stereotype threat not only negatively affects the test taking abilities of women and minorities, but it inhibits major life experiences as well.

(2012, 443)

This issue is not linked solely to technological disciplines. In Chapter 3, for example, Gwen highlighted that there were particular patterns of beliefs about the innateness of musical ability which also made it hard for some students to progress and learn in that discipline. Similar beliefs about innateness of talent or biases about the suitability of particular disciplines for some social groups can be found in many other disciplines.

A number of strategies have been found to be successful in helping to reduce the effects of stereotype threat. A reduced impact of stereotype threat has been found, for example, where students are prompted to see performance as a result of their work and effort rather than as a result of their *innate* abilities (Aronson et al. 2002). Strategies to increase the sense of belonging of minority groups have also been found to be effective. For example, in one study, students in the second semester of their first year were provided with the report of a study which highlighted that most students experienced transition difficulties but eventually became more confident and integrated into university life: challenges were, therefore, represented as a normal and transitory part of university life rather than something which was due to, for example, their 'race' or ethnicity. Students were then followed over the subsequent three years. Participation in the experiment was found to be associated with a halving of the attainment gap between African-American and European-American students as well as with an increased sense of belonging and a reduction in self-doubt as compared to African-American students who had not participated in the study (Walton and Cohen 2011).

This section has highlighted that learning is not solely a function of what a student does alone, but is also a function of their social setting. The right kind of interaction with peers can provide students with support in times of heavy cognitive load as well as opportunities to elaborate and organise ideas. Modelling their thinking on the behaviour of teachers can be productive for students, especially if teachers manage to make implicit strategies and processes explicit for them. Teachers and peers can also influence students' self-esteem, and their beliefs about themselves and about *people like them*. Learning, then, is an integrally social act.

> **REFLECTION POINT 9.3**
>
> Are there stereotypical views about who normally does and does not perform well in your discipline?
>
> Are there ways that you could challenge these implicit biases by emphasising that achievement in your discipline is a result of the right kinds of work, rather than as a result of some kind of *innate* talent?

STUDENTS LEARN MORE WHEN THEY DEVELOP THE ABILITY TO BE INDEPENDENT AND GOAL-DIRECTED

A recurrent theme across these chapters has been that students need to work if they are to learn: they need to be aware of the goals of learning (that is, what an *excellent performance* looks like), and they need to direct their attention towards that. They also need to know which strategies for learning are effective and they need to choose the appropriate strategy from a menu of options which includes techniques like deliberate practice, interleaved practice, spaced practice, retrieval practice, summarising, or organising. When they make mistakes they need to recognise this and fix it. If their motivation declines, they need to find ways to motivate themselves. All of this implies that students need to become able to *manage* their own learning if they are to learn effectively. This idea is one that emerges clearly from all of the reviews of evidence on student learning. In the words of the American Psychological Association, successful learners are "active, goal-directed, self-regulating, and assume personal responsibility for contributing to their own learning" (Lambert and McCombs 1997, 16). This kind of *thinking about thinking* has been repeatedly referenced in this text since Chapter 3. It is known as *metacognition*.

Metacognition includes both knowledge and skills. The *knowledge* component of metacognition refers to what people know about how people think and learn, and about what kinds of thinking are suited to different kinds of tasks. The skills component involves the ability to plan for learning, to monitor their own learning, and to debug when particular strategies for problem solving or learning do not work (Flavell 1999). There is a good deal of evidence that teaching students about metacognition can have a positive impact on learning (Donker et al. 2014). John Hattie and Gregory Donoghue (2016) describe students with heightened metacognitive knowledge and skills as being like their own personal teacher: they knew what it was that they wanted to achieve and they had a repertoire of learning strategies which could be used to achieve that goal: "these students know the what, when, who, where and why of learning, and the how, when and why to use which learning strategies. They know what to do when they do not know what to do" (2016, 3).

Metacognition is important in part because it is not a *innate* attribute of a person – it is something that can be taught and learned. For example, Manita van der Stel and Marcel Veenman (2010) found that students could learn to plan and self-evaluate their learning and that this had an impact upon their performance, independent of their measured intelligence. This finding fits well with the broader data: John Hattie reports on meta-analyses of learning involving 63 studies and over 5,000 participants. These studies tend to show that teaching students to think about what strategy they will use to understand material and solve problems has a strong positive impact on students' attainment (Hattie 2009, 188–189).

> **REFLECTION POINT 9.4**
>
> Do you make the goals of each learning experience clear to students, so that they can plan and monitor their own learning?
> Are there opportunities when starting a task for students to plan how they will approach it, and opportunities afterwards for students to reflect upon how they have managed it? Are these built into the learning (or are students simply left to do this themselves, recognising that many students will not spontaneously do so)?
> Are there periodic opportunities for students to evaluate *how well* they are learning, as well as evaluating *what* they are learning?

LEARNING INVOLVES THE MIND, THE EMOTIONS, AND THE BODY OF THE LEARNER

The picture of learning presented so far in this chapter is of a student engaging in cognitive and physical work as a result of being motivated to do so by a belief that the goal is valuable and that they can achieve that goal. As a description of processes, this image is probably accurate. On the other hand, it also does not sound like much fun. And yet, it is important to consider the role that enjoyment and other emotions play in learning. Recent developments in neuroscience, psychology, and social sciences highlight that humans are fundamentally emotional creatures, and that emotional processes are integrally linked to learning and thinking (Immordino-Yang and Damasio 2007). It is not just when students are acquiring new abilities that emotions matter; emotions also have a role in many of the skills developed by experiential learning. As Chapter 2 noted, expertise across a wide variety of domains also involves experiencing, using, and regulating emotions, and this is true even of disciplines which imagine themselves to be *rational* (such as natural sciences, engineering, or mathematics – for example, see Andrews Wiles' description of being stuck in Chapter 2). Emotions, therefore, are central to the kinds of expertise that higher education seeks to develop in learners, as well as being central to the process through which they develop that expertise.

While an emotional state like interest will play a role in directing learners' attention, and while positive emotions associated with satisfaction and achievement can play a motivational role in encouraging learners to work, other emotions can play a more destructive role in relation to learning. Emotions like fear or anxiety, for example, are associated with a *fight-or-flight* response that directs the brain's resources away from attending to learning goals. The centrality of teacher–student relationships to learning was discussed in Chapter 7. Jeffery Cornelius-White (2007) found that relationship variables related to emotions, such as empathy and warmth, were amongst those most strongly associated with student outcomes. This finding is further supported by a separate meta-analysis undertaken by Debora Roorda and colleagues (2011) which focused specifically on emotional dimensions of student–teacher relationships and which also found substantial associations between teacher–student relationships and both student engagement and achievement. Although studies in higher education were not included by Roorda et al. in their review, they did find "the effect sizes were larger in studies conducted in higher grades" (2001, 513). It is probably not surprising then that the National Academies of Sciences, Engineering, and Medicine have identified that one of the key strategies for improving learning is establishing emotionally supportive environments (2018, 133).

There is also evidence that interventions aimed to reduce student anxiety have a positive impact on learning. John Hattie and Gregory Donoghue (2016), for example, summarise data from almost 250 studies which show, on average, a notable positive effect on learning from efforts to reduce student anxiety. Typically, such strategies are not aimed at reducing the level of stress *per se* but rather at improving the students' ability to manage and cope with stress through coming to see mistakes as a normal part of the process of learning, to ask for support when needed, to improve their self-efficacy beliefs, or to learn about and manage their own emotional processes. This is illustrated in Spotlight 2.2 which looks at how student teachers in practice placements benefit from using techniques to regulate their emotions.

Emotional responses are in part bodily responses: emotions such as fear, anxiety, or excitement involve physiological responses such as changes in patterns of blood flow, as well as the release of different hormones. The body can also impact on learning in other ways. Tiredness, especially mental fatigue, has a negative impact upon a person's ability to pay attention to what they are doing and on their ability to organise cognitive tasks. As a consequence, people who are mentally tired are likely to experience greater learning difficulties and are less likely to spot errors in their work. When beginning a new task (such as switching from studying one subject to another), tired people prepare for the new task less well than rested people (Boksem et al. 2006). People who have had shortened sleep over a number of nights have been found to be slower in completing cognitive tasks and pay less attention to the tasks (and, consequently, have a greater risk of mistakes) than those who are well rested. Where people have been deprived of sleep for periods of 24 hours or more, they have been found to have poorer attention, reduced ability to recall things, and poorer ability to manage their thinking process (Alhola and Polo-Kantola 2007). One study, for example, found that 36 hours of sleep deprivation resulted in a 40% loss in the ability to form new memories (Walker 2006). Students in field settings or on practice placement can end up *pulling an all-nighter* as they prepare their next day's work. Likewise, students working on projects as the deadline looms may also end up losing sleep. These students are likely to suffer a negative impact on learning in two ways: difficulties in directing their attention during the practical learning activity means they are less likely to learn what they need to learn from the task, while, in parallel, their reduced ability to organise cognitive tasks and to plan is likely to impact on their performance on the task. Working while tired is not a productive strategy for students in experiential learning environments.

In addition to reducing tiredness, sleep also plays a more direct role in learning. There is evidence that sleep plays a role in helping people to form long-term memories, specifically that the strengthening of the neural links that encode a memory within the brain happens during sleep. This appears to be true both of motor memories (memories for physical tasks) and cognitive memories. The activation of the brain region called the hippocampus during sleep also seems to play a role in integrating new information with existing memories in ways that allow learners to abstract patterns from specific episodes (National Academies of Sciences, Engineering, and Medicine 2018, 87). Adequate sleep when learning is, therefore, likely to be important. It is worthwhile noting therefore that it appears people are now sleeping a good deal less than was the case only 50 years ago: adults are averaging 1 to 2 hours less daily sleep than in the mid-20th century (National Academies of Sciences, Engineering, and Medicine 2018, 31).

What we consume can also affect our sleep and our ability to direct our attention. While caffeine can have a negative impact on sleep, small or moderate amounts of caffeine may have a positive impact on attention and cognitive performance. On the other hand, researchers have also identified that some so-called *energy drinks* contain high and unregulated amounts of caffeine, as well as other ingredients that have not been subject to rigorous testing. Higher doses of caffeine are associated with increased anxiety, palpitations, and stomach problem, while caffeine overdoses can cause serious health problems – almost 5,500 caffeine overdoses were reported in the US alone in 2007 (Seifert et al. 2011). While many students use caffeine to manage the way their body influences their attention and learning, this strategy is not without its risks.

In addition to *self-medication* with caffeine, there are also various claims made about the effects of drugs, herbal remedies, and specific types of food to enhance either sleep or mental performance. One recent Swiss study found that about 6% of students had taken either prescription drugs or illegal drugs in order to improve their own cognitive performance while studying (Maier et al. 2013). Such *self-medication* is typically based on word of mouth and anecdotal evidence rather than on rigorous medical research evidence. Indeed, Maier et al. found that many of the students surveyed who had used such drugs found that they did not fulfil their learning expectations (2013, 6).

Another way in which the body can impact upon learning is through the role of exercise. Indeed physical exercise has been found to be associated with improvements in cognitive performance as well as in concentration (National Academies of Sciences, Engineering, and Medicine 2018, 87). John Hattie and Gregory Donoghue (2016, 6) found through their review of evidence that exercise had, on average, a small but positive impact on measured learning.

> **REFLECTION POINT 9.5**
>
> Are practical learning activities in your discipline organised to reduce the risk of students having a very heavy workload at particular times with little chance to reflect upon or make sense of their experiences?
>
> Does the culture of your discipline systematically promote or reward those who fail to get adequate rest or who self-medicate using caffeine or other substances?

CONCLUSION

Although learning is principally dependent upon what the learner does, these learning activities are enabled or constrained by bodily, emotional, and social processes. Effective learning requires that learners and teachers also pay attention to these dimensions. Key issues to emerge from research on these contexts of learning are that learning happens best when:

RESEARCH ABOUT THE CONTEXTS OF LEARNING

- The goals of learning are clear and are seen as useful or important to the learner.
- The learner manages their own learning, planning, managing, debugging, and reviewing how they are learning and making changes to their approach if appropriate.
- The learner feels emotionally secure to try things, make mistakes, and try again without fear of being ridiculed or aggressed.
- The learner feels that they, and people like them, belong and can achieve in their programme.
- The learner can work with peers to think about and practice new and challenging ideas or skills.
- The teacher clearly models to the student the ways of thinking of their discipline.
- The learner gets adequate rest and maintains a level of physical fitness.

These findings have a number of implications which have influenced the structure and organisation of this book. Some of the most important of these ideas are:

- As discussed in Chapter 6, when making presentations:
    - being clear with students about learning objectives can aid students' motivation,
    - a lead-in that makes the utility of the material clear can also aid motivation,
    - making explicit the way of thinking of the discipline can provide students with a model to follow.
- As discussed in Chapter 7, managing the class can aid learning through:
    - providing an emotionally safe environment within which everyone can learn,
    - preventing negative interactions between students that may reduce the learning of everyone involved,
    - promoting student interactions which can enable learning of complex concepts and skills.
- As discussed in Chapter 5, feedback plays an important role:
    - in developing students' sense of self-efficacy by clarifying what has been achieved as well as clarifying areas on which to work,
    - in helping students to develop metacognitive skills by encouraging planning how they will improve after feedback.

PART III

The approaches recommended in this book are, then, based not just on the authors' combined decades of teaching experience, but also on the research evidence about learning. The strategies proposed in this book for asking questions, giving feedback, making presentations, and managing classrooms interactions are evidence-informed. Hence there is good reason to think that teachers who follow these strategies will contribute to significantly improving the learning of their students. The next, and final, chapter presents strategies for digesting and applying the ideas from this book in your own teaching practice.

FURTHER READING

This small number of sources is intended to provide further useful information for those who wish to explore the chapter topic in more detail. A full reference list for the chapter is provided below.

Student teams and groupwork

Cohen, E.G., and Lotan, R.A. (2014). *Designing Groupwork: Strategies for the Heterogeneous Classroom*, 3rd edition. New York: Teachers College Press.

Isaac, S. (2018). Supporting Project teams: How do students learn team skills? [video]. *SwitchTube*. https://tube.switch.ch/download/video/344430f1.

Inclusion and equity

Gervais, S.J. (2013). Speak up or stay silent? 5 Reasons to confront prejudice. *Psychology Today* https://www.psychologytoday.com/us/blog/power-and-prejudice/201311/speak-or-stay-silent-5-reasons-confront-prejudice.

Sociocultural factors and structure of learning environments

National Academies of Sciences, Engineering, and Medicine (2018). *How People Learn II: Learners, Contexts, and Cultures*. Washington, DC: National Academy Press. https://doi.org/10.17226/24783.

REFERENCES

Alhola, P., and Polo-Kantola, P. (2007). Sleep deprivation: Impact on cognitive performance. *Neuropsychiatric Disease and Treatment* 3(5): 553–567.

Ambrose, S.A., Bridges, M.W., Di Pietro, M., Lovett, M.C., and Norman, M.K. (2010). *How Learning Works, 7 Research-Based Principles for Smart Teaching*. San Francisco: Jossey Bass.

Aronson, J., Fried, C.B., and Good, C. (2002). Reducing the effects of stereotype threat on African American college students by shaping theories of intelligence. *Journal of Experimental Social Psychology* 38(2): 113–125. https://doi.org/10.1006/jesp.2001.1491.

Bandura, A. (1977). Self-efficacy: Toward a unifying theory of behavioral change. *Psychological Review* 84(2): 191–215. https://doi.org/10.1037/0033-295X.84.2.191.

Beasley, M.A., and Fischer, M.J. (2012). Why they leave: The impact of stereotype threat on the attrition of women and minorities from science, math and engineering majors. *Social Psychology of Education* 15(4): 427–448. https://doi.org/10.1007/s11218-012-9185-3.

Boksem, M.A., Meijman, T.F., and Lorist, M.M. (2006). Mental fatigue, motivation and action monitoring. *Biological Psychology* 72(2): 123–132. https://doi.org/10.1016/j.biopsycho.2005.08.007.

Bransford, J.D., Brown, A.L., and Cocking, R. (Eds) (2000). *How People Learn; Brain, Mind, Experience, and School*. Washington, DC: National Academy Press.

Collins, A., Brown, J.S., and Newman, S.E. (1989). Cognitive apprenticeship: Teaching the craft of reading, writing, and mathematics. In: L.B. Resnick (Ed.), *Knowing, Learning, and Instruction*. London: Routledge. https://doi.org/10.5840/thinking19888129.

Cornelius-White, J. (2007). Learner-centered teacher-student relationships are effective: A meta-analysis. *Review of Educational Research* 77(1): 113–143. https://doi.org/10.3102/003465430298563.

Cotton, D.R.E. (2009). Field biology experiences of undergraduate students: The impact of novelty space. *Journal of Biological Education* 43(4): 169–174. https://doi.org/10.1080/00219266.2009.9656178.

Dillenbourg, P., and Bétrancourt, M. (2006). Collaboration load. In: J. Elen and R.E. Clark (Eds.), *Handling Complexity in Learning Environments: Research and Theory* (pp. 142–163). Advances in Learning and Instruction Series. Pergamon. http://www.elsevier.com/inca/707901, https://www.researchgate.net/publication/32231094_Collaboration_Load, https://telearn.archives-ouvertes.fr/file/index/docid/190700/filename/Dillernbourg-Pierre-2006b.pdf.

Dillenbourg, P., and Jermann, P. (2010). Technology for classroom orchestration. In: M.S. Khine and I.M. Saleh (Eds.), *New Science of Learning* (pp. 525–552). New York: Springer.

Dillenbourg, P., and Schneider, B. (1995). Mediating the mechanisms which make collaborative learning sometimes effective. *International Journal of Educational Telecommunications* 1(2–3): 131–146.

Donker, A.S., de Boer, H., Kostons, D., Dignath van Ewijk, C.C., and van der Werf, M.P.C. (2014). Effectiveness of learning strategy instruction on academic performance: A meta-analysis. *Educational Research Review* 11: 1–26. https://doi.org/10.1016/j.edurev.2013.11.002.

Flavell, J. (1999). Cognitive development: Children's knowledge about the mind. *Annual Review of Psychology* 50: 21–45. https://doi.org/10.1146/annurev.psych.50.1.21.

PART III

Hattie, J. (2009). *Visible Learning, A Synthesis of Over 800 Meta-Analyses Relating to Achievement*. London: Routledge.

Hattie, J., and Donoghue, G. (2016). Learning strategies: A synthesis and conceptual model. *npj Science of Learning* 1: 16013. https://doi.org/10.1038/npjscilearn.2016.13.

Hulleman, C.S., Durik, A.M., Schweigert, S., and Harackiewicz, J.M. (2008). Task values, achievement goals, and interest: An Integrative analysis. *Journal of Educational Psychology* 100(2): 398–416. https://doi.org/10.1037/0022-0663.100.2.398.

Immordino-Yang, M.H., and Damasio, A. (2007). We feel, therefore we learn: The relevance of affective and social neuroscience to education. *Mind, Brain, and Education* 1(1): 3–10. https://doi.org/10.1111/j.1751-228X.2007.00004.x.

Kirschner, F., Paas, F., Kirschner, P.A., and Janssen, J. (2011). Differential effects of problem-solving demands on individual and collaborative learning outcomes. *Learning and Instruction* 21(4): 587–599. https://doi.org/10.1016/j.learninstruc.2011.01.001.

Lambert, N.M., and McCombs, B.L. (Eds.) (1997). *How Students Learn: Reforming Schools through Learner-Centered Education*. American Psychological Association. https://doi.org/10.1037/10258-000.

Maier, L.J., Liechti, M.E., Herzig, F., and Schaub, M.P. (2013). To dope or not to dope: Neuroenhancement with prescription drugs and drugs of abuse among Swiss university students. *PLOS ONE* 8(11): e77967. https://doi.org/10.1371/journal.pone.0077967. PMID: 24236008. PMCID: PMC3827185.

Mazur, E. (1997). *Peer Instruction: A Users Manual*. New York: Pearson Education.

Menekse, M., Stump, G.S., Krause, S., and Chi, M.T.H. (2013). Differentiated overt learning activities for effective instruction in engineering classrooms. *Journal of Engineering Education* 102(3): 346–374. https://doi.org/10.1002/jee.20021.

National Academies of Sciences, Engineering, and Medicine (2018). *How People Learn II: Learners, Contexts, and Cultures*. Washington, DC: National Academy Press. https://doi.org/10.17226/24783.

Pintrich, P. (2000). Multiple goals, multiple pathways: The role of goal orientation in learning and achievement. *Journal of Educational Psychology* 92(3): 544–555. https://doi.org/10.1037/0022-0663.92.3.544.

Rivière, J.-P., Alaoui, S.F., Caramiaux, B., and Mackay, W. (2018). How Do Dancers Learn To Dance?: A first-person perspective of dance acquisition by expert contemporary dancers. In: MOCO 2018: 5th International Conference on Movement and Computing (pp.1–8), June 2018, Genoa, Italy. https://doi.org/10.1145/3212721.3212723.

Roorda, D.L., Koomen, H.M.Y., Spilt, J.L., and Oort, F.J. (2011). The influence of affective teacher–student relationships on students' school engagement and achievement: A meta-analytic approach. *Review of Educational Research* 81(4): 493–529. https://doi.org/10.3102/0034654311421793.

Schwendimann, B., Alberto, A., Cattaneo, A.P., Dehler Zufferey, J., Gurtner, J.-L., Bétrancourt, M.,. and Dillenbourg, P. (2015). The 'Erfahrraum': A pedagogical model for designing educational technologies in dual vocational systems. *Journal of Vocational Education and Training* 67(3): 367–396. https://doi.org/10.1080/13636820.2015.1061041.

Seifert, S.M., Schaechter, J.L., Hershorin, E.R., and Lipshultz, S.E. (2011). Health effects of energy drinks on children, adolescents, and young adults. *Pediatrics* 127(3): 511–528. https://doi.org/10.1542/peds.2009-3592.

Steele, C.M., Spencer, S.J., and Aronson, J. (2002). Contending with group image: The psychology of stereotype and social identity threat. In: M.P. Zanna (Ed.), *Advances in Experimental Social Psychology* (vol. 34, pp. 379–440). Cambridge, MA: Academic Press. https://doi.org/10.1016/S0065-2601(02)80009-0.

van der Stel, M., and Veenman, M.V.J. (2010). Development of metacognitive skillfulness: A longitudinal study. *Learning and Individual Differences* 20(3): 220–224. https://doi.org/10.1016/j.lindif.2009.11.005.

Walker, M. (2006). Sleep to Remember: The brain needs sleep before and after learning new things, regardless of the type of memory. Naps can help, but caffeine isn't an effective substitute. *American Scientist* 94(4): 326–333. http://www.jstor.org/stable/27858801.

Walton, G.M., and Cohen, G.L. (2011). A brief social-belonging intervention improves academic and health outcomes of minority students. *Science* 331(6023): 1457–1451. https://doi.org/10.1126/science.1198364.

Wieman, C. (2007). The "Curse of Knowledge," or why intuition about teaching often fails. *APS News* 16(10): 8.

Zimmerman, B.J. (2000). Self-efficacy: An essential motive to learn. *Contemporary Educational Psychology* 25(1): 82–91. https://doi.org/10.1006/ceps.1999.1016.

Chapter 10

Becoming a better teacher for practical settings

INTRODUCTION

Up to this point, this book has been concerned with one part of your role in practical settings: that of teacher. As a teacher in a practical setting, your interest is in how you can set students on the path to developing the ways of perceiving, thinking, acting, and feeling which are characteristic of expertise in your discipline. But it is probably reasonable to presume that the reason you are reading this book in the first place is that you also see yourself as having a second role in practical settings: that of learner. As a teacher, you are also a learner who is working to develop in yourself expertise in teaching. This chapter aims to help you take some of the ideas about helping students develop expertise which were explored in previous chapters and to apply them to your own development of teaching expertise.

As outlined in Chapter 2, developing expertise in hand-on skills like teaching typically requires many years of deliberate practice in an expert community, which is to say:

- practicing the skills of the discipline that you cannot already perform and constantly moving out of your comfort zone,
- monitoring your performance and getting feedback which helps you to improve,
- taking opportunities to repeat doing the skill correctly (because "practice doesn't make perfect; perfect practice makes perfect" [McFarlane Mirande 2005, 17]),
- developing productive ways of thinking, acting, and feeling, through interaction with other members of an expert community.

It is important to note that learning to teach by teaching is somewhat different than other kinds of learning in practical settings because, while the teacher in a practical setting will often simplify the representative tasks that the students are given, or will have students *walk through it* a number of times before asking them to perform the task in realistic settings, normally no one simplifies the task for the teacher to allow her or him to learn new things. Expertise researchers make a clear distinction between high-stakes *performance* settings (in which it is hard to learn and develop) and low-stakes *practice* settings (in which learning and development are easier because one can try, get feedback, and try again). But higher education teachers typically have to practice *while performing*, and need to try to improve in the full glare of their students' gaze and when the stakes (for learners and sometimes for teachers) can be quite high.

Chapter 2 also noted that teaching is different from other kinds of disciplines because novice teachers have considerable experience of learning situations before they begin teaching. Indeed they have spent well over 10,000 hours as students in classrooms watching teachers teach before they begin their first lesson, all the time developing deeply held assumptions about how teachers should act, sound, and behave. In his classic study of teaching, Dan Lorti (1975) calls this long experience an *apprenticeship of observation* (in Chapter 2 it was referred to as *pseudo-expertise* [Stigler and Miller 2018]). This prior experience, if left unexamined, can continue to impact on the practice of even very experienced teachers. In order to make significant progress towards expertise as a teacher, it needs to be analysed and processed. Indeed, this apprenticeship of observation has been proposed as a key reason why teaching practices have changed so little over the past decades despite significant advances in learning sciences.

So, given these two very specific constraints of learning to teach by teaching, what sort of approaches can a teacher use to develop their practice? In Chapter 3 the experiential learning cycle model was introduced (Kolb 1984). This model proposed that people learn from experience when they can:

- *experience*: be open to fully experience, without bias, their actual experience,
- *reflect*: observe and think about this experience from different perspectives,
- *generalise*: see regularities in these experiences and link them to sound concepts and theories,
- *test*: use these concepts and theories to make decisions and solve problems in the real world.

In this chapter, we describe an approach to doing this which was developed with teaching in mind, taking into account the specific opportunities and constraints of being a practicing teacher: the *critically reflective practice* model of Stephen

Brookfield (1995). Brookfield's model involves investigating our teaching from four perspectives: our own experience, the perspectives of our students, our peers, and the literature of teaching and learning. These lenses can help us to be fully open to our experience, to look at our teaching from different perspectives, to link our practice to sound concepts and theories, and to use this to make decisions about how to proceed (Kolb 1984). In line with the idea of deliberate practice, these lenses also provide us with opportunities to get feedback on and improve our performance, in the context of a community of teachers.

Brookfield's model is only one of a number of possible approaches that have been developed to help teachers develop their practice. Alternatives include, for example, the ALACT model developed by the renowned teacher educator Fred Korthagen (Korthagen and Vasalos 2005), which has been used by Ingrid Le Duc and colleagues in their work on professional development with architecture teachers (Le Duc et al. 2020). While we find inspiration in Brookfield's approach, what is more important than the specific model applied is that you use a structured approach to building expertise through feedback, engagement with peers, and with sound concepts and ideas.

The next section describes some ways of thinking about the process of developing towards expertise in teaching in higher education. The following section describes the overall goal and approach of Brookfield's *critically reflective practice* model. Subsequent sections will then focus on each of the four lenses before a final section which will address how to turn this into action.

DEVELOPING AS A TEACHER IN HIGHER EDUCATION

Chapter 2 described a way of thinking about the journey from novice to expertise, taking nursing as an example. The journey from novice to expert higher education teacher could be described in a similar way. Given the specificities of higher education teaching, however, it is probably not a surprise that there are a number of other ways of describing the development of teachers in higher education. In the UK, for example, the Advance HE fellowship model (https://www.advance-he.ac.uk/fellowship) distinguishes between:

- Associate Fellow, which involves some knowledge of specific aspects of effective teaching as well as some teaching responsibilities,
- Fellow, which involves broad-based effectiveness in substantial teaching roles and a broad understanding of effective teaching,
- Senior Fellow, which implies making a key contribution to high-quality student learning, as well as having an impact on colleagues,

- Principal Fellow, which implies a sustained record of effective strategic leadership in teaching.

As well as providing a model of development towards expertise, the Advance HE framework also can play a role in allowing teachers to document their expertise and thus can contribute to career advancement.

Another model for thinking about the pathway towards expertise in higher education, the Career Framework for University Teaching, was recently developed by a global consortium of research-intensive universities supported by the Royal Academy of Engineering (Graham 2018). The development of the Framework was based on a review of research as well as on interviews with international experts and a survey of higher education teachers. The Framework aims to provide a clear account of what progression towards teaching expertise looks like across a wide variety of academic disciplines in higher education, as well as providing teachers with examples and models as to how they can gather evidence which would allow them to both develop and document their abilities.

One feature of the Framework, presented in Figure 10.1, is that it identifies that higher education teachers may take different pathways towards expertise:

- Level 1: the effective teacher who takes a conscientious and reflective approach to supporting student learning,

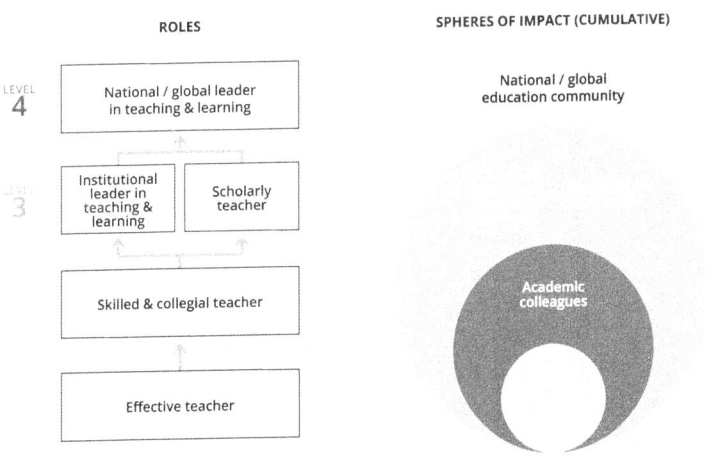

FIGURE 10.1 The Career Framework and teachers' spheres of impact
(Graham 2018 and the Royal Academy of Engineering)

- Level 2: the skilled and collegial teacher who takes an evidence-informed approach and provides mentorship and guidance to colleagues as part of an educational community,
- Level 3a: the institutional leader in teaching and learning who makes a significant contribution to teaching and learning in their institution,
- Level 3b: the scholarly teacher who makes a significant contribution to pedagogical knowledge through engagement in pedagogical research which influences teaching and learning,
- Level 4: the national and international leader in teaching and learning.

The Career Framework project has continued to evolve into an ongoing and growing international network which is developing a broad-based approach to supporting teaching quality in international higher education (https://www.advancingteaching.com/). One particularly valuable aspect of the Framework project has been the development of a range of examples of how teachers can use self-assessment, evidence of student learning, and peer feedback to gather evidence on their teaching practices (https://www.teachingframework.com/framework/evidence/).

> **REFLECTION POINT 10.1**
>
> Where do you place yourself on the trajectory towards an expert teacher in your discipline? To answer this question, it may be useful to review the section "The journey towards expertise" and Case study 2.3 in Chapter 2 (you can use the Career Framework model described above should you wish). What does your current position mean about the teaching skills that should be your focus right now?

Our approach to teaching and to improving as a teacher is often something that teachers are asked to document for hiring or promotion decisions. It is difficult to provide recommendations on how to document teaching practices because there is no clear agreement on how to assess good teaching. This is different from research output, where clear metrics exist despite debate about their value and utility. The lack of cohesion of how to document good teaching is part of what motivated Graham's project with the Royal Academy of Engineering. Four forms of evidence (self-assessment, professional activities, student learning, and peer evaluation) are presented as part of the framework (https://www.teachingframework.com/framework/evidence/), and several are illustrated with case studies. Examples presented on the website include using feedback from former students, contributions to departmental or university-wide pedagogical initiatives, and an extensive section on direct and indirect measures of student learning. Given that each institution has its own human resources procedures and different disciplines are more familiar with different kinds of evidence, it is essential to adapt to the expectations of the department that will be evaluating your dossier.

CRITICALLY REFLECTIVE PRACTICE TO IMPROVE TEACHING

A key idea of this chapter is that one can progress from novice toward competence and expertise in higher education teaching through adopting a critically reflective practice approach. So what makes practice *critically reflective*? The words *critical reflection* often occur in common usage with various meanings, so defining the term precisely will help to prevent misunderstandings (Hammersley-Fletcher and Orsmond 2005). It is worth starting by considering each of the two terms, *reflection* and *critical*.

It is no doubt very evident by now that reflection is central to how people learn from practice. However we noted in Chapter 3 that students are often unclear about what it means to reflect, and we suggested, at that time, that it was possible that the same is true of many teachers. *Reflection* refers to serious thought or consideration and includes thinking that makes "sense of experience in relation to self, others and contextual conditions" (Ryan 2013, 145). A key feature of reflection is that it involves *serious thought* and *sense making*. Having a think about what happened in class while driving home and listening to the radio is not, therefore, reflection in the sense that the term is used here. Reflection involves spending some time and engaging in some structured process to ensure that your consideration is serious.

The term *critical* is also widely used in everyday speech and has a number of different meanings. One common meaning ascribed to the term refers to expressing negative judgements, disapproval, or being exclusively focused on problems. That is not what the term critical is intended to mean in this context. The second meaning of the term refers to the use of an analytical or reasoned approach to arrive at careful judgement or evaluation. This sense of the term is closer to how *critical* is meant here. The term *critical* also implies moving beyond a focus on superficial thinking about teaching (like making the decision about using a blackboard or slides based on your feelings or the stated preferences of students), to trying to evaluate the *deeper* reasons behind these decisions (such as recognising that "I prefer when they don't have slides because they focus on me and I don't feel ignored" may not be a great basis for making such a decision). Superficial thinking about a *nuts and bolts* teaching issue is, therefore, not *critical reflection*.

In particular, Brookfield highlights that power is central to teaching and learning (an idea which we explored in Chapter 7). He argues that critical reflection must seek to understand how power frames and influences interactions in education (social scientists will recognise the influence of the Frankfurt School's critical theory in this approach). Taking power seriously in our classes means making sure we hear from those who may not be otherwise heard from, and Brookfield's approach involves creating opportunities for student voices to contribute to our reflection. As we have discussed in Chapters 5, 7, and 9, implicit biases about particular social groups may also contribute to negative experiences for some students and, indeed, some teachers. Drawing on research literature in this area is therefore also a relevant part of the approach.

Central to the critical reflection approach, then, is the idea that some of our practices as teachers may be driven or supported by ideas, implicit beliefs, or assumptions about our discipline, about learners, or about teaching which are derived from our wider socialisation, our apprenticeship of observation, or from our prior experiences. Part of developing our teaching requires subjecting these ideas or assumptions to serious thought, careful judgement, and evaluation. Brookfield describes critically reflective practice as "a process of inquiry involving practitioners in trying to discover, and research, the assumptions that frame how they work" (1998, 197). Becoming aware of our assumptions is a difficult task, because our assumptions work as filters that influence what we see and the meanings we attribute to what it is that we do see. We can draw an analogy here with the way scientific research works; because humans have a tendency to see information which confirms their prior assumptions and hypotheses, the scientific method is designed to require scientists to look for counterfactual evidence which questions their prior assumptions before reaching judgements. Brookfield's approach is designed to do something similar for teachers; to provide a structured method which requires them to recognise and question their own assumptions before making decisions.

As we noted above, the experiential learning model suggests that, in the *reflect* phase, we learn when we think about our experiences from different perspectives. Brookfield uses the analogy of lenses to illustrate how, when we consider a situation from a different point of view, different parts of the picture become visible to us. You may be familiar with the idea that by using ultra-violet or infra-red filters, for example, photographers can change the light which enters the lens and thereby capture some aspects of an image more or less clearly (using ultra-violet light to allow detectives to see things in crime scenes that are not visible to the naked eye is a common feature of crime movies and TV shows). The analogy of a lens is employed in a similar way here: by looking at a situation through a different lens, it allows you to see something different to what you might see with the naked eye (i.e. your own assumptions).

Brookfield recommends employing four *lenses* (or perspectives) to look at our teaching:

- our own perspective,
- our students' perspectives,
- our peers' perspectives,
- perspectives from literature.

Using multiple lenses increases the range of things that we see in our teaching, allowing us to become more aware of how our own assumptions and biases may be influencing what we see and how we interpret it. The different lenses are important for illuminating different aspects of your teaching and of students' learning. If you rely too heavily on self-reflection, you may overlook the experiences of your students who live and study in a context that is very different from yours. If you rely too much on your students' experience, you may be limited by their naïve perspective of the discipline and of learning. It is only by juxtaposing different lenses that a more nuanced picture of teaching starts to emerge.

SPOTLIGHT 10.1 – DELAYED ALIGNMENT OF TEACHING INTENTIONS AND ACTIONS

While pursuing graduate studies in chemistry, Siara (one of the authors of this book) participated in a few teaching development workshops and felt that she had embraced the importance of active learning in exercise sessions. Siara had received lots of positive feedback about her teaching – the professors were pleased that she was well prepared and organised, students said that she gave clear and detailed explanations, and a good class dynamic meant that there was always someone ready to volunteer an answer to her frequent questions.

However, a reflection activity during a course in the faculty of education caused her to recall an experience from her first-year physics class. A few days before the midterm exam, the physics professor helped students prepare by demonstrating how to solve each problem from the previous year's midterm exam. There were about 500 students in the lecture hall, all watching and carefully copying down the professor's work, when he admonished them to pay careful attention. He recounted that he had made a mistake the previous year when, rather than taking a previous year's exam to solve in front of the class, he had actually mistakenly solved the exam the students were to take a few days later. Since the professor only discovered this on the night of the exam, and with 1,200 students distributed across campus, he could do nothing about it. So the students ended up taking the exam he had solved for them only days previously. The professor told the class, with hilarity, that their grades were nevertheless pretty average and that we should be more attentive than they were. It was a funny story as a first-year student.

Later, as a teaching assistant responsible for the first-year chemistry exercise sessions, Siara realised that by promoting passive learning in her own teaching she was replicating the same failed experiment. Each week, she carefully demonstrated to students how to solve the assigned problems, asking students to contribute occasionally, while students took diligent notes. Siara was replicating what she had internalised from her experience as a student and neglecting what she had learned about active learning and effective teaching in the various workshops and courses. This lag between a teacher developing their thinking about teaching and actually enacting coherent strategies has been identified as a recurrent issue (Norton et al. 2013). The reflective exercise prompted Siara to recognise the mismatch between her ideas about good teaching and what she was actually doing. This became an important motivation for her to actually change.

Each of Brookfield's four perspectives will be explored in the following sections, with specific attention to how to engage in critical reflection about teaching in practical settings.

LENS 1: THE AUTOBIOGRAPHICAL PERSPECTIVE

The first of Brookfield's lenses is the autobiographical lens. As we have noted a number of times, teachers have a lot of experiences of teaching to draw on before they ever teach a class. These can have a major influence on the kinds of practices, and beliefs, teachers develop. In many disciplines, practitioners are encouraged to start by first learning the theory of the discipline before putting it into practice. But a teacher's understanding of teaching, on the contrary, normally starts with experience. As David Kolb noted, the first relevant skill in learning from experience is to be open to fully experience, without bias, what actually happens. Our experiences are not simply the stories we can recount. Our experiences of teaching are often felt in an emotional, visceral way. These deeply felt experiences will often have a more powerful and long-lasting influence on us than the results of a research study which we have read.

There are two angles to our autobiographical perspective: as a learner and as a teacher.

- Our experiences as a learner can include models of what teaching looks like in our discipline, but also our ideas about what it feels like to be a learner. A teacher who remembers fighting back tears and frustration as they tried to get an answer right in school will often think about teaching and learning differently than a teacher who has largely experienced being one of the most competent in their class, for example.
- Our experiences as a teacher (the classes we felt went well and those which we feel left a scar) can also deeply affect our assumptions and beliefs about teaching and learning.

Exploring these two aspects of your own perspective can help you clarify how your mental models of competent teachers, or a well-run class, contribute to the assumptions that guide your teaching. Brookfield argues that if we do not explore the role of our personal experience in how we teach, these experiences will continue to exert an unexamined influence on our teaching and potentially prevent us from enacting teaching practices that are coherent with our intentions. While you are probably not often a student, it is useful to reflect on your experiences in situations where someone else is leading the group. For instance, listening to keynote speakers at conferences, taking ski lessons, or following cooking class are all interesting opportunities to explore how you respond to different teaching approaches. Reflection point 10.2 provides a few questions to organise your reflections about participating as a learner or audience member.

> **REFLECTION POINT 10.2**
>
> Next time you are sitting in an audience, take a moment to note how engaged you feel and how comfortable you would be asking

questions. What makes you feel like the speaker is really addressing you? What makes you feel that your questions would be appreciated?

REFLECTION POINT 10.3

1. Think back to a course or a teacher that you particularly enjoyed as a student. What characteristics made this a positive learning experience for you?
2. What assumptions about teaching did you make based on these experiences? How could you check the validity of these assumptions?

Brookfield recommends that we leverage our experiences of trying to learn things that are particularly difficult or unfamiliar to us, and that we seek to identify the emotions and feelings that these experiences brought out in us. Brookfield stresses that situations where we struggled to learn can provide an important insight into teaching and learning. For Brookfield himself, this was swimming – and thinking about learning swimming was therefore a valuable way of understanding learning *from the inside* for him. For you, it might be something else, like navigating new software, achieving a fine emulsion in your salad dressing, or assembling flat pack furniture. Revisiting practical situations that were difficult for us as learners can be useful to reconnect with what it feels like to struggle, something that can be hard to see when we are comfortably navigating in our own discipline. This discomfort can help us identify points of surprise and therefore to hunt our assumptions about our teaching.

REFLECTION POINT 10.4

1. Did you complete the Reflection point activities in previous chapters? Why or why not? How did being asked to do these activities make you feel? How did having sample answers influence how you felt and undertook the activities?

> 2. How do your personal views, reflected in your responses to the questions above, influence how, when, and what tasks you assign to your students?

Having identified some of your own assumptions and implicit beliefs (that is, having *experienced*) using the autobiographical lens, the next stage in the process of critical reflection is to start to question those assumptions by thinking about your experience from different perspectives (that is, to *reflect*). To do this, you can draw on the perspectives of others around you: in particular students (lens 2) and peers (lens 3). The next section looks in more detail at gathering students' perspectives on your teaching.

LENS 2: STUDENTS' PERSPECTIVES

We noted in Chapter 7 that students' and teachers' perceptions of incivility in classes can differ significantly from each other. You may have seen this mutual misrecognition in other areas too: a teacher who ask questions instead of giving answers can be accused of not knowing the material well enough to provide answers, giving detailed feedback to help students learn can be interpreted as a tool for negotiating or contesting a grade, and an open-ended project statement which is designed to help students learn to scope a project can lead to a teacher being described by students as disorganised and unclear (these are all examples from our personal experiences).

Understanding how students interpret your course, then, provides valuable information. This section presents three types of student perspective data that we can collect from students in order to reflect on their experience, specifically:

- students' experiences of your teaching,
- students' reflections on their experience as learners,
- data on student learning.

Student evaluations of teaching, typically collected with questionnaires, are the most common type of feedback on teaching (European University Association 2015; Wieman 2015). While these evaluations tend to come late in the term and focus on macro-level experiences (i.e. was the course well organised?), surveys can be used any time during a course. For instance, the first session could conclude with asking students about the pace and the adequacy of their background knowledge. Before reading students' answers, take a moment to write down the response you expect students to give and then compare your perception with their experience.

The second angle on the student perspective involves students' experiences of their own learning. One way of collecting this information is to use reflective questions, like those reproduced in Figure 10.2, as writing prompts for students that will help you better understand what moments or activities made them feel particularly engaged, anxious, or surprised (and can also have the added benefit of helping them to develop metacognitive abilities by thinking about their own learning). We noted above that power is an integral part of the relationship between teacher and learners. While lots of leaders say they welcome criticism, this is not always borne out in how they behave when criticism is actually expressed. Even if you are incredibly open-minded about student feedback and welcome their implied or stated criticism with open arms, their prior experiences with other teachers may still mean that it feels risky to them to voice their opinions. Given that students' answers to these questions are intended to help you improve the course, you should collect their responses anonymously (for example, with an online questionnaire). Prefacing this activity with an explanation for students of your motivations and also how you will use their responses will likely encourage students to provide you with more relevant information.

It is important to remember that students are not all the same. Indeed, the possibilities for diverging student experiences are increasing as the population now participating in higher education broadens, and not all students

---

Dear student – The goal of this short questionnaire is to enable me to understand what it is like to participate in my course as a student. Please do not write your name – your anonymous answers will help me improve conditions for learning my course. Thank you for your participation.

When during the session did you feel most engaged?

When during the session did you feel most anxious or stressed?

What surprised you most about the session?

FIGURE 10.2 Brookfield's Student Experience Reflection Prompts
(Brookfield 1995)

will be seeking the same things from a course or bringing the same experiences to it. This means that we should anticipate diversity in our students' perspectives and think about what the spread of students' views or grades means about their experience. In practical terms, assigning a numerical scale to student responses (i.e. one to five) and calculating an average has the effect of reducing the full range of experiences to a single data point and, consequently, of hiding diversity. If you do ask questions with an ordered set of responses (such as *strongly agree*, *agree*, *disagree*, *strongly disagree*), it is more productive to represent this in terms of the percentages of the class who give each response (e.g. a bar chart) than as a single numerical summary (e.g. the mean average). The *average* student doesn't actually exist, and so a course that is designed entirely with this fictional character in mind, rather than with the variation of the actual student group, will fall short of its potential.

The final angle to explore your students' perspective on your teaching comes from what students have learned. Students' grades on their reports, practical exams, or placement reviews can each offer some insight into their learning. One important limitation for practical courses is that this data tends to be macro-level and may not be adequately focused on process skills. There may however be data you could collect during term which might give you a more fine-grained picture of students' learning. For example, the results to a polling question or an analysis of your comments on students' weekly lab reports may help you see obstacles to learning that were not immediately apparent. If there are process skills, or values, that are hard to observe on formal assessment tasks, teachers can employ a wider range of strategies to collect students' experiences, such as having students self-report on their confidence in their skills level. See Spotlight 10.2 for an example of how students' self-report on process skills was used to complement the information available to the teaching team about student learning. The Career Framework project also provides additional ideas as to how to gather data related to student experience: https://www.teachingframework.com/framework/evidence/.

SPOTLIGHT 10.2 – TEACHING MEASUREMENT TECHNIQUES IN INQUIRY-BASED LABS

One way of getting feedback from students is to ask them how confident they are about their ability to carry out the tasks and procedures which the course intends to teach. Dominique Pioletti and colleagues (2019) describe using this approach in designing a new biomechanics lab course for mechanical engineering students.

The lab was intended to teach a number of discipline-specific skills related to the mechanical behaviour of tissues and fluids. A review of the literature about labs led him to also explicitly identify the importance of students learning the skills of defining the problem, creating a research protocol, and determining what data to collect. These skills are often underdeveloped in lab courses where students are given protocols to follow, and these skills are not readily observable from the written reports that are typically used to grade students' experimental work.

Pioletti therefore designed a course that had students work in small groups, guided by a teaching assistant trained in teaching with question strategies (see Chapter 4), on lab assignments that consist of only two to three questions rather than a detailed protocol to follow (see Figure 10.3). To get more insight into how well students had learned the skills that were not directly assessed or were assessed at the level of the team, students were asked to anonymously rate their own abilities.

Constructing an experimental protocol was entirely novel for students, so it was important information for the teaching team that over 80% of students reported that they had acquired the ability to do this.

While Pioletti and his teaching assistants argue that the right amount of guidance for students requires constant attention, their approach allowed them to keep students focused on the *process* of doing experimental work rather than obtaining the correct result for any particular experiment.

Lab: Regenerative treatment of cartilaginous lesions of the knee by injecting cells.

What are the different *biomechanical events* that the cells will undergo during the injection through a syringe and its needle?

How can you determine the effects of these *events* on cell viability?

What is the optimal solution for injecting cells into a patient's knee ?

FIGURE 10.3 Example of an inquiry lab assignment

> **REFLECTION POINT 10.5**
>
> Keep a list, over a number of weeks, of what questions your students ask you during your practical course.
> After a few weeks, review the questions. What do they tell you about your course? What do they tell you about the things that your students are able to do and the things for which they need further guidance? Can you see any patterns that emerge over a few weeks?

Students' perspectives are valuable and can help you start to question some of the assumptions and beliefs that derive from your own autobiographical experience. But students often have naïve assumptions about your discipline, about what expertise in your discipline looks like, and about how they should be learning. Juxtaposing student perspectives and your own with those of peers can, therefore, be helpful.

LENS 3: PEERS' PERSPECTIVES

It is strange to think that, for such a social activity, teaching is often a solitary affair, in which the teacher is alone with students in a closed room, rarely being observed by peers and rarely having the chance to observe other teachers. We noted above that expertise is developed through interaction with an expert community. The third lens provides a framework for engaging in this kind of interaction.

In fact, teachers in practical settings in higher education, given the applied nature of the skills they teach, may have a wide circle of people who could be considered peers, including other teachers in their department, institution, or discipline, or practicing experts in their field. When reading the word *peer* in the following section, keep this broad definition in mind and consider how you could make use of the richness of experience of this broader group to advance your teaching. Opportunities to discuss, with peers, or others, about teaching can have a strong and lasting effect on teacher behaviour (Hattie 2009, 112). The section presents a few recommendations to make the most of exploring the perspective of your peers:

- choose peers who you trust,
- focus on mastery, not performance,
- communicate what you want from them and your motivation for seeking their feedback,
- schedule a debriefing or discussion when you know you have time.

Many teachers enjoy talking to other people about their teaching; however there is a certain amount of exposure involved in inviting a peer to provide feedback on your teaching or teaching resources. Choosing a person with whom you have, or can establish, a context of confidentiality and trust will make it more likely to be a constructive experience for you. Being attentive to context and power relations has been shown to make peer observations more effective for improving teaching (Hammersley-Fletcher and Orsmond 2005).

It is worth being clear with yourself about your motivations for discussing your teaching with peers. In Chapter 9 we distinguished between being motivated by the desire to perform well (*performance goals*) and being motivated by the desire to increase your competence (*mastery goals*). While there is nothing wrong with being proud when you consider you have done your job well, it is worth being clear with yourself that the purpose of discussing your teaching with peers is not to have them confirm your expertise, but rather that they help you to develop it further. Being ready to be open-minded when colleagues have a different perspective to you, or when they criticise a practice that you are content with, is likely to be helpful.

Just like you, your peers have their own autobiography, beliefs, and assumptions, and it may be that the things they naturally pay attention to in teaching are not all that interesting to you. This can be particularly relevant in the case of peer observations where the things your peers look at in a class may not match the questions that are motivating you. Communicating your interests and sharing what you hope to gain is a good idea. This might involve meeting together before a peer observation. When peer feedback does not work well, it can sometimes take a limited vision of teaching and may focus only on visible behaviours while neglecting the teachers' underlying philosophy (Hammersley-Fletcher and Orsmond 2005). In this case, peer observations may work to reinforce traditional teaching norms. One way to avoid this is to focus on understanding the thinking behind your observer's perspective rather than on asking her or him to recommend particular behavioural strategies to you. Another type of peer observation is to organise to teach to peers with the exclusive goal of getting feedback, as illustrated in Spotlight 10.3.

BECOMING A BETTER TEACHER

The final phase of peer feedback is the discussion or debriefing. Chapter 3 noted that reflection requires some detachment from the event. This means that you should ensure that there is some time between the observation and the debriefing, for both you and your peer to reflect. Choosing a time when you have the emotional and cognitive capacity to discuss your teaching is also important – there may be some months of the year or days of the week where you are unable to make the most of the experience. You can set good groundwork for a productive discussion by being clear before the observation about the type of feedback that will be useful to you. Suggesting that your observer record what surprises them will set up the discussion to focus more on underlying assumptions and ideas than on *nuts and bolts*.

The Career Framework project also provides additional ideas on how to collect evidence from peers that can contribute to teaching development: https://www.teachingframework.com/framework/evidence/.

SPOTLIGHT 10.3 – TEACHING FOR PEERS AND PRACTICE

Siara and Cécile teach a course for novice university teachers that devotes about 50% of class time to participants teaching each other using a mini-lesson activity derived from the Instructional Skills Workshop model (Johnson 2006). This means that for each day of the five-day course, each participant prepares and teaches a short lesson for a group of their peers. Each day the teaching activity has a different focus. On the first day, for example, participants are asked to include a lead-in, objective, and summary (see the full description of the LOAFS structure in Chapter 6). As the course progresses, participants build up to a full integration of the LOAFS structure for their mini-lessons.

The mini-lesson cycle has four parts (see Figure 10.4) and starts with a few minutes for the mini-lesson *teacher* to set up for their lesson. During the mini-lesson, the peers' role is to participate as students. At the conclusion of the mini-lesson, the *teacher* responds to a short, written questionnaire that prompts them to think about what they felt went well, what did not go as planned, and what they think students learned from the lesson. The peer *students* also respond to a questionnaire, and they record their take-away from the mini-lesson in terms of skills or content from the mini-lesson itself.

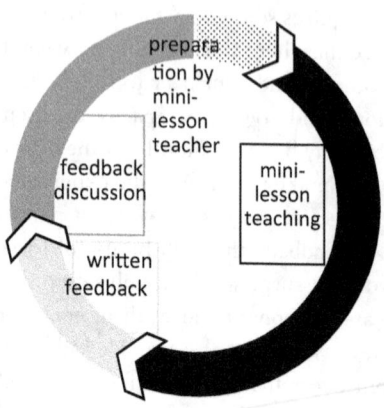

FIGURE 10.4 The mini-lesson cycle

Each mini-lesson cycle wraps up with a discussion, where the *teacher* seeks to understand the experience of the mini-lesson *learners* without justifying or defending their pedagogical choices (Pendleton et al. 2003). The next cycle then starts, and a new *teacher* teaches their mini-lesson.

On the first day, mini-lesson teachers are frequently surprised at the gap between what they think that have communicated to *students* and what their *students* report having learned. Each day offers another chance to practice teaching, get feedback, and reflect again. This format generates multiple occasions for *teachers* to confront their own experience with their *students'* feedback, and to compare their impressions while teaching with those of being a student only minutes later. Part of each day also involves Siara or Cécile facilitating activities about evidence-informed strategies for teaching engineering.

Siara and Cécile do not observe the mini-lessons, or read the self and peer feedback that participants produce and exchange with each other about their mini-lessons. They made this choice to encourage participants to stretch and try new teaching strategies without concern that their grade depends on the successful execution of their teaching.

While students' and peers' inputs can allow us to reflect on teaching and see things from multiple perspectives, experiential learning also involves identifying regularities in these experiences and linking them to sound concepts and theories (i.e. the *generalise* phase in the cycle). It may be that peers (or even some students) can direct us to some sound concepts and theories. However it may also be that we can more reliably find such ideas by engaging with the fourth lens: drawing on perspectives from literature.

LENS 4: USING DISCIPLINARY AND GENERAL LITERATURE ON HIGHER EDUCATION TEACHING

In this book, we have taken an evidence-informed approach and proposed teaching strategies that have been demonstrated to be effective for learning the types of skills targeted in practical courses. This section extends this approach and illustrates how to use the literature as a lens for critical reflection about both what should be taught and how it should be taught in your course. Earlier in this chapter, Reflection point 10.3 asked you to think back to a course or a teacher that you particularly enjoyed as a student and to identify what characteristics made this a positive learning experience for you. Looking back now on your answer to that question, was it a unique characteristic of the course or the teacher's personality that made it a particularly positive learning experience for you, or can you also recognise more general features of good teaching and learning that were present in the class such as how the teacher created a relationship with a class, provided feedback, stimulated thinking, or explained well? Developing an ability to see how general teaching concepts apply in a particular case helps us transfer good practice into other situations. Brookfield describes this as using theory to "name our practice by illuminating the general elements of what we think are idiosyncratic experiences" (1995, 36).

On a number of occasions in this book we have noted that there are popular theories and common-sense ideas about teaching and learning which are widely shared by higher education teachers (and learners) but which do not align with evidence. Perhaps the most obvious example of this is the idea of learning styles which, as we discussed in Chapter 2, is not well supported by empirical evidence (Coffield et al. 2004). It may be worthwhile to ask yourself if there were particular ideas or research findings presented in this book that surprised you or which contradicted your own experiences of or beliefs about teaching and learning. Confronting your own experiences and beliefs with research evidence can be a fruitful way of thinking through and developing your own teaching practices.

Books about higher education teaching, providing that they take an evidence-informed approach, are often a good place to start with this process. The resources recommended in the *Further reading* sections of Chapters 8 and 9 should be particularly useful as a starting point. As you engage more with the language of educational researchers, you may find that journal articles allow you to delve deeper into a particular topic. Research on teaching and learning in higher education is published in both domain general journals like *Studies in Higher Education* or *Teaching in Higher Education* and in journals at the nexus of your discipline and teaching: journals like *Teaching Sociology*, the *Journal of Chemical Education*, and the *Journal of Engineering Education* are only a small sample of the discipline-based educational research sources available.

> ### REFLECTION POINT 10.6
>
> Is there a specific research finding, concept, strategy, or idea from this book that surprises you?
> Why does it surprise you (for example, does it contradict a particular belief you hold or an experience you have had)?
> Is there data you could gather or observations you could make that would be useful to enable you to think further about how this should impact on your own teaching practice?

FROM REFLECTION TO PRACTICE

Thus far this chapter has introduced the ideas of critically reflective practice and the way in which the use of multiple *lenses* can help a teacher to authentically engage with their own experiences (*experience*), identify different perspectives on an issue (*reflect*), and to link this to sound concepts, ideas, or theories (*generalise*). Improving as a teacher will mean going one step further, to follow through on this to generate some ideas for how you might act differently, and *testing* out those ideas in practice. Ultimately your goal will be to develop some new habits, which means that these strategies move from conscious and intentional decisions into automated routines that allow you to navigate in the busy practical situations in which you teach. This section proposes four ways to help teachers integrate the results of their critical reflection into their teaching, namely:

- start small,
- share your motivation with students,
- use an iterative, deliberate practice approach,
- be kind to yourself.

Starting small means being realistic about the time required for you to develop strategies that work for you. Starting small could mean identifying a few weeks in which you will consistently focus on integrating just one new thing in your teaching. For example, you could decide you want to prioritise questioning strategies during your one-to-one interactions with students. Over a period of weeks you could focus on this one issue: writing some autobiographical notes, getting input from students on how they see your questions, discussing with peers, trying to ask questions, monitoring how well you are doing so, and then trying again.

Starting small could also mean making a more significant change to a particular part of the course. For example, you could decide to completely revise how students learn one set of skills (in the way in which Dominique Pioletti sought to target skills for designing experimental protocols in Spotlight 10.2). Again, you might want to write some notes on your own experiences in labs, gather some self-assessments from students about their relevant skills, have a peer sit in on your lab, read some papers on designing labs, and try out a new approach. Given the multiple demands on academics' time and attention, starting small is important for sustainable change.

Once you have determined what you want to change in your teaching, you should consider how to share your motivations with your students. Students arrive in higher education with well-established expectations about what they will learn, how teachers will teach, and what they should do to demonstrate their learning. Some of these expectations are quite general and come from their own experience, while others are passed down from senior classmates about your specific course. Making big changes can cause uncertainty and instability, and make students less receptive to unfamiliar teaching methods. Explicitly telling students why you employ a specific teaching strategy, particularly in terms of the advantages for their learning, as well as your expectations for their behaviour, will help both you and them make the most of your class. It can also play a role in aiding students' metacognitive development.

Building new teaching habits will require you to repeat the new habit or procedure a number of times in order to develop some degree of automaticity. In the early stages of using a new skill, it can take a great deal of attention and effort. It also may not go well the first time. You should expect to try, fail to some degree, give yourself feedback, and try again. When you are under pressure it is normal to revert to pre-existing habits, so giving yourself timely reminders when practicing is a useful strategy. By paying attention to the situational factors that cue your existing habits, you can plan to initiate the new practices you wish to develop. If you recognise, for example, that you are in the habit of responding to a question with an explanation, and if you wish to try responding with a question, you can visualise these exchanges in advance so that when you hear a student say "Excuse me, I have a QUESTION ...", it reminds you to practice asking a good question in response. With each repetition it becomes easier as the new practice starts to become automated. However it is important to remember that it is "perfect practice that makes perfect", so monitoring and reflecting on your practice will help you to continue to improve.

At the beginning of this chapter we noted that learning to teach by teaching is unlike learning in other practical settings because it means having to practice *while performing*. Under these circumstances, it takes determination to persist with less familiar teaching strategies when it feels like things are not going well or that students do not appreciate the approach (Norton et al. 2013). You have seen that becoming an expert means developing the emotional awareness and regulation skills that will help you to use your emotions productively in your practice. So it will be important to be gentle with yourself by acknowledging when things do not go well with a class but also recognising that the reasons for this are multiple and that some reasons may not be related to your skills as a teacher. Issues that are related to your teaching can be used as opportunities to grow and develop. In Patricia Benner's work with nurses, she noted that unless nurses are emotionally engaged and can accept the joy of a job well done and the guilt and shame of mistakes, they stagnate, and risk burnout (Benner 1984). Something similar could well be said of higher education teachers.

CONCLUSION

Developing expertise in teaching comes from having and reflecting on experiences which allow you to build the perceptions, knowledge, understanding, habits, and emotional responses that are required to consistently generate high-quality learning opportunities for students. This chapter has reviewed many of the key ideas of this book (expertise, metacognition, feedback, power, social identity, evidence-informed practice, and feedback to name just a few) and looked at how you can apply them to yourself as well as to your students, to help you develop your practice as a teacher while you are helping them to develop towards expertise in your discipline.

Improving as a teacher involves giving yourself the same opportunities to experience, reflect, theorise, plan, and practice as you create for your students in their labs, field work, projects, and studios. Using Brookfield's four *lenses* to analyse your teaching and to hunt the assumptions and beliefs that might be limiting your development as a teacher is a useful way of creating these learning opportunities for yourself. It is important to remember that students learn when they feel safe to try, fail, get feedback, and improve, and the same is true for teachers; it will be necessary to be kind with yourself so that you have permission to try something challenging, fail, get feedback, and improve.

Finally, remember that developing as a teacher is an ongoing process that can take years. What appears relevant and important to you as you read this today may not be the same things as in a few months or years. It is useful to return and revisit concepts and issues as your experience, your students, and the world change. Being a critically reflective teacher is a skill, which means that you should seek to incorporate and improve the practice in an ongoing way.

ACTION SUMMARY – BECOMING A BETTER TEACHER FOR PRACTICAL SETTINGS

- Teaching expertise is developed through experiential learning, so create opportunities for you to experience, to reflect, to theorise, and to test new ideas about teaching.
- Pay attention to the way your own autobiography influences your thinking about teaching.
- Find ways to see things from your students' perspectives – they may not always be right but they will often help you recognise aspects you had not considered.
- Expertise is developed in a community of experts, so find peers to share and discuss with.
- Concepts, ideas, and sound theories from the literature on learning in higher education and in your discipline can help you to see things that might otherwise have remained hidden.
- Anticipate that deep changes to your teaching will take time and effort.
- Allow yourself permission to try new things, to get feedback on how to improve, and to try again.

PART III

FURTHER READING

This small selection of sources provides further useful information for those looking for more guidance on using reflection to improve their teaching. A full reference list for the chapter is provided below.

Ashwin, P., Boud, D., Calkins, S., Coate, K., Hallett, F., Light, G., Luckett, K., McArthur, J., MacLaren, I., McLean, M., McCune, V., McLean, M., and Tooher, M. (2020). *Reflective Teaching in Higher Education*. London: Bloomsbury Academic.

Brookfield, S. (2014, August 27). *Becoming a Skillful Teacher*. Keynote Fall Perspectives on Teaching Conference Held at Western University [Video]. YouTube. https://youtu.be/JaOwYqj57BY?t=1165.

Cowan, J. (2006). Chapter 4. On what models can we base reflective learning and teaching? *On Becoming an Innovative University Teacher: Reflection in Action: Reflection in Action, 2nd edition* (pp. 44–61). Maidenhead: McGraw-Hill Education.

Kahn, P., and Anderson, L. (2019). *Developing Your Teaching: Towards Excellence*. London: Routledge. https://doi.org/10.4324/9780429490583.

Moffatt, K. (2017). Chapter 5. Teaching social work as a reflective practice. In: N. Gould and I. Taylor (eds.), *Reflective Learning for Social Work: Research, Theory and Practice*. London: Routledge. https://doi.org/10.4324/9781315245058.

REFERENCES

Benner, P. (1984). *From Novice to Expert: Excellence and Power in Clinical Nursing Practice*. Reading, MA: Addison-Wesley.

Brookfield, S.D. (1995). *Becoming a Critically Reflective Teacher*. San Francisco: Jossey-Bass.

Brookfield, S.D. (1998). Critically reflective practice. *Journal of Continuing Education in the Health Professions* 18(4): 197–205. https://doi.org/10.1002/chp.1340180402.

Coffield, F., Moseley, D., Hall, E., and Ecclestone, K. (2004). *Learning Styles and Pedagogy in post-16 Learning: A Systematic and Critical Review*. London: Learning and Skills Research Centre.

European University Association (EUA). (2015). Trends 2015: Learning and teaching in European universities. Edited by A. Sursock. Brussels: European University Association. http://www.eua.be/publications/.

Graham, R. (2018). *The Career Framework for University Teaching: Background and overview*. London: Royal Academy of Engineering. https://www.raeng.org.uk/publications/reports/career-framework-for-university-teaching-backgroun.

Hammersley-Fletcher, L., and Orsmond, P. (2005). Reflecting on reflective practices within peer observation. *Studies in Higher Education* 30(2): 213–224. https://doi.org/10.1080/03075070500043358.

Hattie, J. (2009). *Visible Learning: A Synthesis of over 800 Meta-Analyses Relating to Achievement*. Routledge. https://doi.org/10.4324/9780203887332.

Johnson, J.B. (2006). *Instructional Skills Workshop Handbook for Participants*. Vancouver, BC: The Instructional Skills Workshop International Advisory Committee. http://www.iswnetwork.ca/.

Kolb, D.A. (1984). *Experiential Learning: Experience as the Source of Learning and Development*. Englewood Cliffs, NJ: Prentice Hall.

Korthagen, F., and Vasalos, A. (2005). Levels in reflection: Core reflection as a means to enhance professional growth. *Teachers and Teaching* 11(1): 47–71. https://doi.org/10.1080/1354060042000337093.

Le Duc, I., Dietz, D., and Guaita, P. (2020). An experiential learning approach to educational development: Responses to teaching architecture through the lenses of reflective practices. *ETH Learning and Teaching Journal* 2(2): 422–427. https://learningteaching.ethz.ch/index.php/lt-eth/article/view/177.

Lortie, D. (1975). *Schoolteacher: A Sociological Study*. Chicago, IL: University of Chicago Press. https://doi.org/10.1177/019263657505939422.

McFarlae Mirande, T. (2005). *Championship Swimming: How to Swim Like a Pro in Thirty Days or Less*. Frankfurt: McGraw-Hill Education.

Norton, L., Norton, B., and Shannon, L. (2013). Revitalising assessment design: What is holding new lecturers back? *Higher Education* 66(2): 233–251. https://doi.org/10.1007/s10734-012-9601-9.

Pendleton, D., Schofield, T., Tate, P., and Havelock, P. (2003). *The New Consultation*. Oxford: Oxford University Press. https://doi.org/10.1093/med/9780192632883.003.0001.

Pioletti, D., Bourban, P.-E., Poupart, O., Isaac, S.R., and Hardebolle, C. (2019). *Teaching Measurement Techniques in Biomechanics Through Inquiry-Based Labs*. Zurich: Swiss Faculty Development Network. http://infoscience.epfl.ch/record/273571.

Ryan, M. (2013). The pedagogical balancing act: Teaching reflection in higher education. *Teaching in Higher Education* 18(2): 144–155. https://doi.org/10.1080/13562517.2012.694104.

Stigler, J.W., and Miller, K.F. (2018). Expertise and expert performance in teaching. In: K. A. Ericsson, R. R. Hoffman, and A. Kozbelt (eds.), *The Cambridge Handbook of Expertise and Expert Performance* (pp. 431–452). Cambridge: Cambridge University Press. https://doi.org/10.1017/9781316480748.024.

Wieman, C. (2015). A better way to evaluate undergraduate teaching. *Change: The Magazine of Higher Learning* 47(1): 6–15. https://doi.org/10.1080/00091383.2015.996077.

Index

Note: Page locators in italics refer to figures and bold refer to tables.

Adshead-Lansdale's Dance Analysis model **117**
Aeby, Prisca (et al.) 54, **173**
ALACT model (Korthagen) 242
Alberts, Heike (et al.) 178
Ambrose, Susan (et al.) 218, 219; *How Learning Works* 196
American Psychological Association review of evidence 195, 197, 209, 230
Andrade, Heidi (et al.) **116–117**
apprenticeship comparisons: cognitive apprenticeship 224–225; of observation or pseudo-expertise 33, 241, 246
approaches to learning and teaching *see* teaching and learning approaches
architecture examples 132, **180–183**, 242; IT systems architecture **42**, **48**, **51**, **54**, **58**, 131
Aristotle 169
art students examples **18**, 32–33
asking questions *see* questioning as learning/teaching approach
assessment literacy 109
assumptions *see* prior knowledge or misconceptions
attention and cognitive load 200–204, 222

Beasley, Maya 228
Beckett, Samuel 102
Benner, Patricia **30**, 33, 262
biases (implicit): in analogies and metaphors 132; curse of knowledge 223; in design 26; within diverse teams 54; ethnicity biases 26, 54, 90, 171–173, 227–228; evidence of implicit 113–114; gender biases 54, 90, 113–114, 171–173, 228; managing learning climates 171–174; in offering help 90, 113; social identities and 227–228; Spotlight **173–174**; stereotype threat 227–229; *see also* power relations
Biggs, John 13
Bjorklund, Wendy 164, 185
Bloom's cognitive learning outcomes 7
bodily responses 232–234, **234**
Boice, Bob 161–164, **166–169**, 174, 186
Brookfield, Stephen 241–242, 246–250, 252, 259, 263; *see also* critically reflective practice model

caffeine and learning 233–234
Career Framework for University Teaching 243, 243–244, 253
Case, Jennifer 14

266

INDEX

Case studies: about 9; analysing risk in emerging markets 73–74, 84–85, 95–96; building productive relationships in a studio 180–183; create a habit or wait for it to happen 178–180; designing a social research project 100–101, 108, 110–113, 121, 122; disruptions threaten lab safety 157–158, 166–167, 175; explaining how to give feedback to physiotherapy clients 147, 148–149, 154, 155; explaining priorities and deadlines for a project 133–134, 141, 152–153; how to kill bacteria 117–119, 122–123; questioning in social work field placements 92–93, 97–98; Rockin' the explaining 125–126, 133, 144–146, 152, 153
Cepeda, Nicholas (et al.) 206
chemistry *see* science examples
chess examples 17, 23, 27, 28, 33, 206
Chi, Michelene (et al.) 198–199; *The Nature of Expertise* 25
Clark, Cynthia 165, 166, 168, 169
class environment/climate *see* managing learning climate
cognition: ways of thinking 40–41, 67; *see also* metacognition
cognitive apprenticeship 224–225; *see also* observational learning or modelling
cognitive load 202–203, 202–204, 222
cognitive reappraisal 28
Colbeck, Carol (et al.) 54
collaboration *see* team work and collaboration
Collins, Allan (et al.) 224–225
Collins, Harry 28
common-sense ideas 210–212, 222; *see also* biases (implicit); prior knowledge or misconceptions

community of practice and expertise 28, 30–32, 255–259
complexity and cognitive load 200–204, 202–203, 222
computer science example: IT system architecture 42, 48, 51, 54, 58, 131
concept inventories 212
conditionalised knowledge 23, 207–208
context, response to: conditionalised knowledge 23, 207–208; questions to stimulate 82–83; reflection point 24; role in expertise 16–17; spotlights 41–44, 45–51, 56–60; transfer of skills 45, 50–51, 208–210; ways of thinking 40–41; *see also* experiential learning/teaching
Corcoran, Roisin 27–28, 166
Cornelius-White, Jeffery 232
Cotton, Debby 218–219
critically reflective practice model: about 103, 241–242, 245–248; action summary 263; aligning learning to action 247–248; autobiographical perspective 248–251; definitions 245; literature on teaching 259–260; peers' perspective 255–259, 258; Reflection points 249–250, 250–251, 255, 260; *see also* experiential learning/teaching
Crouch, Catherine (et al.) 138–139, 211–212
Csikszentmihalyi, M. 46
cultures of critique 116–117

dance examples: cognitive load 202–203; observational learning or modelling 225; peer feedback 115–117
Darling-Hammond, Linda (et al.) 160

267

decision making: learning strategies for **59**, **106**; model of expertise as **21–22**
deep processing 210
deep/surface model 13–15, 208–210
De Jong, T. 208
design students examples **18**, 32–33
digital tools to build community **226–227**; *see also* social dimensions of learning/teaching
Dillenbourg, Pierre 223
disciplines: disciplinary inquiry *see* investigatory techniques; educational research sources 260; educational trajectory differences 32–33; *see also* experts, becoming one
discovery learning 66
disruptive class behaviour *see* managing learning climate
Donoghue, Gregory 66, 222, 230, 234
Dreyfus, Hubert **30**
Dreyfus, Stuart **30**
drug use to enhance learning 233–234

Edison, Thomas 218
educational theories *see* evidence about learning
Ellefson, P. William **87–88**
emotional competence: bodily responses 232–234, **234**; questions to stimulate 82; role in expertise 24–26, 30, 231–232, 262; reflection points **29**, **170–171**, **234**; students' accounts 5–6; teacher immediacy (warmth) 167–170, **170–171**; teacher-student relationship 158–159, 160, 169, 232; when learning to teach **27–28**; *see also* managing learning climate; social dimensions of learning/teaching

engineering examples: decision making 21–22; edge cases 132; illustration tools 131; modelling thinking and processes 142–143; negative impacts' response 26 *see also* emotional competence
Entwistle, Noel 15; *Teaching for Understanding at University* 13
environment of class *see* managing learning climate
Erfahrraum **227**; *see also* social dimensions of learning/teaching
Ericsson, K. Anders 34
ethnicity biases 26, 54, 90, 171–173, 227–228
Evans, Robert 28
evidence about learning: about 10, 195–197; approaches to research on learning 12–13; cognitive load, and complexity 200–204, 222; *deep/surface* model 14, 208–210; demonstrating as teaching approach **138–139**; disruptive class behaviour 161–164; engaging and interacting **198–199**; explaining as teaching approach **128–129**; feedback on students' work 102, 107, 121; implicit bias 113–114; learning as effortful 197–200, *199*; learning styles models 64; memory and remembering 205; metacognition, teaching of 230; misconceptions 211–212, 222; practice 206–207; questioning as a teaching method 75–76, 76, **87–88**, 207; reviews of research 195–196; reflection points **200**, **201**; simulations 208; spotlights **87–88**, **128–129**, **138–139**, **198–199**
exercise to enhance learning 234
Exley, Kate (et al.) 143–144

INDEX

experience, role in expertise: deliberate practice 33–35, **35**, 206; experiential learning cycle model 62–64, *63*, 241; *see also* practicing; prior knowledge or misconceptions

experiential learning/teaching: approach of this book 7–9, 200, 213, 235–236; contextualised knowledge 23, 207–208; *deep/surface* model and 14, 208–210; diversity and similarity of 44; experiential learning cycle model 62–64, *63*, 241; expertise framework 15; inter-related levels of **46–47**; model of 62–64, *63*, 241–242; motivation of learner 218–220, 225–226; performance settings 241; process-focused teaching **253–254**, *254*; reflecting on doing 62–63; safety protocols **60**; spotlights **41–44, 45–51, 56–60**; student experiences of 4–6; students' accounts of challenges 4–6; terminology 7; transfer 45, **50–51**, 208–210; ways of thinking 40–41; *see also* emotional competence; investigatory techniques; learning models; pattern recognition (perception); practicing; problem solving; processes; social dimensions of learning/teaching; teaching and learning approaches

experts, becoming one: about expertise (definition) 15–17; community of practice 28–29, 30, 255; conditionalised knowledge 23, 207–208; curse of knowledge 223; decision-making practice **21–22**; *deep/surface* model and 13–15, 208–210; emotional competence 231–232; expertise not transferable 20, 23; five-stage adult learning model **30–32**; literature on teaching 259–260; motivations and types of goals 219–220, 256; questions to stimulate 82; from reflection to practice 260–262; 10,000 hours 13, 34; reflection points **20, 22, 24, 29, 35**; *see also* novices compared to experts

explaining as learning/teaching approach: action summary **150**; analogies and metaphors 132; case studies **125–126, 133–134, 141, 144–146, 147, 148–149**, 152–153, 155; evidence supporting **138–139**, 213; five-step template (LOAFS) 126–127, 134–141, **135**, 144, **148–149, 154**, 257; how-to procedures (steps for explaining) 143–144; illustrations and demonstrations to support 131–132, 135–136, **138–139**; Jigsaw activity 137; keep it short 130; managing student discomfort 128; match students' needs (know audience) 129–130, 135, 219; modelling how experts think 127, 141–143, 144, 204, 224–225; reflection points **147, 150**; spotlights **128–129, 138–139**; when to explain 127–129; *see also* managing learning climate; questioning as learning/teaching approach

feedback as learning/teaching approach: about 62, 213; action summary **119**; assessment literacy 109; case studies **100–101, 108, 110–113, 117–119**, 121, 122–123; clarify expectations 103–104, 120, 136, 219; evidence of effect of 102, 107, 121; feedback from students 86, 151, 251–255, *252*; how to

INDEX

give feedback 114–115, 220, **221**; implicit biases 113–114; in LOAFS structure 137, 140–141, **148–149, 154**; managing or problem-solving level 106–107, 120; marks, effect of 121–122; by peers **115–117**, 252–259, *258*; personal level 107–108; practice and 206, **208**; process level 105–106; as a question 109; in question-friendly environment 79; reflection points **104, 108–109**, 121; self-efficacy and 225–227; task-level 105; spotlights **105, 106, 106–107, 115–117**
Felder, Richard 81, **81**
Fischer, Mary 228
five-stage adult learning model **30–32**
Ford, M. 54
forgetting, practicing, and repetition 205–208; *see also* practicing
formative assessment (LOAFS) 139–140
Frankfurt School's critical theory 246
free body diagram 131; *see also* explaining as learning/teaching approach
Freeman, Scott (et al.) 75

Gainsburg, Julie 75
Gaspard, C. 75
gender biases 54, 90, 113–114, 171–173, 228
geography courses examples 64, 177–178, 218–219
geology examples 76, **125–126, 133, 144–146**
German Intercity express train crash 26
Gestalt task **18**
goals: of experiential learning 55–56, 67; explicit learning 66, 136, 219–220; of higher education 12, 13;

motivation and types of 218–220, **221**, 256; self-directed 229–231
grading students' feedback 253
group work *see* team work and collaboration

hands-on learning *see* experiential learning/teaching
Hattie, John 52, 66, 102, 115, 121, 206, 219, 222, 230, 234
Healey, Mick 64
higher education's goal 12, 13
How Learning Works (Ambrose et al.) 196
How People Learn II (National Academies) 196
Hughes, Michelle **87–88**

ICAP classification **199, 200**
implicit bias *see* biases (implicit)
independent and goal-directed learning 229–231
intelligence: role in expertise 16
interleaved practice 206–207; *see also* practicing
interpersonal skills *see* social dimensions of learning/teaching; team work and collaboration
investigatory techniques: explicit learning goals 66, 136, 219–220; goal of experiential learning 56, 67; misconceptions and 211–212; stepwise process 52–53
Isaac, Siara **174**
IT system architecture examples **42, 48**, 51, 54, **58**, 131

Jenkins, Alan 64
Jenkins, Jennifer 167, 168
Jigsaw activity 137

Karpicke, Jeffrey 207
Kelsey, Louise **117**
Kent State University, Ohio **176–177**

INDEX

Kirschner, Femke (et al.) 222
Klingberg, Torkel **201**
Kolb, David 62–63, 67, 98, 249
Korthagen, Fred 242
Kozbelt, Aaron **18**, 32–33

learning by doing *see* experiential learning/teaching
learning in practical settings *see* experiential learning/teaching
learning models: advance HE fellowship 242–243; ALACT model (Korthagen) 242; Career Framework for University Teaching *243*, 243–244; critically reflective practice *see* critically reflective practice model; decision making **21–22**; *deep/surface* 13–15, 208–210; experiential learning cycle 62–64, *63*, 241; five-stage **30–32**; learning outcomes 12; learning styles model 64, 259
learning process: as effortful 197–200, *199*
Le Duc, Ingrid (et al.) 242
literature on teaching 259–260
LOAFS five-step structure 126–127, 134–141, **135**, 144, **148–149**, **154**, 257
Long Island parkways 26
Lorti, Dan 241

Maier, L.J. (et al.) 234
managing learning climate: about 62; achievement goals **221**; action summary **183**; case studies **157–158**, **166–167**, 175, **180–183**, 184–185, 186–188; corrections, direct and later 177–178, 184, **185**, 186–187; data on new teachers and 158–159, 160; disruptive class behaviour 160–167, *163*, **180–183**, 186–188;

implicit biases 171–174, 187–188; in online courses **176–177**; participation **178–180**; power relations (teacher-student) 169; preventing disruption (strategies) 174–176; question-friendly environment 77–78, **79**, 97–98; reflection points **161**, **170–171**, 185, **185**, **220**; safety and 159–160; spotlights **165–166**, **173–174**, **176–177**, **178–180**; warmth and trust 167–170; *see also* explaining as learning/teaching approach; feedback as learning/teaching approach; questioning as learning/teaching approach
Marshall, Delia 14
mastery goals 218, 220, 256
mathematics examples 14, 25–26, **128–129**
Mazur, Eric 222
McCormack, Orla 65
McCroskey, James (et al.) **171**
McFarlane Mirande, Tracey 34
McGarr, Oliver 65
measurement techniques for teaching **253–254**, *254*
medicine examples: decision making **21–22**; emotional competence 25; incivility in practical settings **165–166**; microsurgery environment 23; modelling thinking and processes 142–143; nursing, becoming an expert **30–32**
memory and remembering 205–208; *see also* practicing
Menekse, M. (et al.) **199**, *199*
metacognition: critical reflection 252; explicit learning goals 66; feedback to develop 106–107; group work 90; practical learning 15; principles for teaching 55, 56; reflection

271

point **231**; teaching students about 230–231, 261; ways of thinking 67; *see also* critically reflective practice model
Miller, Kevin **27**, 33
misconceptions or prior knowledge 208–212, 222
models *see* learning models
monitoring of self: by experts 24, 30; independent and goal-directed 229–231, 261–262; questions to stimulate 82; teaching of 54–55, **56–58**, **59**; teaching with questions 77; *see also* experts, becoming one
Morice, J. 54
Moss-Racusin, Corinne (et al.) 113–114
motivation of learner 217–220, **221**; self-efficacy 225–226
musicians: deliberate practice 24; explaining as learning/teaching approach 131; music studio example **41–42**, **45–47**, **56–58**; self-monitoring 24, 54

National Academies' (US) reviews of evidence 195–196, 227, 232
note taking 199–200
novices compared to experts: contextualised knowledge (recall) 23 *see also* context, response to; emotional competence 24–26, **27–28**, 30; pattern recognition (perception) 17–18, **18**, **20**, 29; problem solving (decision making) 20–21, **21–22**; processing as linked and automated 18–19, 29; self-monitoring by 24, 30; *see also* experts, becoming one
nursing examples: educational trajectory 33; emotional competence 25; spotlights **30–32**, **165–166**

Oatley, Keith 168, 169
observational learning or modelling 127, 141–144, 204, 224–226
O'Donovan, Berry (et al.) 109, 114
Oetzel, John **171**
online courses: student incivilities **176–177**

passive compared to interactive learning **198–199**, *199*
pattern recognition (perception) 17–18, **18**, **20**; deep processing and rich encoding 44; *see also* problem solving; processes
Peer Instruction **139**
perception: novices compared to experts 17–18, **18**, 29; questions to stimulate 82
physical skills and expertise 16–17
physics examples: classroom demonstrations **138–139**; illustration tools 131; knowledge recall example 19, 209; misconceptions 210–211
physiotherapy example **147**
pianist examples 24
Pioletti, Dominique (et al.) **253–254**, 261
Polya, George 51
power relations: among peers 256; interactions in education **57**, 169, 246; *see also* biases (implicit); managing learning climate
practical learning *see* experiential learning/teaching
practical settings: about 7; *deep/surface* model and 14, 208–210; spotlights **41–44**, **45–51**, **56–60**; transfer of skills 45, **50–51**, 208–210; ways of thinking 40–41; *see also* experiential learning/teaching

practicing: conditionalised knowledge 23, 207–208; deliberate practice 34–35, 206, 218; evidence supporting 206–207; from reflection to practice 260–262; reflection points **35**, **208**; strategies for 205–208; *see also* experience, role in expertise; experiential learning/teaching
Predict – Observe – Explain **139**
Prescott, Renate **176**
Price, Argenta (et al.) **21–22**
prior knowledge or misconceptions 208–212, 222, 246–247, 249–250, 261; *see also* biases (implicit)
problem solving: decision-making strategies **21–22**, 59, 105–106; *deep/surface* model and 14, 208–210; defining problems **48–50**; experts and novices compared 20–21; explicit learning goals 66, 136; goal of experiential learning 56; modelling to students 127, 141–143, 144, 204, 224–225; process or stages of 51–52; reflection point **22**; sketches in 131; ways of thinking 40–41, 67; *see also* pattern recognition (perception); processes
processes: decision making **106**; deep processing and rich encoding 44; feedback targeting 105–106; as linked and automated 17, **18**, 19, 29, 130; modelling for students 141–143, 144, 204, 224–225; questions to stimulate 82; *see also* pattern recognition (perception); problem solving
Project Implicit (Harvard) 114
psychology *see* social scientist examples

questioning as learning/teaching approach: about 74–76, 94; action summary **93**; case studies **73–74, 84–85, 92–93**, 95–96, 97–98; cognitive load and 204; diagnostic questions 80, 86–87, **87**, 95–96; evidence supporting 75–76, 76, **87–88**, 207, 213; examples of 61–62, 130, 139–140; feedback in question format 109; goals/types of questions 80, 80–81; hints with questions 80, 87, 88–90, **89**, 96; how to ask questions 76–80, **79**; incorrect student answers 77–78, 107–108, 122, 212, 220; question-friendly environment 77–78, **79**, 97–98; reflection points **90–91, 91–92**, 96–97; responding to students' questions 91, 97–98, 261; spotlights 81, **87–88, 253–254**; stimulating questions 80, 81–84, **83**, 95–96; thinking time and debriefing 78–79, **79**; *see also* explaining as learning/teaching approach; feedback as learning/teaching approach; managing learning climate
Quinlan, Kathleen 159

Ramsden, Paul 13
recall *see* context, response to; processes
reflection 62–65, *63*; about reflection points 65; definition 245; *see also* critically reflective practice model
Reflection points: attention/cognitive load **201**; becoming an expert teacher **244**; bodily responses **234**; cognitive load and complexity **204**; critical reflection **249–250, 250–251, 255**; developing disciplinary expertise 20, 22, 24, 29, **35**; explaining as learning/teaching approach **147, 150**; interactive learning **200**; managing

273

learning climate **161**, **170–171**;
metacognition, teaching of
231; misconceptions **210**, **212**;
motivation **220**; practice **208**;
questioning as learning/teaching
approach **90–91**, **91–92**, **96–97**;
stereotypes and implicit biases **229**;
teams and group settings **224**
Rehling, Diana **164**, **185**
relationship with a class *see* managing
learning climate
remembering and repetition **205–208**;
see also practicing
representative tasks: ability to complete
16–17, **18–19**; reflection point **20**;
utility value of **219**
research on learning *see* evidence about
learning
research techniques *see* investigatory
techniques
responding to students *see* feedback as
learning/teaching approach
retrieval practice **207**; *see also* practicing
Reupert, Andrea **159**
Rivière, Jean-Philippe (et al.) **225**
Roediger, Henry **207**
Roorda, Debora (et al.) **232**
routines, development of **14**; *see also*
experiential learning/teaching
Royal Academy of Engineering **243**,
243–245

safety and class management **159–160**;
see also managing learning climate
Schneider, Bertrand **223**
Schoenfeld, Alan **128–129**
Schwendimann, Beat (et al.) **226–227**
science and technology example **132**
science examples: chemistry labs
43–44, **50–51**, **60**; decision making
21–22; emotional competence
25–26; how to kill bacteria

117–119; inquiry lab assignment
253–254; misconceptions **210–212**;
self-monitoring **24**
self-efficacy **225–226**; *see also* social
dimensions of learning/teaching
self-medication **233–234**
Shell, Duane (et al.) **205**
simulations **208**
sleep and tiredness **232–234**
social dimensions of learning/
teaching: community of practice
28, **30–32**, **255–259**; digital tools
to build community **226–227**;
explicit learning goals **66**; goal of
experiential learning **56**; interactive
learning **198–199**, **200**, **221–223**;
metacognition **15**; modelling or
observational learning **127**, **141–
143**, **144**, **204**, **224–226**; problem
solving and **22**; reflection point **224**;
social identities and **227–229**; *see
also* emotional competence; team
work and collaboration
social scientist examples: discussion
participation **178–180**; managing
open-ended projects **43**, **48–50**,
58–59; misconceptions **210**;
problem solving **20**; sociology
research project **100–101**
spotlights: about **9**; classroom
demonstrations (explaining)
138–139; cognitive load (in ballet
studio) **202–203**; decision making
(science and engineering) **21–22**;
digital tools to build community
226–227; disruptions/incivility
in online courses **176–177**;
disruptions/incivility in practical
settings **165–166**; enacting teaching
active learning **247–248**; explaining
as learning/teaching approach **128–
129**; feedback by peers **115–117**,

257–258; feedback targeting task, process, and thinking **105, 106, 106–107**; five-stage adult learning model (nursing) **30–32**; implicit bias **173–174**; interactive learning **198–199, 247–248**; IT system architecture (practical settings) **42, 48, 58**; lab investigations (practical settings) **43–44, 50–51, 60**; managing emotions (teachers) **27–28**; managing open-ended projects (practical settings) **43, 48–50, 58–59**; music studio (practical settings) **41–42, 45–47, 56–58**; participation, managing class **178–180**; perception (visual arts) **18**; questioning as teaching (evidence for) **87–88**; teaching measurement techniques **253–254**, *254*; using literature on teaching **260**

Stel, Manita van der 230

stereotypes: stereotype threat 227–229 *see also* biases (implicit)

Stigler, James **27**, 33

strategic approach to learning 14–15; *see also* learning models

student experiences of practical learning 4–6; *see also* experiential learning/teaching

student-teacher relations *see* managing learning climate

Studies in Higher Education 260

talent: role in expertise 16

teachers, becoming experts: Advance HE fellowship model 242–243; action summary **263**; ALACT model (Korthagen) 242; Career Framework for University Teaching *243*, 243–244; critically reflective practice model 241–242, 245–262; documenting good teaching 244–245; experience as students 33, 241, 248–251; explaining as learning/teaching approach 127–128; feedback from students **86**, 151, 251–255, *252*; immediacy (warmth) 167–170, **170–171**; lesson study practice 35; novice teachers' assumptions 33, 241, 246, 249–251; novice teachers' practical settings 240–241; peers as community of practice **30–32**, 255–259, *258*; peer teachers 222, 223, **257–258**; perceptions 17–18; reflection points 244, 255; spotlights **27–28, 30–32, 41–42, 45–47, 253–254**, *254*, **257–258**; teacher-student relationship 158–159, 160, 169, 232; *see also* critically reflective practice model

teaching and learning approaches: about 61; focus on learner's activity 74; student-/ teacher-led continuum 60–61, *61*; *see also* evidence about learning; explaining as learning/teaching approach; feedback as learning/teaching approach; learning models; managing learning climate; practicing; questioning as learning/teaching approach

Teaching in Higher Education 260

team work and collaboration: active learning (LOAFS) 137, 257; community of practice and expertise 28, **30–32**, 255–259; evidence on 221–223; guiding of 53–54, **59**, 66; heterogeneous and homogeneous 50, **58–59**, 223–224; implicit bias **173–174**; interactive learning **198–199, 200**, 221–222; Jigsaw activity 137; in

INDEX

problem solving 22; reflection point 224; *see also* social dimensions of learning/teaching
10,000 hours 13, 33–35, 241; *see also* experts, becoming one
theory/practice divide 226–227
thinking skills: cognitive apprenticeship 224–225 *see also* observational learning or modelling; cognitive load 202–203, 202–204, 222; cognitive reappraisal 28; ways of thinking 40–41, 67; *see also* metacognition
Timperley, Helen 121
Tormey, Roland 14, **27–28**, 159, **166**, 167, 169, 170
transfer: definition 45; elaboration and organisation of ideas 209–210; expertise not transferable 20, 23; explaining as learning/teaching approach 132; goal of experiential learning 55, 67; questions facilitating 86; *see also* metacognition
trust 168–170; *see also* managing learning climate

understanding or expertise 13; *see also* experts, becoming one
university/workplace divide **226–227**
using questions *see* questioning as learning/teaching approach
US National Academies' reviews of evidence 195–196, 227, 232
utility value 219–220
Uytterhoeven, Lise **117**

value and utility 219–220
Van Joolingen, W.R. 208
Veenman, Marcel 55, 230
violinists example 24
visual artists example **18**
Voss, James (et al.) 20

Warburton, Edward (et al.) **203**
Wenger, Etienne 28–29
Wieman, Carl **21**
Wiles, Andrew 25–26
Woodcock, Stuart 159
writers, example of professional 25

Zhang, Qin **171**
Zimmerman, Barry 225–226